RINGSIDE 2

Also by Doveed Linder

Ringside: Interviews with 24 Fighters and Boxing Insiders (McFarland, 2016)

RINGSIDE 2

More Interviews with Fighters and Boxing Insiders

DOVEED LINDER

Foreword by "Iceman" John Scully

McFarland & Company, Inc., Publishers
Jefferson, North Carolina

ISBN (print) 978-1-4766-8697-4
ISBN (ebook) 978-1-4766-4743-2

LIBRARY OF CONGRESS AND BRITISH LIBRARY
CATALOGUING DATA ARE AVAILABLE

Library of Congress Control Number 2022035728

Front cover: Evander Holyfield (left) and Dwight Muhammad Qawi in their July 12, 1986, championship fight in Atlanta, Georgia (Boxing Hall of Fame Las Vegas/Official Boxing Gods)

Printed in the United States of America

McFarland & Company, Inc., Publishers
Box 611, Jefferson, North Carolina 28640
www.mcfarlandpub.com

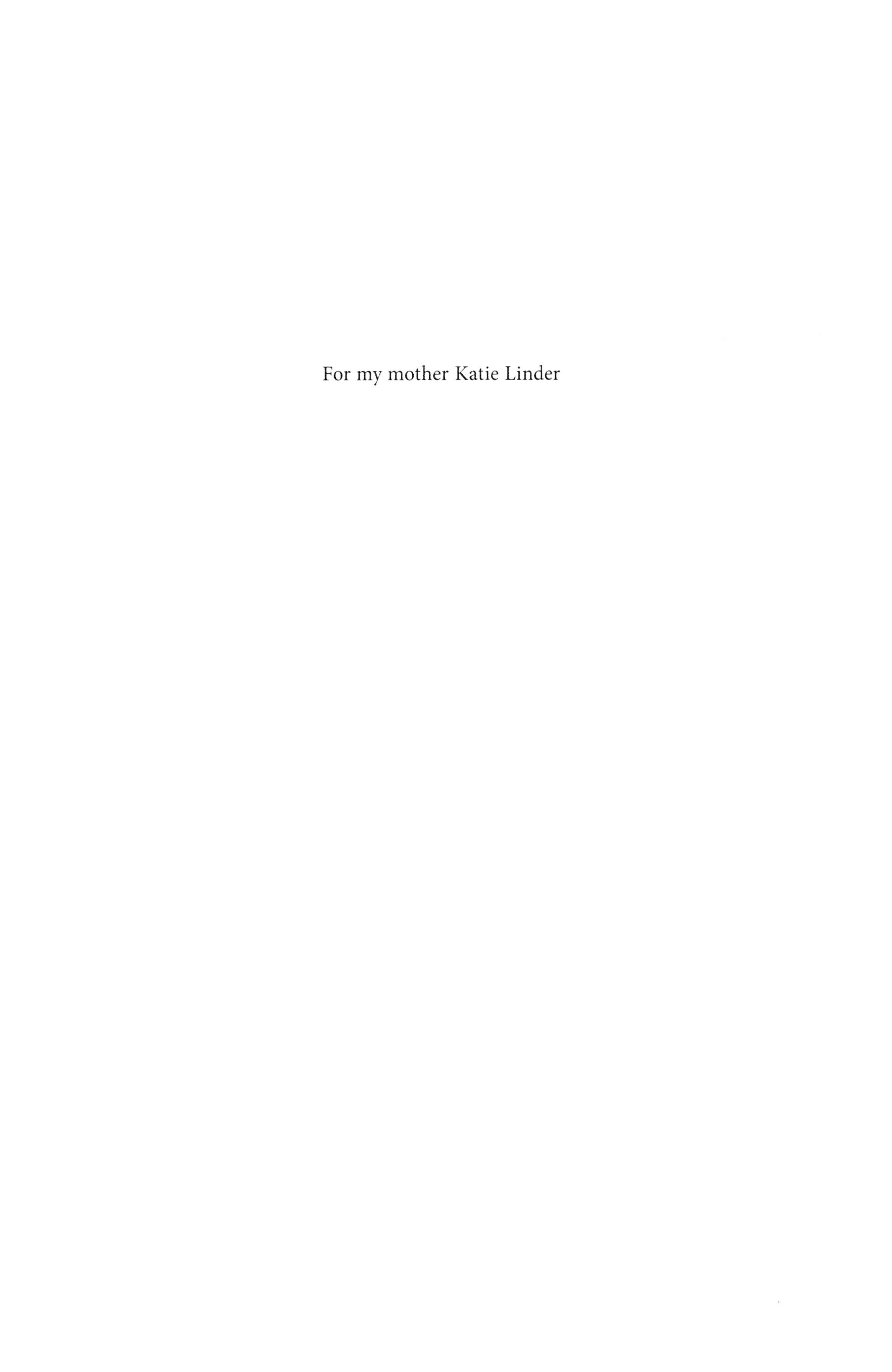

For my mother Katie Linder

Contents

Announcers and Officials

Acknowledgments

This is now my second book of boxing interviews. Projects like this wouldn't be possible without the help and support of a number of generous people.

Individuals and companies who either arranged interviews, provided me with contact information, or contributed photographs from their personal collection include Jean-Christophe Courreges, Marvin Elkind, James Akhir Fisher, James Gibbs, Dan Graschuck, Tim Hallmark/timhallmark.com, Jackie Kallen, Dr. Stuart Kirschenbaum, Greg Leon/Boxingtalk.com, Main Events, the Nevada State Athletic Commission, Tom Patti, Ray Rodgers, Michael Schmidt, Ronnie Shields, and Steve Smoger.

Photographers whose work is featured include "Sugar" Ray Bailey, Claudia Bocanegra, Tim Cheatham, Chris Cuellar, Dan Graschuck, Ray Flores, Andrew Kerman, Jimmy Range, Bob Ryder, and William Trillo.

Bret Newton/ThreatPhoto.com & Pound4Pound.com, and Marty Rosengarten/RingsidePhotos.com, contributed a large number of photos to this book, as well as the first book.

Steve Lott, who is credited as "Boxing Hall of Fame Las Vegas/Official Boxing Gods," contributed a number of historic photographs to this manuscript, as well as the first *Ringside*, including images that were used for the cover of both books. Like many of the people who contributed to this project, he didn't know me personally, but he was willing to help because of his love of boxing. Lott died before the publication of this book.

John Scully has devoted a big part of his life to helping people in boxing and keeping old friends in touch. He was an interviewee for my first book, wrote the foreword for this book, helped arrange a number of interviews, and contributed photographs.

Barbara Madison and Rick Perez were especially generous and supportive during this process.

Barry Hamilton helped organize and deliver the photos for this book, as well as the first book.

During this process, I lived through some boxing stories of my own, which involved training a few St. Louis-based professional boxers. These fighters include Raymond Handson, Vaughn Alexander, Juzzton Hill, and Nick Reeder, as well as amateur boxer Zach Gong. Butch Gragg's pro debut fell apart at the weigh-in, but we had fun training together.

St. Louis trainers and cutmen who helped me in the corner include Winston "Buddy" Shaw, Nick Reeder, and Jerry Leyshock. Yeshai Gibli, Shimon Ohana, and Steven Fitzpatrick Smith came out to all of the local fights and were a huge source of support while I was training boxers. Rob Donaker and Jesse Finney of Shamrock FC gave my boxers a slot on their cards and always put on a classy event.

While writing this book, I worked as a boxing instructor/personal trainer. I always loved telling the people I trained about the interviews I was getting and some of the stories I was told.

Other people and companies I want to acknowledge are Steve Cakouros, the Fuchs Family, Grafica Fine Art & Custom Framing (Lary and Lynn Bozzay), Nathan Hershey, Performance Lab (David and Renae Lazaroff), Jan Roberg, Dave Rutherford, and Jeff Schnuck (Volunteer Lawyers and Accountants for the Arts, St. Louis).

My father, Daniel Linder, didn't live to see this book published, but his faith and encouragement was a motivating factor.

Most of all, I want to thank the people who allowed me to interview them. They are the true authors of this book.

Foreword
by "Iceman" John Scully

In the 1990s, there was a street in my hometown of Hartford, Connecticut, where everybody hung out on the weekends. There were clubs, a pizza place, a barbeque place.... We would be there until three or four in the morning, talking, laughing and having a good time. Across the street was a train station. One cold winter night, I noticed these faces in the window. Every now and then, a head would pop up and look out at the street. I was a little curious, so I went over there and saw about thirty homeless people inside. Apparently, they would go there at night when the station closed. I just thought it was crazy to see people living like that, so I went back across the street, bought a couple of pizzas, and brought them back over.

It was actually a pretty good time. I ended up talking to some of the people there and staying all night. One guy told me how he had been a doctor. He was married and had two kids, but he got hooked on drugs and lost everything. Another guy told me he was a Red Sox fan. Can you imagine that? There he was, homeless and starving, and he liked the Red Sox. It just goes to show you that everybody has a story to tell, even a homeless person.

I talk to people everywhere I go. My daughter and stepsons are amused by this. If I'm standing in line at an amusement park, I might strike up a conversation with the guy who runs the ride. Of course, it sometimes comes up that I'm involved with boxing. When they ask me about it, I try not to make a big deal of it. I just say that I used to box and that I train fighters now.

In actuality, I'm a pretty well-rounded boxing guy. I turned pro around the same time as guys like Roy Jones, Jr., Gerald McClellan, Riddick Bowe, and Ray Mercer. I fought Michael Nunn on ESPN. I went to Germany to challenge Henry Maske for his IBF world light heavyweight title. I trained Chad Dawson when he beat Bernard Hopkins for the WBC light heavyweight championship, and Jose Antonio Rivera when he won the WBA junior middleweight title by defeating Alejandro Gonzalez. I've been a commentator, I've interviewed fighters, and I've written about the sport. The only thing I won't do in boxing is manage or promote fighters. I have nothing against managers or promoters, but I'm a little sour on the business side of the game. I just stick with what's best for me. The gym is where I'm most comfortable. That's the place I call home.

I first learned about boxing because my father had these boxing books that I used to read. Namely, they were biographies of "Sugar" Ray Robinson, Muhammad Ali, and Willie Pep. When I read those books, I would get pictures in my head of what it must have been like to be them. It made me want to be a boxer and to be able to tell stories of my own. A lot of the values I have about boxing came from Archie Moore, who I was good friends with before he passed away. Despite a lack of formal education, Archie was a very intelligent person. One thing he always told me is that the media is our friend. Without them, boxing doesn't exist. I had never thought of that before, but he was right. The media is who lets the world know what we're doing. You could be the best fighter in the world, but nobody will know unless somebody writes about it.

After a while, I compiled a database of all the members of the media who I was familiar with. I did this because any time there's an issue or something I think they should know about, I'll write an e-mail and send it en masse to all of my contacts.

In 2009, I trained cruiserweight Matt Godfrey when he out-boxed this undefeated knockout artist on ESPN. Teddy Atlas was one of the commentators during the broadcast and he was a little critical of the fight. According to Atlas, Godfrey should have been more exciting and aggressive-minded. In response to what Atlas said, I sent out an e-mail and voiced my opinion on the matter. I didn't expect anything to come of it, but I got an e-mail back from Doveed Linder of Boxingtalk.com, asking if I wanted to do an interview.

Former light heavyweight world title challenger John Scully (left) and former world light heavyweight champion Archie Moore, 1988 (courtesy John Scully).

As I recall, Doveed was new to the scene at that time. When I talked to him, he didn't come across as a writer; he was more like a regular guy who was interested in boxing. I could tell that he had a lot of respect for the sport and he seemed to have this humble way about him. The questions he asked were a little off the center line—different than the kind of questions I was used to. He wanted to dig deep into the sport and talk about the psychology behind it.

A couple years later, Doveed e-mailed me again and asked if he could interview me for a book he was writing. Of course, I was more than happy to help him out. I just assumed he wanted some technical input. But as I answered his questions, all of these personal and humorous stories kept coming up. I started telling him how I used to wrap my hands with toilet paper when I was a kid and put Halloween blood on my face, so I could pretend that I was a boxer. After a while, I realized that the interview wasn't about boxing; it was about me.

When the interview was over, I asked Doveed if there was anyone else he wanted to interview for his book. I was friends with some of the people he wanted to speak with, so I ended up helping him secure a number of interviews. This sport doesn't get as much coverage as it used to, so I figured here was a chance for other people to tell their stories, too. Five years later, he sent me a copy of his book, *Ringside: Interviews with 24 Fighters and Boxing Insiders.*

Since that time, I've continued helping Doveed get interviews. Whether a person is a three-time champion, a journeyman, or just somebody who has helped the sport in some way, I want them to be recognized. There are a lot of people in boxing who aren't famous, but they've impacted the sport more than anyone will ever know.

One of the most beloved boxing people from Hartford, Connecticut, was a trainer by the name of Johnny Duke, who passed away in 2006. Fans generally don't know who he is, but I guarantee you that you've never met anyone quite like him. Not long after his death, I raised $4,000 so we could purchase a plaque which was placed at the site of his former gym, located in the Bellevue Square projects on the north end of the city. To this day, the people on the street still cherish that plaque, because they know and remember the name Johnny Duke.

They say that boxing is a poor man's sport and I would have to agree with that. I know boxing trainers who've slept in their gyms and sold their belongings, so the kids can have the equipment they need and the finances to go to the tournaments. We wouldn't have a boxing world if it wasn't for these people. If you really want to know about boxing, you need to know about everybody who's involved. There's much more to it than what you read in the headlines.

One of the main reasons that I'm a lifelong boxing person is because of the people who happen to be a part of the game. They're genuine, they're strong, they're compassionate.... There's nobody in the world like them.

"Iceman" John Scully is a former super middleweight/light heavyweight contender and trainer of world class boxers, based in Hartford, Connecticut.

Prologue: Why I Write About Boxing

Like John Scully, I'm a lifelong boxing person because of the people who are a part of the game. They're everything he described and more. But when I first started meeting people in boxing, I was kind of intimidated. This is a sport where the objective is to inflict damage on the guy in the opposite corner. Boxers, trainers, promoters, and officials all work together to carry on this tradition of organized warfare. Who *wouldn't* be intimidated? I had admired boxing from a distance, but being up close and personal was a different experience.

The first time I walked into a boxing gym, I thought it would be like that scene in *Rocky III* when Rocky Balboa goes to Apollo Creed's gym, and all of the fighters stop training and give him a dirty look. Instead, most of the people there treated me with a lot of kindness and took me seriously as a potential fighter. That's just how boxing people are. If you're willing to put on the gloves and give it a try, you'll have their respect.

Having grown up in the suburbs of St. Louis, Missouri, I never heard people talk about boxing, nor had I ever met anyone who was involved with it. My only connection was through the movies. But as I learned about boxing and as I became familiar with the culture of the sport, I found myself becoming part of the tribe.

I haven't been involved with the game quite as extensively as Scully. But like Scully, I would also consider myself as a pretty well-rounded boxing guy. I boxed a little bit as an amateur. I've trained numerous amateur boxers and a few professionals. I've been a boxing writer for over ten years. And as of this writing, I support myself as a boxing instructor/personal trainer. Basically, I'm a die-hard fan who wanted to get involved in any and every way.

I started following boxing in the mid–1990s. At that time, the heavyweight division was thriving with fighters like Lennox Lewis, Evander Holyfield, Mike Tyson, George Foreman, Riddick Bowe, and Michael Moorer. Going into the late '90s and early 2000s, the star power of Oscar De La Hoya brought a lot of attention to the welterweight and junior middleweight divisions, where Shane Mosley, Felix Trinidad, Winky Wright, Fernando Vargas, and Vernon Forrest were all in a number of great match-ups.

During that time, Bernard Hopkins proved to be a dominant middleweight champion. Multi-division champion Roy Jones, Jr., put on a mind-blowing

Doveed Linder (left), middleweight Raymond Handson, and trainer Winston "Buddy" Shaw after Handson's 2016 unanimous decision victory over Joel Blair. This victory was dedicated to Raymond's close friend Michael Williams, a professional boxer with a record of 6–1, 5 KOs, who was shot and killed two weeks before the fight (courtesy Jimmy Range).

performance every time out. Kostya Tszyu was the man at junior welterweight. Fans were treated to an epic battle between super bantamweight champions Marco Antonio Barrera and Erik Morales, who went on to have an historic trilogy. The emergence of featherweight Manny Pacquiao made a strong impression, not to mention a talented junior lightweight by the name of Floyd Mayweather, Jr., who was off to an excellent start. This was a great time to be a fan and I'm proud to have discovered the sport when so many special fighters were in the mix.

I started writing about boxing by posting on message boards and engaging in discussions with other fans. My words first went to print when *KO Magazine* published a paragraph I wrote in a section where they featured submissions by readers. Eventually, I began contributing articles, interviews, and fight reports to Boxingtalk.com. It was a lot of fun, but I didn't find what I was looking for as a boxing writer until I managed to secure an in-person interview with now retired HBO boxing analyst Larry Merchant. Over lunch, I spoke with Merchant about his career and got to know him as a person. Instead of getting caught up in the hustle of current events, I found that I like to take my time with interviewees and listen to them reflect on the lives they lived.

Gaining boxing information isn't what compelled me to write this book, although there is a lot of information to be found. These interviews are meant to give the reader a chance to meet some interesting and inspiring people, and to discover the colorful personalities and strength of character that exists in the sport. To bring my point home, I'll borrow a quote from the Michigan Boxing Commissioner Emeritus, Dr. Stuart Kirschenbaum. In his interview, Dr. Kirschenbaum said, "The people in boxing are what made the sport what it is. They're part of the fabric of life, and the history in a country growing out of social injustice, racial discrimination, and inhuman tolerance. We need to remember who these people are and what they meant. That's been my mission and I'm not letting go."

FIGHTERS

1

Lennox Lewis: The Emperor

> "I didn't wait four years to be in that position. If I was going to lose, I had to lose big. If I was going to win, I wanted to win big. That was my mindset."

At one point in time, winning the heavyweight championship of the world was said to be the greatest accomplishment in all sports. As far as many boxing fans are concerned, it still is. The undisputed heavyweight champion stands above everyone in the game and is looked at as royalty.

Born in London, England, later relocating to Kitchener, Ontario, Canada, Lennox Lewis won the gold medal at the 1988 Olympic Games in Seoul, South Korea, as a super heavyweight, before turning professional in June 1989.

In October 1992, Lewis defeated Donovan "Razor" Ruddock by second-round TKO in an eliminator for the WBC world heavyweight title, which was held by Riddick Bowe. When Bowe relinquished the title, Lewis was awarded the championship.

Lewis defended his title three times before losing to Oliver McCall via second-round TKO in September 1994. After the fight with McCall, Lewis returned to his winning ways, eventually facing McCall in a February 1997 rematch. This time, Lewis defeated McCall via fifth-round TKO, winning the vacant WBC world heavyweight title.

Lewis defended his title four times before facing WBA and IBF world title holder, Evander Holyfield, in a bout that was ruled a split draw. In November that year, he defeated Holyfield in a rematch by unanimous decision, becoming the undisputed heavyweight champion.

After the two fights with Holyfield, Lewis defended his WBC and IBF titles three times before losing to Hasim Rahman by fifth-round knockout in April 2001. He faced Rahman in a November rematch that year, regaining his titles via fourth-round knockout.

In June 2002, Lewis defended his IBF and WBC titles against former world heavyweight champion Mike Tyson by eighth-round knockout. In June the following year, he defended his WBC title against former WBO world heavyweight champion, Vitali Klitschko, winning the bout via sixth-round TKO due to a cut suffered by Klitschko.

Lewis retired in 2003 with a record of 41–2-1, 32 KOs. He holds victories over every man he ever faced, including Tyrell Biggs, Tony Tucker, Frank Bruno, Tommy Morrison, Ray Mercer, Henry Akinwande, Andrew Golota, Shannon Briggs, Michael Grant, Frans Botha, and David Tua. This interview took place over the phone in July 2018.

When did you first put on the gloves? How old were you and what were the circumstances?

The first time I put on the gloves, I was at a boarding school in London. I was about thirteen. It was a situation where I was the most aggressive kid there. The headmaster said, "Put on these gloves and throw some punches at me." At that time, I didn't really know boxing or how to throw straight punches. I would just swing wild. That's how I generated power. I remember throwing punches at him and he said, "Hit me harder!"

When I was younger, I used to fight all the time. People would call me names, and there would be words, and it would be a matter of respect. I didn't know anything about conflict resolution. I would just go to war. I grew up around east London, which was one of the roughest places in England at the time. We went through a number of different time warps there—the years of the gangs, the years of footballism.... I think the good thing about the rough times in England is that the weapon of choice was fist fighting.

But that particular incident with the headmaster wasn't really what got me started with boxing straight away. I was an athlete. My first sports were soccer and cricket. When I came over to Canada, I was given a lot of different sports to look at—basketball, volleyball, hockey, street hockey.... It wasn't until I was at a school dance that I really got involved with boxing.

There were these guys who wanted to fight. We realized that if we fought them that we would get expelled, so we invited them down to the police boxing club, thinking that we could beat them up and not get in trouble. So, we went down there and these guys never showed up. At the next dance, we said, "Hey, you guys never showed up. Maybe you forgot. Make sure you're at the police station at such and such time." They said, "Yeah, we'll be there." But again, they didn't show up.

The trainer there at the time, Arnie Boehm, said to me, "Hey, you. Come over here. I want you to move around with this guy." The guy they put me in with was way smaller than me, but he was good. Because of my size, I thought I could beat him up. When I stepped in there, he danced around me. I couldn't even touch him. Again, I was just swinging wild. He gave me a couple jabs to the nose and my eyes started watering. I said, "No, no... This ain't for me." I didn't like getting hit in the nose. Then the trainer, Arnie Boehm, said, "I want you to move around with this other guy." He was my size and he was a novice as well. The only boxer I remember seeing before was Muhammad Ali. So, when I got in there, I started acting like Muhammad Ali.

When I was younger, we used to play a game called tag where you're supposed to get the last touch. Boxing felt like a game of tag and it was exciting for me. I was using my athleticism, moving around, and staying away from the guy who was trying to hit me, while I was trying to hit him. It was fun.

Vitali Klitschko and Lennox Lewis at a press conference for their 2003 bout, which was arguably the best heavyweight fight of the 2000s (courtesy Bret Newton—ThreatPhoto.com/ Pound4Pound.com).

At this time, I was still playing all sports. I was on the football team, but there are fifty guys on a football team. It's a team effort and you're only as strong as your weakest link. In football, we would win every game in the season, but when we got to the championship game, two guys would drop the ball and then we would lose. What I loved about boxing is that everything is up to you. If you go into the last round and somebody says that you're losing, it's up to you to step it up. You tell *yourself* to step it up. I realized that I would be better at a sport where I can control what happens. It's up to me to be able to deal with any situation that erupts in the ring.

Boxing became my life, because trainers started to tell me, "Hey, you could be really good at this." I started winning my fights, and when I won, people would suggest that I go to the different tournaments. So, I started winning all of Ontario, all of Canada.... I was getting spoken about, and then I was getting written about.... The biggest thing was traveling. I got to travel and I realized that my talent was bringing me to all these different places.

At the 1984 Olympic Games, you lost a decision in the quarterfinals to Tyrell Biggs, who ended up winning the gold medal at super heavyweight. Instead of turning professional, you honed your craft in the amateurs for four more years, eventually winning a gold medal at the 1988 Olympics. In the final fight of that tournament, you faced Riddick Bowe, now a former two-time world heavyweight champion, and defeated him by second-round TKO. Bowe out-punched you in the first round of that fight. After waiting four years to get another shot at Olympic gold, what went through your mind between rounds one and two?

I didn't wait four years to be in that position. If I was going to lose, I had to lose big. If I was going to win, I wanted to win big. That was my mindset. In the second round, I was upset because he had hit me with an uppercut. When you look at his career, that was really his main punch. I wasn't aware of that at the time. I used to have a habit of putting my head down. People would tell me not to do that, and I was pissed off that I got hit with something a big man like me wasn't supposed to get hit with. And he bloodied my nose. So, I came out like, yo, I'm going *all* out! When I hit him with that left-right, he walked away and the referee was saying, "Turn around! Turn around!" He wouldn't turn around because he was trying to straighten himself out mentally, and because he was a bit concussed. So, the referee stopped it because he couldn't continue.

Do you think the fight with Bowe in the Olympics influenced his team to relinquish the WBC heavyweight title instead of face you?

I think it did. I took that as he didn't want to fight me. I took that as his manager didn't have the *confidence* in him to fight me. He wanted to keep his gravy train alive. But we're gladiators. And if I was in the position that he was in and I lost to a man who I felt I should have beat, I wouldn't hesitate to get back in the ring.

In November 1991, you faced Tyrell Biggs as a professional, defeating him by third-round TKO. Did your 1984 loss to Biggs in the Olympics give you additional motivation for this fight?

One hundred percent. When I first fought Tyrell Biggs, I was young and lacking experience. At that time, the American team was going to different countries and getting experience fighting all over the world. We didn't have that in Canada. When we fought in the pros, I had the Olympics under my belt and I had almost three years as a pro. You dare fight me now? Don't you know what you're gonna get? When I looked at the fight between me and Biggs from the Olympics, I realized that I had a bigger heart than him. I wanted to mix it up. We were gonna go toe-to-toe. I had the experience and the exposure, and I just wanted to go after him. I was a menace in that fight. I didn't really give him any room. I was coming from a great training camp and I knew there was no way he was in better shape than me. I knew that his will would weaken before mine.

In October 1992, you scored a second-round TKO over Donovan "Razor" Ruddock, who was best known for being competitive with former heavyweight champion Mike Tyson in two previous fights. The fight with Ruddock was an eliminator for Riddick Bowe's WBC world heavyweight title. After the bout, Bowe relinquished his WBC title and the belt was awarded to you. What do you recall about the fight with Ruddock?

That was a great fight for me. And he motivated me before the fight when he said that he still had my blood on his shoes from when we used to spar. You came to England to say that to me? Don't you know I'm the king of England? I looked at the fact that he went nineteen rounds with Tyson. Now, he's thinking he can do the same to me and hit me with that "Smash" punch? Yeah, try it! I trained hard for that fight,

Lennox Lewis and David Tua face each other, surrounded by team members, at the weigh-in of their 2000 fight (courtesy Rick Perez).

because I really wanted him. I was in training camp each time he fought Tyson. I'd watch them and I'd be like, "Put me in there. I'll beat both of them." In the fight, he did something that a heavyweight shouldn't do and that's duck low. He put his head down. As soon as I saw him do that, I was like, bam-bam! I just seized the moment. I didn't hit him to knock him out; I just hit him because I saw the opening. But the knockout came.

In October 1993, you faced Frank Bruno, who later went on to win the WBC world heavyweight title. Held at the National Stadium, Cardiff Arms Park in Wales, this was a competitive scrap that you won by seventh-round TKO.

In that particular fight, England was kind of separate on who they wanted to win. The young cats were saying that I was the best. The elderly people were saying, "Frank Bruno is a lovely person." They didn't know who to go for. For me, I was the young kid coming out, saying that I could beat everyone. I had been watching Frank Bruno's fights for a while and I was like, "Yo, this guy's had some easy opponents and they say he's good. Give him somebody like me!" I was prepared, I was focused, I was confident....

Early in the fight, somehow, he was one step ahead of me. I thought he must have been more warmed up than me, but I realized that it was because he had hate for me. He wanted to get me. He was like, "Who is this guy? He's been calling me names and saying this and that. I want to get him!" He was fighting upset to a degree.

He actually hit me with a good shot and I reacted with a wild hook that caught him. I saw him do this wobbly thing, so I went after him. I wasn't doing it in a constructive way; I was just trying to blast him out of there. Looking at the fight, I'm actually glad the referee stopped it. At one point, he was just taking shots for no reason. There was one uppercut I threw and it's a good thing that it missed him. It would have been a jarring one. But everything ended correctly and I'm glad nobody got hurt badly.

In September 1994, you lost your WBC title to Oliver McCall via second-round TKO. What happened that night from your perspective?

When you start knocking people out, you think you're invincible. We all go through it if we've been there. Who is this guy? I'm going to knock him out, too. There's a technical thing you start doing wrong that catches up to you. It's called, letting the guy know that the punches are coming. If you let the guy know that the punches are coming, he's going to prepare for it and come back with something. That's what Oliver McCall did—a slip and a right hand. Another thing I did wrong was that I leaned in when I threw my right hand. So, there were a number of things I changed after that fight, which helped me to improve my game.

The late trainer Emanuel Steward was in McCall's corner when you faced him the first time. Ironically, you ended up working with Steward, who played a big part in guiding you to become a dominant heavyweight champion.

I first met Manny at the North American Championships in Canada. He said that I was a good fighter and that he would be watching me. I was supposed to work with Emanuel Steward for a long time. When I reached out to him, I think he was working with Oliver McCall. And I think he realized that McCall had some serious issues that were going to break him down. Did he want to stay there for that? Or did he want to work with this other guy who has all the talent in the world, but just needs a little tuning up?

So, he basically came over to my side and we started a relationship from there. What I liked is the way he communicated with me. I was able to break down and do exactly what he wanted. It was a challenge for me at first, but once I got what he was telling me, it was like clockwork. After I started working with Manny, the commentators started talking about me differently. Before, they would say that Lennox is lacking this and Lennox is lacking that.... But when I got together with Manny, they

Trainer Emanuel Steward, who helped bring Lennox Lewis's game to a new level, 2000s (courtesy Marty Rosengarten/RingsidePhotos.com).

were saying how I was starting to do some good things and that I was looking better as a fighter.

In May 1996, you faced former WBO world heavyweight champion Ray Mercer in a toe-to-toe war that you won by majority decision.

The day before the fight, we measured the ring. I went in there and danced around a bit. The next day, we go there and it was about a fifteen foot ring. It was smaller. One or two steps and my back was hitting the ropes. There was nothing we could do at that point. Nothing. So, I said to myself, okay, they're trying to test my gangsta. What they didn't know is that I was prepared for this. I knew that Ray Mercer was a fighter, a battler. Most of my sparring partners were his size and we went toe-to-toe in the gym.

Before the fight, one of my trainers had said to me, "You have to be the best on the outside *and* the inside." That always stayed in my head, so I was ready. What surprised me about Ray was how he fought the fight. He was pretty smart. He would throw punches and then lean on me, not allowing me to throw any punches. So, after he finished throwing his punches, I would push him and start throwing combinations. He would start and I would finish. I wanted to make it look good for the judges, because my trainer said, "We couldn't get any first-row tickets for our people. His manager bought out the first row, so all the noise will be for him. They're against you, Champ. They're against you." I kept thinking, "They're against me."

We were in New York and it was like I was boxing in his backyard. After winning the fight, they were booing. I got out of the ring and some guy goes, "Lennox Lewis, you're a bum! You're a bum! You're a bum!" I'm a bum? I just boxed a guy on his home turf and they put me in a dodgy ring with a dodgy ref. That means I have to over-beat him to beat him, which was uncanny for my style of boxing.

In February 1997, you had a rematch with Oliver McCall for the vacant WBC world heavyweight title, defeating him by fifth-round TKO. The fight was stopped due to McCall having an emotional episode in the ring, when he broke down in tears.

I had come from a good training camp and I was like, I'm coming for this guy. He took what I had. I had to chase him all around the world for two years. Once he gets in the ring, he's mine. But he threw me for a loop. I was prepared for everything he would bring, but I was not prepared for him to break down in the ring like that.

Before the fight, Don King wouldn't let anyone interview Oliver. There were whispers that something was wrong with him, that he was having psychological problems. But they were trying to build this mystique around the fight, as if he was just so focused that he didn't want to talk to anybody. The first time I fought him, he played possum and I thought he was playing possum again. I thought that I had better be careful. But after one of the rounds, I went back to the corner and Manny said, "What are you doing?" I said, "Manny, he's crying." Manny said, "So, beat him up!"

In March 1999, you put your WBC title on the line in a unification bout with Evander Holyfield, who held the WBA and IBF titles. Many regarded Holyfield as the best heavyweight at that time, because of his longevity at the elite level, and because of his 1996 and 1997 victories over Mike Tyson. The bout with Holyfield was ruled a split draw, though the boxing public felt that it should have been a victory for you. You faced Holyfield again in November of that year, winning a unanimous decision.

Holyfield was a great warrior. I always wanted to fight him, because I felt he would enhance my boxing. With me fighting him, he brought me in a new light. Holyfield had a disadvantage, which he overcame with hard training. His disadvantage was that he was not a natural heavyweight. If he was a heavyweight, then the rest of us were super heavyweights. I always admired his appetite for boxing. He was a student of the game. He had different defenses, he was always in great shape, and he had a technical side to him.

Holyfield also used his head as part of his offense. You've seen it in his other fights and I don't believe in that type of fighting. When I fought Holyfield, I would throw a one-two, and he would throw a one-two-three. The third punch was his head. I would block his one-two and his head would be coming towards my face. I could see he was using his head, so I had to make sure I didn't duck into it or we would have a head-to-head situation.

In order to be a great fighter, you have to be ready for any situation. You have to be able to adjust. I'm a five-dimensional fighter—a boxer, a mover, a puncher.... I can fight inside *and* outside. When I fought Holyfield, I had all this experience that I built up over the years and I had to resort to that. Because of all my other fights, I knew what to do.

Lennox Lewis and Max Kellerman sit ringside at a 2000s fight, working as commentators for HBO (courtesy Marty Rosengarten/RingsidePhotos.com).

2

Winky Wright: Undisputed

> "Everybody's got a chance to shine one time in their life. When you get that time, you've got to do it. That was my time."

In the late 1990s and early 2000s, several talented fighters with big names competed around the welterweight and junior middleweight divisions, including Oscar De La Hoya, Shane Mosley, Felix Trinidad, Vernon Forrest, and Fernando Vargas. Having these boxers in the mix led to a number of exciting matchups. But there was another fighter who had just as much potential as this group, though it took him a bit longer to make his mark.

Born in Washington, D.C., later relocating to St. Petersburg, Florida, Ronald "Winky" Wright started boxing simply because he liked the sport and it was something fun to do. Despite the fact that he cut corners with his training, Wright excelled as an amateur. He turned professional in October 1990, winning his first twenty-five fights.

Wright's first shot at a world title came in August 1994, when he faced WBA world junior middleweight champion, Julio Cesar Vasquez, losing a unanimous decision. After this bout, Wright took his training to a new level.

In May 1996, Wright captured his first world title when he won a split decision over WBO world junior middleweight champion, Bronco McKart. He defended his title three times before losing a majority decision to Harry Simon in August 1998.

Wright regained his status as a world champion in October 2001, when he defeated Robert Frazier by unanimous decision for the vacant IBF junior middleweight title. He defended his IBF title four times before facing WBC and WBA world junior middleweight champion Shane Mosley in a March 2004 unification bout. Wright defeated Mosley by unanimous decision, becoming the undisputed junior middleweight champion of the world.

In November 2004, Wright defended his WBC and WBA titles against Mosley in a rematch, winning via majority decision. He then moved up to face former multi-division champion, Felix Trinidad, in a May 2005 WBC middleweight eliminator, winning a unanimous decision.

In June 2006, Wright fought to a split draw against Jermain Taylor, who was defending his WBC and WBO middleweight titles. Following the bout with Taylor,

Wright finished his career at middleweight with the exception of a July 2007 encounter with former undisputed middleweight champion Bernard Hopkins, which was fought at a catchweight of 170 pounds. Wright lost the bout with Hopkins by unanimous decision.

Throughout his career, Wright has also faced Fernando Vargas, Juan Carlos Candelo, Angel Hernandez, Sam Soliman, Ike Quartey, Paul Williams, and Peter Quillin, retiring in 2012 with a record of 51–6-1, 25 KOs. This interview took place over the phone in October 2013.

When did you first put on the gloves? How old were you and what were the circumstances?

I started boxing when I was two months from my sixteenth birthday. I always wanted to box, but I was busy playing other sports. When one sport ended, the next sport began—football season to basketball season, basketball season to baseball season.... When I moved from Washington, D.C., to Florida, I didn't really know too many people. I heard about a boxing club, so I figured I might as well go. I was just looking for something to do. I had no idea that I would be a professional fighter, let alone a world champion.

Being from Washington, D.C., I was a big "Sugar" Ray Leonard fan and I watched him with that slick boxing style. I had boxed before in the neighborhood without gloves. It was just slap boxing and body punching, but that led to me knowing what to do. I had been in fights before, but I've never been the type of person who started fights. I was more of a laugher and a joker. When I first went to the gym, I just watched. I came back the next day, and two weeks later I won the Golden Gloves. It was just a novice tournament, but things started happening real quick. I was an amateur boxer for only two years, but I had like sixty fights. Back then, we used to fight every week.

I started becoming one of the top amateur boxers in the United States, but I wasn't thinking about turning professional. It was just fun to me, something I loved to do. I was winning tournaments, but I wasn't training like I should. I liked to spar and do the speed bag and all that, but I hated running. Mark Breland, who was a world champion at the time—he used to train at our gym. He told me, "You could be pretty good if you would train right." I was like, "Man, I don't want to be no boxer."

When I graduated from high school, I had to figure out what I wanted to do. A local businessman came to my gym and said he would pay me to turn pro. I didn't have any other plans, so I figured I would just take the money and see what happened. When I had my first pro fight, I didn't even run. I was training, but I didn't do my roadwork. I thought my natural ability would get me through it. The dude I fought was a world champion kick-fighter. I hit this dude with everything and the kitchen sink, and he wouldn't go down. We went all four rounds and I got tired. After that, I started running every day!

Your first sixteen professional fights took place in the state of Florida. After that, most of your fights began taking place in Europe. What was going on with your career at that time?

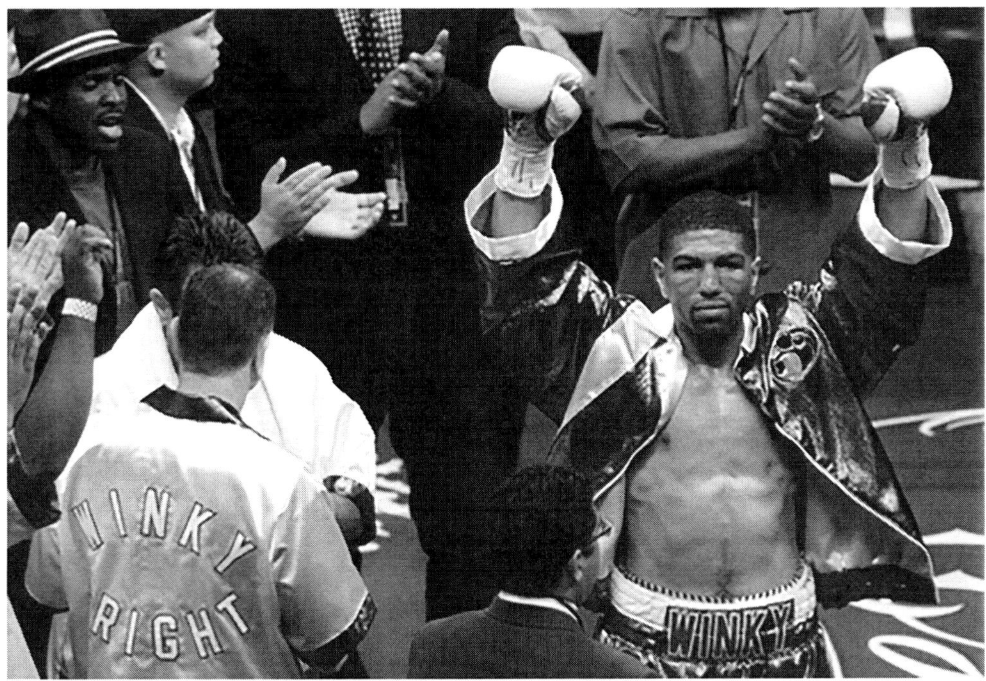

Former undisputed world junior middleweight champion Winky Wright acknowledges the crowd, 2009 (courtesy Bret Newton—ThreatPhoto.com/Pound4Pound.com).

I was with a local promoter and he couldn't do anything else but get me local fights. It was cool, though, because I was fighting on the undercard of a lot of *Tuesday Night Fights* and I got to meet some of the big names like James Toney and Roy Jones. Once I got like twelve fights, I was like, man, I could beat these guys I see on TV.

Somehow a European manager reached out to my coach and asked if we would like to do some fights in Europe. My coach told me, "They're gonna pay you $5,000 to have a six-round fight." I was like, "What?!" I had just made $1,200 for a ten-round fight. I knocked the dude out in the first round, but it was only $1,200. I was like, "Yeah, let's go." I knew God was with me the whole time, because there were a lot of things I did that I know I couldn't do without Him. I wasn't training, I wasn't preparing right.... There were a lot of things I should have been doing that I didn't do, but I got through it unscathed.

Your first shot at a world title came in August 1994 when you faced WBA world junior middleweight champion Julio Cesar Vasquez, a fight you lost by unanimous decision.

This was my first time staying in Europe. Before that, I would come a week before the fight. This time, we decided we were going to stay there a full month and train over there. In training, I had worn my shoes down. So before the fight, I had to put a new sole on the bottom of my boxing shoes and they weren't compatible with the boxing ring. When they paint it and it gets wet, if you don't have the right sole, you'll slip. That's what kept happening. I was slipping and sliding and couldn't get my balance. But if you watch the fight, I was killing Vasquez. If they hadn't given me all those knockdowns, I would have won the fight.

This was my first time going twelve rounds. I had never gone past eight before. He didn't hurt me, but I was tired. I was exhausted. The last two knockdowns, he just pushed me down. I accept that loss, but that fight right there let me know that I could be a world champion. I was just doing boxing for the fun of it, but that was a world class fighter and I felt that I beat him on my worst night.

You won your first world title in May 1996 when you defeated WBO world junior middleweight champion Bronco McKart via split decision.

When I won the world title from Bronco, I was like, okay, I'm a world champion. But it was the WBO. It wasn't the WBA, WBC, or IBF. Those were the key belts. The WBO was new. I wanted one of those other belts. It felt great, but I wanted to be a *real* world champion. If you want to be the best, you need the other belts. I saw "Sugar" Ray Leonard having all those belts and I wanted them, too.

In December 1999, you lost a majority decision to IBF world junior middleweight champion Fernando Vargas in what was your highest profile fight up to that point.

Vargas had been knocking everybody out, and they were expecting me to stick and move and run. But I changed my game plan on them. That was the first time I stood there and fought. In any fight before that, I always boxed. I would stick and move like "Sugar" Ray Leonard, but I was having problems getting on the networks. They were like, "They're not hitting you. It's not exciting." I thought that's what it was supposed to be. I'm supposed to win and not get hit, but they wanted to see a fight. So, I changed my game plan right there on national TV just to give them some excitement, and they cheated me. I definitely know I won the Vargas fight. That was all politics. They were looking past me, and I came out and shocked them. That's the bad part of boxing. It's frustrating that you can beat somebody and they just take the decision.

In March 2004, you defeated Shane Mosley in a junior middleweight unification bout via unanimous decision. You put your IBF title on the line, while Mosley was defending his WBC and WBA titles. That night, you became the undisputed junior middleweight champion and you were recognized as an elite level fighter for the first time in your career.

Everybody's got a chance to shine one time in their life. When you get that time, you've got to do it. That was my time. When I got there, I had trained hard and there was all this stuff built up inside me. I had been cheated before and I was like, if you're gonna lose, you're gonna die in this ring. I won all the belts and that was another good thing for me. It wasn't just one belt, it was *all* the belts. That right there showed me that I came a long way. I was an undisputed champion.

In November of that year, you defeated Mosley in a rematch by majority decision. In May 2005, you moved up to middleweight and won a unanimous decision over former multi-division champion Felix Trinidad.

Before the Trinidad fight, we saw Tito just destroy Ricardo Mayorga. Everybody knows Mayorga is tough. He's strong, he comes straight forward, and Trinidad just

Winky Wright mixes it up with Shane Mosley in their 2004 rematch (courtesy Bret Newton—ThreatPhoto.com/Pound4Pound.com).

dismantled him. Everybody was like, "You're fighting Tito? That's a tough fight. I don't know if you should do that." Me, myself, I like fighting the best. The best brings the best out of me. True champions want to fight the best. I looked forward to that and I was ready.

This was my first Pay-Per-View fight. We did press tours, and me and Tito became friends during the tour. It was kind of hard for me to really want to hurt him, but I knew he had a heck of a punch. I didn't want him to catch me with that punch. Once I knew I was winning the fight and I knew he couldn't hurt me, I just kept the jab on him and moved around. We knew what we had to do. It's a business; it wasn't anything personal. Me and Tito became friends before the fight, but we became *good* friends after the fight.

You followed the Trinidad fight up with a unanimous decision over Sam Soliman in December of that year. In June 2006, you fought to a split draw with Jermain Taylor, who was defending his WBC and WBO world middleweight titles.

I clearly beat Jermain Taylor. In the first couple rounds, I got in there and just worked. I knew he was strong and that he was going to try to throw that right hand. Once I started getting inside him, I hit him with more punches. He threw one or two big punches at a time. They weren't landing clean, but they were giving him the rounds. You got to connect. I was jabbing him, working his body, I got his eyes closed.... When we got to the twelfth round, I was just moving and keeping him off, because I thought he was going to come out wild and try to score a knockout. He didn't do that, though. He didn't do anything.

How did you give him the twelfth round? I did more than he did. People say I lost the fight because I took the twelfth round off, but a fight is supposed to be judged round by round. You can't go back and erase the scorecards. If you were gonna cheat me, you were gonna cheat me in the first place. I'm telling you we got to stop letting these judges judge these fights. People train hard to come in there, and win, and give it their all. It doesn't matter who the favorite is. If you win, you deserve to win.

I could have done more in boxing. I could have broken records. If they hadn't cheated me with Jermain Taylor, I would have been the undisputed junior middleweight champion *and* middleweight champion at one time. I never lost my junior middleweight belts; I gave them up.

After the fight with Jermain Taylor, I felt like I didn't want to do this no more. I was tired. I was ready to get out. That's why I took so long between fights. I couldn't get the fights I wanted. They were offering me fights with people I never heard of and I couldn't get up for those fights. I had to move up two divisions to fight Bernard Hopkins. He was supposed to be bigger than me, and all he did was head butt and hold. When I fought Paul Williams, I was like, who is Paul Williams? He was a welterweight. Why am I fighting him? What does this mean to me? That was the only fight they were giving me. If I didn't fight him, I wasn't going to get a fight that year or the next year.

They say I'm the one who was always turning down money, but I was always the one getting the less amount of money in every fight. People say, "Why didn't you

Winky Wright and former world light heavyweight champion Chad Dawson, who was in training for his 2011 bout with Bernard Hopkins (courtesy Bret Newton—ThreatPhoto.com/ Pound4Pound.com).

take the rematch with Jermain Taylor?" They say I asked for too much money, but they only offered me $300,000. Why would I take $300,000 when we just fought for a million and I beat you? They knew I was going to say no. They made me an offer, but they didn't give me a *legit* offer. This is a great game, but it's so corrupt. There are a lot of young fighters who aren't educated and need money, and there are people taking advantage of them. It's hurting the sport.

In June 2012, you lost a unanimous decision to Peter Quillin, who later won the WBO world middleweight title. Shortly after the Quillin fight, you announced your retirement.

The last couple of weeks before the fight, I hurt my hand and I couldn't hit the bag. I didn't feel ready, but I couldn't postpone it. I said to myself, "If I don't fight this fight, I'm done. Period." Plus, the training killed me. I should have stayed in shape when I wasn't fighting. I guess I was too old to train like that. It wore out my body. I gave everything I had to make the weight and I felt flat. When I got in the fight, I could see what he was doing, but my punches just wouldn't come off. I thought maybe I just needed a couple rounds to shake it off, but I couldn't get anything going.

I had a hard time getting up for this fight. I'm saying to myself, "Who was this kid?" I had never heard of him before. I'm glad he's winning now. I have nothing but respect for him for getting in the ring, but it was hard for me to take a fight like that. At the end of my career, I was doing it just to be doing it. I was doing it for the wrong reasons. People were telling me I was too young to retire, but I didn't have it in me to do it no more. But I was never gonna be one of those fighters who shows up, and gets knocked out, or doesn't even try. I always gave it everything I had. I always wanted to stand for something that was good. When I got to that point where I felt I couldn't be what I was redeeming, I said that's it.

When I became undisputed at junior middleweight, that division was the hottest division in boxing. Go look at junior middleweight in 2004. When I won the titles, everybody either moved to 160 or 147. Everybody in those weight classes would blow up when they fought Oscar De La Hoya—Shane Mosley, Manny Pacquiao, Floyd Mayweather.... They got their name when they beat him. I was the only one in their group who beat the guys that he lost to. I did it on my own and I know that God was with me the whole way. No matter what, He stayed behind me, pushed me, and gave me the heart.

When the fans came to see me fight, they always knew that Winky Wright was gonna give it his all. My grandmother gave me the name Winky when I was two months old and it stuck with me ever since. All through school, nobody called me Ronald. Even the teachers called me Winky. I should have changed it legally, but I never did. People get confused sometimes about what they should call me. I say, "Just call me Winky." It's always been that way—Winky Wright. Hopefully that name goes down in history.

3

Ivan Robinson: Fight of the Year

"How many guys do you know who would get beat up, cut, eyes shut, and still fight? I don't know many. I know one, but I don't know many."

In 1998, former IBF world junior lightweight champion Arturo Gatti was looking to bounce back from a loss. He had just been defeated by Angel Manfredy by eighth-round TKO, though he was still considered one of the best fighters in the lightweight division. In order to get back to his winning ways, Gatti's team sought an opponent who would be a safe bet.

Born and raised in Philadelphia, Pennsylvania, "Mighty" Ivan Robinson was one of the top amateurs of his time, having a career that included a stoppage victory over Sharmba Mitchell and three competitive fights with Oscar De La Hoya, which he lost by decision. As professionals, Mitchell won the WBA world junior welterweight title and De La Hoya was a multi-division champion.

Robinson turned professional in October 1992 and remained undefeated in his first twenty-three bouts, before losing a unanimous decision in December 1996 to IBF world lightweight champion, Phillip Holiday.

Inspired by his idol, "Sugar" Ray Leonard, Robinson always dreamt of having one night where he could show the world what he was made of—where he could rise to the occasion and give the fans a night that they would remember for years to come.

On August 22, 1998, with Philadelphia trainer English "Bouie" Fischer in his corner, Robinson's dream came true. That night, he defeated Arturo Gatti by split decision in what turned out to be the Fight of the Year in '98, as well as the biggest upset of that year.

After beating the odds the first time, Robinson went on to win a unanimous decision over Gatti in a December 1998 rematch.

Having faced the likes of Emanuel Augustus, Israel Cardona, Angel Manfredy, Antonio Diaz, Vivian Harris, Jesse James Leija, Michael Stewart, and Julio Cesar Chavez, Sr., Robinson retired in 2008 with a record of 32–12–2, 12 KOs. This interview took place over the phone in July 2013.

When did you first put on the gloves? How old were you and what were the circumstances?

We're gonna have to give away my age, but I don't care. I ain't that old. My dad took me to the gym in 1976. I was five years old. My dad said I was a little Energizer Bunny. I would hit the bag, run around, hit the bag, run around, hit the bag.... After a while, a young man by the name of Johnny Settles asked my dad if he could train me. My dad said, "Yeah, 'cause he don't listen to me." He grabbed me, took me, and we started working. From '76 to '79, I developed as a boxer. In '80, I started having amateur fights. I used to beat everybody here in the Philadelphia area and in the state of Pennsylvania, but I wasn't old enough to go nowhere.

My first national trip was in '86. I went to the JO nationals in North Carolina. It was the first time I ever got on an airplane. When they called my name to get on the airplane, my mom and dad didn't go. They were just sitting there looking at me. I said, "I have to get on this plane by myself? You must be crazy!" I cried my little heart out, but I had to go because I had to meet my team. My mom and dad talked to one of the flight attendants, and she stayed with me the whole time. She let me have soda, water, peanuts....

We eventually got to North Carolina and I got off the plane and did what I had to do. I beat everybody up to the finals. When I got to the finals, I fought a kid from Tacoma, Washington. He was the '85 JO national champion. We fought a real, real close fight. He told me after that I was a good fighter and that he expected good things from me. Who would have guessed that me and him would turn out to be great friends?

As a young kid, I wanted to do so many different things. My dad let me try every sport there was—football, baseball, basketball.... I tried every sport except for tennis and hockey. Boxing was the sport I was best at. My mom and dad's basement is filled with so many boxing trophies, it's crazy. Boxing was something that was good for me. It propelled me to be the man I am today. My mom didn't want me to do it, but my dad was the man of the house. They had great communication though. As long as my mom made sure I did right in school and came home and did my chores and ate that day, I was allowed to go to the gym with my dad.

One day in elementary school, I was acting up and being bad. The teacher called the house and told my mom, so my mom called my dad at work. They never even told me. The next morning, I got up to get dressed. My dad used to always have my clothes out for me, but that morning I looked at my clothes and I was like, "I'm supposed to wear this?!" He had me wear a pair of slacks, a short sleeve-shirt, a short-sleeve sweater, and these Converse shoes which were known as "Bobos." I had to wear that because I was a class clown. The kids made fun of me and I cried all day. When school let out, I was the first one home. Kids nowadays think that what they do now is mean, but they don't know nothing about when I came up.

When I was little, I was the smallest kid in the gym. Everybody called me "Mighty Mouse." They were making headgear with our names on them. We couldn't fit Mighty Mouse on the headgear, so we just put "Mighty." From then on, they just started calling me "Mighty."

In '86, I turned open and I went to Washington, D.C., to fight in a regional tournament. That was the first year I fought Sharmba Mitchell. He beat me that year. He had fought in the nationals the year before, and was good, and had a lot of experience. After the fight, I said that I was going to knock him out the next time we fought. The next year, I went to DC again and who did I have to fight? Sharmba Mitchell. I knew he was a great fighter and it was going to be a tough fight, but I was up to the task. My dad and Mr. Settles trained me hard, and I went out there and we stopped him!

I also had three great fights with Oscar De La Hoya. For a guy to be so young, and for me to never be on a stage that was so high, the Oscar fights put me there. Oscar was a young up-and-coming amateur and I thought I was better than him. I didn't get to beat him, but people that know boxing know that I showed a lot. Those fights said a lot about me and about the city I'm from.

Philly is a big fight town and my dad was a big boxing fan. Growing up, I heard all about Bennie Briscoe, "Cyclone" Hart, Tyrone Crawley, Matthew Saad Muhammad, Joe Frazier.... We looked at them like icons, which they are. I used to see these guys every day in the gym. It's good to be in those lanes with those guys and to share that we grew up in the city of Philadelphia.

What led to your decision to turn pro?

Honestly, it was in '87 when I saw Leonard–Hagler. I was just so amazed by what Leonard was doing. He was my idol. I loved him to death. When I met him in '88, it was just crazy. I knew around that time that this was what I wanted to do. I knew I was going to turn pro. I didn't know when it was going to happen. I was never worried about how much money I was going to make. I just wanted to be in the spotlight like Leonard. My time came in '92. I had two options. I could have been an alternate for the Olympic Team and spar with the number one guy, or just turn pro. So, I decided to turn pro.

There was a gentleman by the name of Eddie Woods, who was like me and my dad's shadow. He was always around us since I was about fifteen. He was like, "I like your son. He's going to be a great pro. All I ask is that when he gets ready to turn pro, please give me the first shot to manage him." When I got ready to turn pro, we had a couple offers. Top Rank wanted us and the Duvas were pressing us hard, but my daddy is a man of his word. Eddie knew with me being a top amateur that it was going to cost him a little money for us to turn pro with him. He gave me more money than I had ever seen before and he became my manager.

We also had another manager named Cassie. She was a millionaire. She owned Margaret's Kitchen in Jersey, which was a big cake factory. If you see my fights, she always wore a cowboy hat into the ring with us. Her and Eddie helped me get to bigger and greater things. In my first pro fight, I had a first-round knockout. By '95, I was 20–0 and I was already fighting for my first USBA title. I didn't expect my career to move as fast as it did, but I was loving it. I was fighting regularly, I was living good, I was married.... Everything was great.

At what point did English "Bouie" Fischer begin training you?

Bouie didn't come along until '97. I knew Bouie my whole life. Bouie Fischer, Quinzell McCall, Jimmy Archer, "Slim" Jim Robinson—all those guys were the great trainers in Philadelphia. When I was kid, Bouie always thought I was going to be a great fighter. It's kind of ironic how we started working together. He happened to be in the same gym as me at the time. Champs. He was training Bernard Hopkins, and they were on like a cool down because it was hard for Bernard to get fights.

Bouie was coming into the gym every day. I was getting ready for Arturo Gatti and I needed a trainer. I needed someone who wasn't just going to be there for the pay. I needed somebody who was going to work with me—somebody who knew me and knew how to beat Arturo Gatti. Bouie Fischer was definitely that guy. Bouie knew boxing and he was more than just a trainer. He was a friend. He was a father figure. He told me things that I needed to do to win.

In December 1996, before your first fight with Arturo Gatti, you lost to IBF world lightweight champion Philip Holiday via unanimous decision. In July of the following year, you lost to Israel Cardona by third-round TKO. At this point, it appeared that you were not a threat to a world class professional. Tell me about your August 1998 fight with Gatti.

One thing everybody knows about me—I never sugarcoat anything. Everything I do and everything I talk about, I always tell the truth. Before the fight, Gatti had just fought Angel Manfredy. I thought he was on the verge of beating Manfredy, but they stopped it because he was bleeding so much. For his next fight, they wanted somebody who was gonna be an easy fight—somebody who wasn't gonna be a threat that he could just knock out in a couple of rounds. I always gave my manager permission to put me in the mix and make fights. That's just me. I'll fight anybody. I'll fight a dude in his backyard if they wanted me to.

One night, Eddie called and said he needed to come over and talk to me. He sat me down and said, "I got a fight for you." I said, "How much is the fight for?" He said, "$51,000." At the time, I'm looking at it like it's good money. I figured it would just be some guy we beat. I said, "Who are we fighting?" He said, "Arturo Gatti." I said, "Who?! You're not talking about 'Thunder,' are you?" He said, "Yes." I said, "Oh, my God! Okay, let's go!" We took the fight and people were like, "Your manager is trying to get you killed. That's a bad fight for you." I said, "Okay, no problem. If you think I'm gonna get beat, go buy a ticket and see!"

Trainer English "Bouie" Fisher and Ivan Robinson after Robinson's 1998 Fight of the Year with Arturo Gatti (courtesy James Akhir Fisher).

At press conferences before fights, I never ever got into confrontations with any of my opponents. For this one, I did. When I spoke, I said that Arturo Gatti is a good fighter and that it's gonna be a great fight. He got up on the podium and said, "He can't beat me. I bring guns to a fight, he brings knives." I didn't know what he meant by that. What do guns and knives have to do with it? I was puzzled the whole time.

As we got back to Philly to get ready for the fight, I said to my partner, "Yo, what did he mean that I bring knives and he brings guns?" He said, "Well, he's a puncher and he said he can knock you out at any time." I said, "What did he mean by I have knives?" He said, "You just have quick hands, but you can't hurt him." I was like, "Oh, okay. No problem. I got you." I thought about that the whole time I was training.

When we were in camp, all we did was box, box, box.... Hit and not get hit. That was the plan. But the night of the fight, right before we left to go to the ring, something just hit me—BOOM! I'll never forget it. The guy told us it was our time to go, but I was like, "No, wait a minute." I said to my team, "I just want you to know that I love you all and I know you all love me. But this ain't gonna be no boxing match. I'm gonna go in there to kill him!" Everybody was like, "No, no, no.... Wait!" That was the last thing they ever said to me. When I got into that ring and they announced my name and put my mouthpiece in, I said, "That's it. This is war!"

Gatti was gonna have to kill me. I knew he was a great body puncher and that's what he was gonna do to try to slow me down. I knew I was gonna have to take a lot of punishment to win, but I didn't take as much as I thought because I was quicker than him. I hit him four times for every one time he hit me. But when he hit me with that one, it hurt. It was life-threatening. It was one of those nights where you have to rise to the test. I was always the guy who could rise. I rose to the occasion that night and that fight put me where I needed to be.

I always dreamt that somewhere in my career, I would have one of those fights that people would talk about. Honestly, I thought it was back when I fought Oscar De La Hoya those three times. I didn't think it could get no better than that, but the Gatti fight was a thousand times better. After the fight, Larry Hazzard walked up to me and said, "Man, you did a hell of a thing tonight." I was so overwhelmed with the performance I had done that I didn't care what anybody said. The judges could have been wrong, but I still felt that I fought a great fight. Even with a loss, it still would have been a fight that everybody talked about.

The ring announcer said something about "Fight of the Year." I didn't hear him when he said it. I didn't even notice it was such a good fight till I saw the tape. People were surprised, but I already knew what I could do. My team knew what I could do and my manager knew what I could do. If he didn't, he wouldn't have made the fight—not with a dangerous guy for that little money any goddamn way.

The night of the fight, I sat and talked to Gatti down at the bar. He told me he was sorry for what he said about the guns and knives. I understand that he was just trying to hype things up, but at the time I didn't know. I wasn't into making threats and insults to people. Way before the fight, me and Gatti were friends. We were in different training camps together. We went to movies, went shopping, hung out....

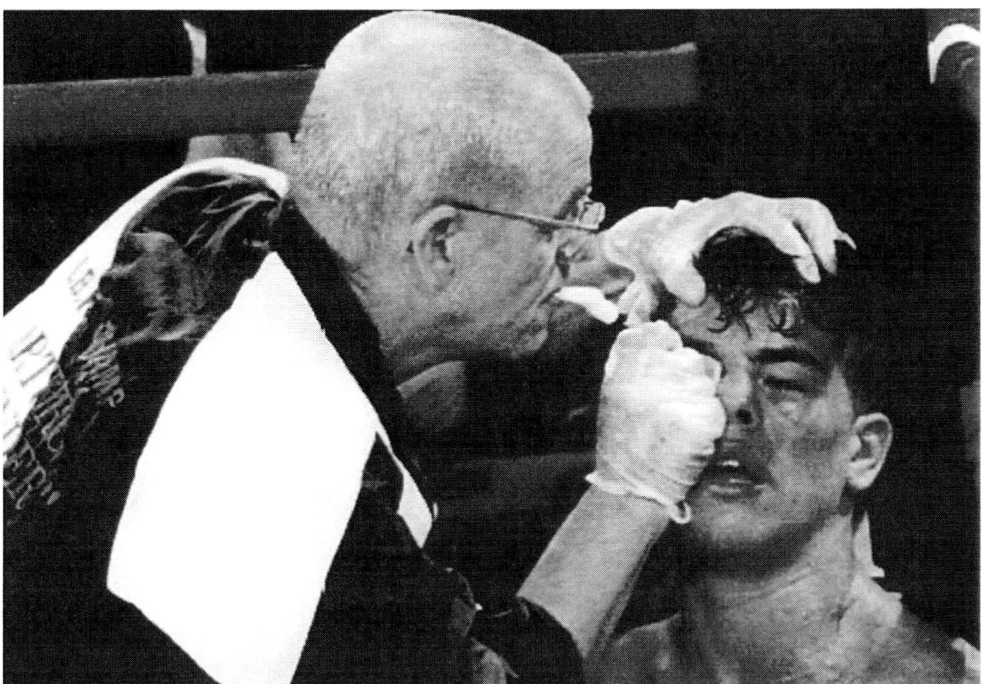

Former world junior lightweight and junior welterweight champion Arturo Gatti sits on his stool between rounds as cutman Joe Souza goes to work, 1990s (courtesy Rick Perez).

I look at Gatti like an icon. He gave me a shot when nobody else would. He gave me the opportunity to do the things that I always wanted to do. But I had to dig down deep to do it. I may not have dug as deep as Gatti, though. God knows that Gatti always dug down deep. I think there were times when he dug to the bottom of the Earth in some of his fights. I don't think I could have ever, ever, ever dug that deep. Gatti did, though.

How many guys do you know who would get beat up, cut, eyes shut, and still fight? I don't know many. I know one, but I don't know many. He had a lot of hard roads in his fight game and he's the king of coming back. I'm always gonna commend him till the day I die. I'm always gonna love him.

When I heard that Gatti died, my whole world came to an end. I was upset by the things that were being said about him. They were saying that he killed himself, but I knew Gatti as a fighter. For Gatti to kill himself, that just wasn't in his repertoire. Gatti was Gatti. He didn't have any quit in him. He would have never done that.

Me and Gatti fought on the same card once. I fought Juan Negron. That was my first ten-round fight. Gatti was the main event. Me and my daddy took pictures with him. Who would have thought that me and Gatti would have fought back then? Nobody.

When I started in boxing, the fight game was real tight. People really loved to come to the fights and I was just happy to be a part of that era. I had a great amateur and professional career, but I don't like to toot my own horn. I'm a humble dude.

I'm only talking about it now because you asked me. You'll never see Ivan Robinson bragging about himself. No, sir. I have a son, Ivan Robinson, Jr. He plays basketball and that's where I'm at. When he was born, I told his mom that he's never gonna look at a pair of gloves. I know what I had to go through and I never wanted him to go through that. Being a basketball player is good enough for his daddy.

4

Jose Antonio Rivera: The Rooster

> "Roosters fight until they can't fight anymore. Sometimes it's to the death. That was my mindset going into all of my fights."

The idea of winning a world championship belt is often a motivating factor for a kid to get into boxing. They see their idols putting belts around their waist, dreaming that one day they will do the same. Sometimes these belts inspire so much desire that kids are able to turn their whole lives around, finding a sense of discipline and accountability that they never had before.

Born in Philadelphia, Pennsylvania, later relocating to Worcester, Massachusetts, Jose Antonio Rivera was once an orphan in the streets. Without any parents to look after him, he would get into fights, abuse drugs and alcohol, and bounce around from home to home.

Despite the fact that Rivera's life was heading in a bad direction, he always declared that he would one day be a world champion boxer. As a kid, Rivera was only familiar with boxing because he watched it on television. But at age fifteen, he walked into a boxing gym and began taking the first steps toward his goal.

After a brief amateur career, Rivera turned professional in November 1992. Having won the majority of his bouts as he climbed the ranks, he captured the vacant WBA world welterweight title in September 2003 with a majority decision over Michel Trabant. In April 2005, he lost his title to Luis Collazo via split decision.

In May 2006, Rivera moved up to take on WBA world junior middleweight champion Alejandro Garcia, sending Garcia to the canvas five times en route to a unanimous decision victory. In January the following year, Rivera lost his title to Travis Simms by ninth-round TKO.

In addition to the aforementioned fighters, Rivera has also faced Teddy Reid, Robert Frazier, Patrick Byrd, Frankie Randall, and Daniel Santos.

Rivera retired in 2011, but returned to the ring in 2018. As of this writing, Rivera's most recent fight was in 2019 and his record was 43–6-1, 25 KOs. This interview took place over the phone in August 2011.

When did you first put on the gloves? How old were you and what were the circumstances?

Boxing was something I was attracted to when I was eight years old. My mother was a single parent. She left my father when I was about a year and a half. One time when my parents had an argument, my dad got mad, and grabbed me, and threw me off the bed. I had a cut on my head, so DFS (Division of Family Services) came in and took all the kids away. I ended up in an orphanage.

At that point, my mom had to decide if she wanted her kids or if she wanted to stay with my dad. She decided to be with the kids. My dad moved back to Puerto Rico, so I was living with my mom, and my uncle, and my cousins. We used to watch boxing on TV. There was something that intrigued me about seeing a fighter win a world championship belt and put it around his waist. When I saw that for the first time, right away, I knew it was something I wanted for myself.

When I was ten, my mother passed away. At that point, I lost all of my dreams and desires. I lost all of my hope. My life was over and I didn't think I was going to make it. Between the ages of ten and fifteen, I got into a lot of trouble. I quit school and roamed the streets. I was already an angry kid and I was fighting a lot. When we were living in Florida, my mom gave all the kids gold necklaces with their names on them, but I didn't get one. My mom said it was because I was always fighting. She said that when I got older and stopped fighting that she'd get me a necklace. A little while after that, she passed away.

Former world welterweight and junior middleweight champion Jose Antonio Rivera surrounded by team members, 2000s (courtesy Marty Rosengarten/RingsidePhotos.com).

At that point, I really didn't care anymore. I would live with an aunt and uncle, and then go and stay with another aunt and uncle. I smoked cigarettes, I was drinking, I was smoking weed, I had done cocaine, I tried mescaline.... I was just going in a direction that was taking me further and further away from my dream of being a champion. But even though I was up to no good, I still talked about boxing all the time.

When I was fifteen, a

friend of mine told me about this gym. We went there to check it out and the trainer there put us in to spar one of his best guys. Me and my friend went in there and we beat this guy. We just lit him up. That was my first time at a gym. When I was sixteen, I went to Worcester to visit one of my sisters. She told me about this other gym that was nearby, and she showed me this newspaper article that said how these local kids were doing good things and traveling all over the country.

I went down there, and talked to the trainer, and asked him if he would train me. I lived in Springfield at the time and I told him that I could come every weekend. He kind of laughed and told me that he couldn't help me if I only came on the weekends. But he said that if I lived in Worcester and came every day, he would definitely work with me.

That was all I needed to hear. I went home, packed my bags, and moved to Worcester. My goal had always been to become a world champion. But I knew that if I wanted to be a serious boxer, I couldn't be drinking and doing drugs and that type of stuff. So, I just stopped. It was easy for me. I never missed the partying, because I was living the life of a boxer. That meant running and training and eating good. At the time, I had no concept of what eating good was, but I learned. I wanted to know everything I had to do to be a world champion. This was a must. This was how it was supposed to be. There was never any question. From that point on, boxing completely took over my life.

I had a short amateur career, from sixteen to nineteen. My coach didn't put me in the novice division. He had me fighting open right away. He saw my heart and desire, and he wanted to test me. My first amateur fight was actually at the Harambee Festival in Springfield, Massachusetts. I was just walking by and I saw the ring. It was a thing where you show up and they match you by age and weight. I just jumped right in. I didn't care who they put me in there with. I just wanted to fight. I got in there and I ended up stopping the kid in the second round.

A couple fights later, my coach put me in with a kid who won the Golden Gloves the year before. I beat him, so he kept stepping me up every fight. In my fourth or fifth fight, I fought a kid who was ranked number three in the country. At the time, I didn't know the rules of boxing that well and I got disqualified for holding. That experience ended up hurting me in the long run, because I never held or clinched again. I never used any of those tactics in the pros. All I did was punch. In my final year in the amateurs, my third year, I started to get a lot of confidence in my boxing and I took a bronze medal at the PAL tournament in California. At that point, my coach let me turn pro. I wasn't a great amateur standout, but my coach knew I would be good in the pros because I had a pro style.

What stands out in your mind about your first few years as a professional?

At the beginning, they picked the right opponents for me. The guys I was fighting were in way over their head. When I was 7–0, a manager came into the picture. He thought I needed a big-time trainer, so he sent me to California to train with Jesse Reid. I had a little son at the time and I wanted to be a father to my kid, so my manager let me come back home. Sending fighters off to training camp is supposed to be a way of keeping them away from all of the distractions, but I never needed that kind of isolation. I always trained hard no matter where I was.

For me, boxing was breakfast, lunch, and dinner. There was no going out, no partying, no women.... That's how it had to be. That's what I needed to succeed. I wanted to win that belt and make my mom proud. I'll be the first to admit that I wasn't the most talented fighter in the world. I wasn't the fastest and I wasn't the strongest. But come fight time, I knew that the guy I had to face didn't work harder than me. He wasn't as hungry as me. He didn't want it more than me.

My nickname is "El Gallo." That means "The Rooster." In Puerto Rico, cock fighting is legal. My older brother and I used to help my uncle raise and train roosters, and prepare them for the fights. In one particular fight, one of our roosters was losing bad. He was on his belly, looking like he was about to surrender. The other rooster walked up to him like he was going to finish him off, but then our rooster jumped up and clawed the other rooster's throat. Roosters fight until they can't fight anymore. Sometimes it's to the death. That was my mindset going into all of my fights.

I remember the fight I had with Frankie Randall. At the time, he was trying to get back into the title picture. He was almost in the same boat I'm in now. I'm thirty-eight; he was thirty-nine. He was a veteran and he was doing things in the ring that I hadn't seen before. He caught me with some punches where if it had been

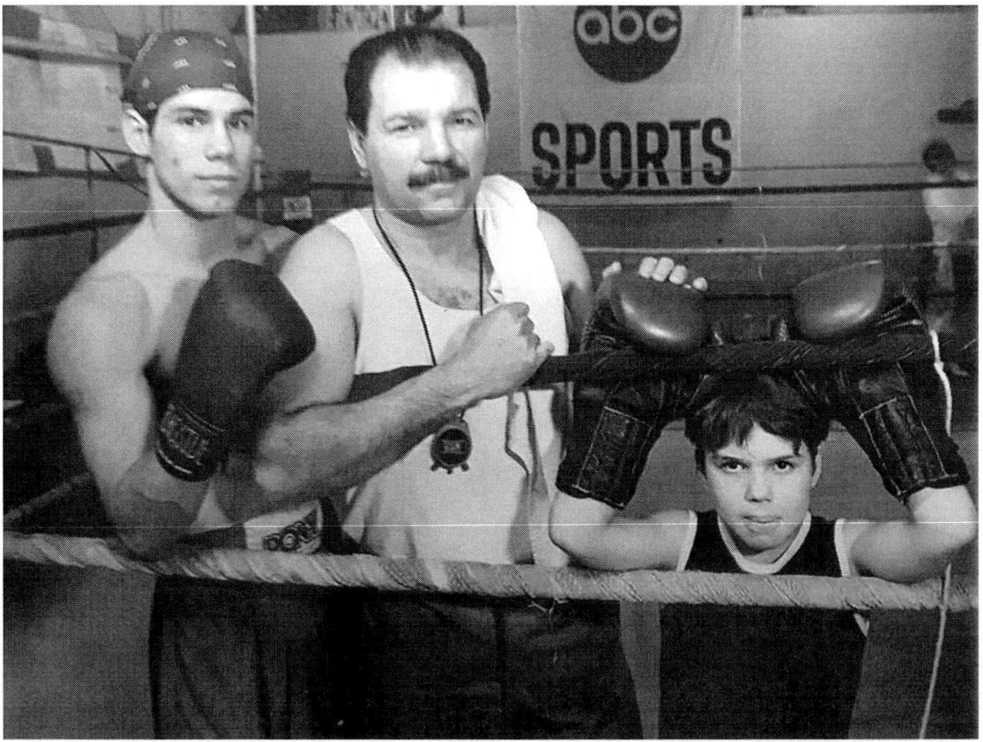

Jose Antonio Rivera (left), trainer Carlos Garcia, and a nine-year-old boy, Nicholas Aghapour, at the Ionic Avenue Boys & Girls Club, 1991 (courtesy Jose Antonio Rivera).

another fighter, he probably would have knocked them out. But my determination and my drive weren't going to allow that to happen. I just kept putting on that pressure, pressure, pressure.... In the tenth, I hit him with a combination. He went down and didn't get back up. To me, that's what I take pride in. I never gave up in the ring and I always put it on the line.

At one point in your career, you were promoted by Don King, which led to opportunities on a world-class stage. Tell me about that experience.

Being promoted by Don King got me to two world championships, but it wasn't a prosperous situation. I wasn't his top priority and I didn't get any big paydays. But winning a world title was all I really wanted out of boxing anyway. I was never the guy who was fighting for just the money. As I started to move up and get involved with some of these bigger fights, I really learned about the politics of boxing, especially after the Ricardo Mayorga travesty.

I was supposed to fight Mayorga at Madison Square Garden and defend my WBA welterweight title. I weighed in at 147 on the dot and he came in at 153 and ¾ pounds. We were supposed to go forward with the fight anyway. Since Mayorga came in over the limit, they were going to make it a ten-rounder. I was going to keep my title win or lose, but Don King already had Mayorga's other opponent at the weigh-in. He ended up fighting Eric Mitchell who was already there, waiting and ready. They knew Mayorga couldn't make the weight. That whole time, they strung me along. It's mind boggling how they got away with that. I was scheduled to make

Jose Antonio Rivera mixes it up with Larry Smith en route to a 2018 seventh round TKO victory (courtesy Jose Antonio Rivera).

$250,000 for that fight. Instead, they gave me a $50,000 settlement and half of it went to my manager.

I was out of the ring for over a year after that. When I came back, I lost a split decision to Luis Collazo. It got to the point where boxing wasn't that fun for me. I was having managerial issues, promotional issues, personal issues, and a lot of things all at once. Me and my manager went to court because I split with him. I didn't feel like Don King was sticking to his word, and me and my wife were going through a separation. After my fight with Alejandro Garcia, I started having problems with the WBA and I was in the middle of all these lawsuits. They were offering me no money for my fights and I just felt like I was being taking advantage of.

When things like that happen, no matter how hard you train, if you're not there mentally, it's all for nothing. I went from my best performance against Garcia to my worst performance against Travis Simms. I just didn't care anymore. This wasn't why I got into boxing. This wasn't what it was for. I wasn't going to keep going on like this, so I hung 'em up.

As you said, your best performance came in May 2006 when you defeated WBA world junior middleweight champion Alejandro Garcia by unanimous decision. Tell me about that night.

That fight with Garcia was the kind of moment I always dreamed of when I was a kid. For some reason, everything just came together for me. I made some changes before that fight. I got rid of some people I felt were holding me back and I put together the perfect team. John Scully was my trainer and I also had a conditioning coach from Boston named Radovan Serbula. Training camp went really good. I actually enjoyed being in the gym again. But what made things come together for me, what made my victory inevitable was that the day before the fight at the press conference, Garcia and his team made a big mistake. They brought the belt with them. Right then, right when I saw the belt, I knew it was my time.

My motivation as a boxer was always to win that belt. Every time I traveled as a pro, if there was a champion fighting that night, I would find a way to get into his dressing room so I could see his belt. I didn't want to meet him or get my picture taken with him. I just wanted to see his belt, because I knew that one day it would be mine. Throughout my whole career, throughout my whole life, people always told me I couldn't do it. That always drove me. I always believed in myself and I never lost that. It didn't matter what other people thought. When I saw that belt the day before the fight, it motivated me to put on the best performance of my career.

When I walked out of the dressing room and heard the crowd cheering, it was like that feeling I had when I first walked into the gym. It felt like I belonged there. It's what I was destined for. In the first round, I stuck my jab out there to put a stop to whatever he was doing, and I caught him flush. He went down, and from that point on, things just rolled for me. I was in the zone. I was flawless. I dropped him five times in that fight, including a knockdown in the final round. That was like an exclamation point.

When they announced the decision, I dropped to my knees and thanked God. After everything I had been through in my life, I saw my dream come true in the

Jose Antonio Rivera with friend and former trainer John Scully after sparring each other in 2018 (courtesy John Scully).

ring that night. It's something I can't even explain and I never felt like that again. It's easy to give up on yourself when you think the world is keeping you down. There were times when I thought my life was over, but I always knew that something better was waiting for me. I always believed that. I'm an orphan from the streets who wasn't afraid to dream. For some reason, God saw it fit to bless me.

5

Dwight Muhammad Qawi: The ABC Plan

"I had plans for my life, but boxing for some reason just pulled me to it. It wouldn't let me go. I didn't find boxing; boxing found me."

Destiny is defined as a hidden power that is believed to control what will happen in the future. It's a questionable idea, considering the variety of choices people face. But sometimes a person has their entire future mapped out, yet life pulls them in another direction.

Born in Baltimore, Maryland, later relocating to Camden, New Jersey, Dwight Muhammad Qawi, formerly known as Dwight Braxton, didn't put on the gloves till he was a young adult.

After serving around five years in prison for armed robbery, Qawi intended to get a formal education. He had only a casual interest in boxing, but it was boxing that kept showing up in his life.

Qawi started his professional career in April 1978 at age twenty-five, with no amateur experience. Nicknamed "The Camden Buzzsaw," Qawi built up a record of 15–1-1 before defeating WBC world light heavyweight champion, Matthew Saad Muhammad, via tenth-round TKO in December 1981.

Qawi defended his title three times before losing a unanimous decision to WBA world light heavyweight champion Michael Spinks in a March 1983 unification.

In July 1985, Qawi captured a world title in a second weight class with an eleventh-round knockout of WBA world cruiserweight champion Piet Crous. He defended his title twice, before losing a split decision to Evander Holyfield in July 1986. Later in his career, Qawi competed at heavyweight.

In addition to the aforementioned fighters, Qawi also faced Johnny Davis, Theunis Kok, Mike Rossman, James Scott, Jerry Martin, Eddie Davis, Leon Spinks, George Foreman, Everett Martin, Robert Daniels, and Nate Miller, retiring in 1998 with a record of 41–11-1, 25 KOs. This interview took place over the phone in January 2012.

When did you first put on the gloves? How old were you and what were the circumstances?

I put the gloves on when I was fourteen or fifteen. I was just messing around, slap boxing in the streets like kids do. Sometimes we didn't even use gloves. We were just kids acting like we were boxers. I had a lot of street fights, but I was never serious about boxing. Boxing was just something that kept coming into my life. I'd meet somebody and they'd show me how to hold my hands. I'd meet somebody else and they'd show me how to throw a left hook. People just kept introducing me to it. I wasn't one of those kids who stayed in the gym since he was fourteen. I didn't plan on making a career of it.

I had the ABC Plan. Plan A was to go to college. Plan B was to have a trade. Plan C was boxing, but my C Plan became my A Plan. I did a little time when I was younger. When I was nineteen, I was locked up and I had my mind made up that I wasn't going back to prison. I had plans for my life, but boxing for some reason just pulled me to it. It wouldn't let me go. I didn't find boxing; boxing found me. When I was in prison, I'd hit the bag, and hit the speed bag, and run around the yard. It was just something to pass the time. Sometimes I'd spar a little. One time, I was laying in bed and a friend of mine asked me to get in the ring with this guy. They were having a little tournament. They needed somebody and he begged me to get in. So, I went in there and knocked him out in the first round, and went back to my bed and went to sleep.

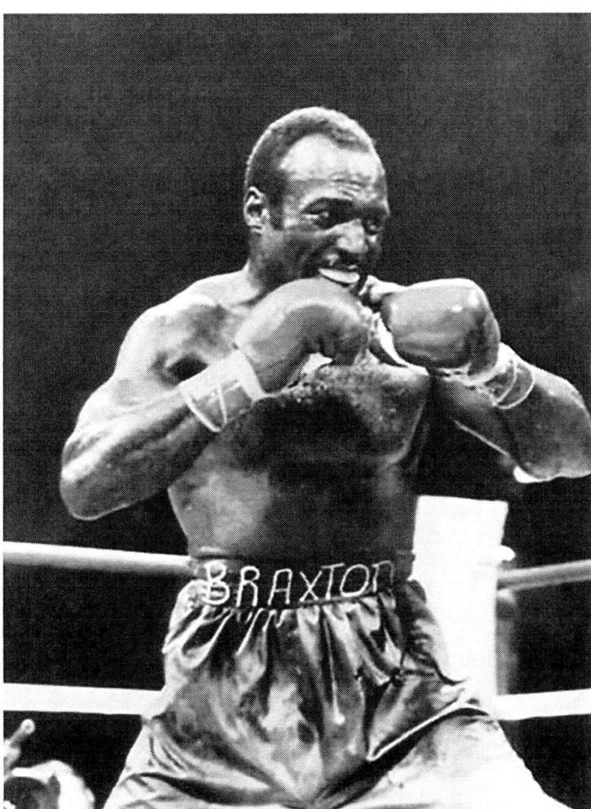

Former world light heavyweight and cruiserweight champion Dwight Muhammad Qawi, born Dwight Braxton, early 1980s (Boxing Hall of Fame Las Vegas/ Official Boxing Gods).

I was about twenty-five years old when I was released from prison. I entered programs where they help you get a job and a career and all that. When I was out, this guy saw me, who I knew from back in the day. He knew I could fight, because he had seen me street fight. He told me I should start boxing and he took me to Joe Frazier's Gym. They eventually put me in the ring, and they challenged me and dared me to come back. I came back every day and I was always competitive. They were watching me and helping me a little bit.

After about a month, they said, "Do you want to have a fight?" I said I did. They told me that I was too old to do the amateurs, so they asked me if I wanted a pro fight. I said, "I don't care. I'll do it." Before you know it, they were calling me "The Camden Buzzsaw." I got the name because I fought with a lot of aggression and a lot of ferocity. I'd chop them up. I was a 5'7½" light heavyweight and I was knocking people out. Three and a half years after my first fight, I became champ.

In February 1980, with a record of 5–1–1, you faced Theunis Kok in his homeland of South Africa. He was 8–0 and you were brought there as an underdog, but you won by tenth-round knockout.

I believe in destiny. I believe there are certain things that are meant to be. That night, it was materializing. I didn't know it at the time, but that's what it was. I couldn't have planned it better. All I did was stay in shape. That's an old adage in boxing—just stay in shape. My trainers told me that all the time. They told me that opportunities would present themselves, but I had to be ready. If you're not ready when that opportunity comes, you'll miss it. I was ready. I was on top of my game. When I was in South Africa, it just happened for me. The fighters of today could learn a lot from the fighters of my time. In my day, you had the Marvin Haglers and the John Mugabis. They trained hard back then and they had skills. They were hungry. I think boxing meant more back then than it does today.

After three and a half years as a professional, you captured your first world title in December 1981 with a tenth-round TKO of WBC world light heavyweight champion Matthew Saad Muhammad.

I knew that fight was coming. I beat Mike Rossman and I beat James Scott, so I knew I was going to fight one of the Muhammads. I wanted to fight Matthew Saad Muhammad and Eddie Mustafa Muhammad, because they were the champions. I didn't care which one. My camp for that fight was only for like three weeks. It was a low-budget training camp. They set up a little place for me and I stayed by myself. I'd get up in the morning and run. Come back. Rest. Go to the gym and train. Training and resting. That's what it was. I was just focused, because I knew it was going to be a tough fight. I knew I was going to have to take some to give some.

I did a lot of learning before this fight. My trainers Wesley Mouzon and Quinzell McCall did a lot of inside stuff with me to get me ready. They showed me how to do certain things, how to get around and slide. They had been trying to show me how to do these things two or three fights before this. I struggled in the gym and looked bad when I was doing it, but I liked learning and I was a good student. On the night of the fight, it all came together.

I was always shorter than my opponents, but I beat these bigger guys with my jab. I wish I did more of that. In the beginning I did. That's what I did with Saad in the first fight. I took his jab away with my jab. I'd slip to the left and come up. They thought I was going to throw a hook, but I threw a jab. It was a *hard* jab! I'd take their head off with my jab! You've got to be able to slip. You can't just dip to the side, 'cause they'll time you. You gotta slip the punch and come up—BAM! It's like hitting them with a 2 × 4. Cus D'Amato saw me one night and he said, "I've got this boy I'm training. You've got to see him. I have him watching your fights and I'm showing him what you're doing."

The fight with Saad was an intense fight. Before that, the guys I fought would always punch themselves out, but I knew I had to be prepared. That was my mindset.

I acted like I had to go thirty rounds with this guy, because no matter what I did, he kept coming back. He was always coming back. Even in the tenth when I stopped him, he was coming back. That was a hard fight, but the rematch I had with Saad was the best fight of my life. I went to California and ran in the mountains. I was the champion, so I had better accommodations. I was ready for that one. I couldn't miss. I was in great, great shape and I stopped him sooner the second time.

You defended your title three times, including a sixth-round TKO of Matthew Saad Muhammad, before facing WBA world light heavyweight champion Michael Spinks in a March 1983 unification bout which you lost via unanimous decision.

My nose was broken before that fight with Michael Spinks. I was in there with an amateur and my trainer said, "Stop playing with him! Make him respect you! Hit him!" I should have been more defensive, because he stuck a right hand in there and broke my nose. I had a deviated septum and it was hard to breathe. It's like when you have a stopped-up nose. You can't get oxygen and you get tired quicker. If you see the fight, I buckled him in the fourteenth round. Somebody told me, "You had him!" I should have jumped on him, but I was pacing myself too much and I felt like I couldn't fight my fight.

We were supposed to have a rematch. I signed for the fight, but everything was going wrong at the time. My father passed away when I was in training and I was going through a divorce. I tried to block everything out and be mentally tough, but I wasn't feeling it. My head just wasn't right. Butch Lewis came to my camp and tried to tell me I had to do it. He was trying to force me, and I got mad and kicked over

Dwight Muhammad Qawi catches Michael Spinks with a right hand in their 1983 light heavyweight unification bout (Boxing Hall of Fame Las Vegas/Official Boxing Gods).

the spit bucket. I was real upset, so we didn't fight. After a while, I tried to get the rematch again. They wouldn't give it to me, so I moved up and became champion at cruiserweight.

In July 1985, you captured a world title in a second weight class by knocking out WBA world cruiserweight champion Piet Crous in the eleventh round. You defended that title twice before facing Evander Holyfield in July 1986, a fight you lost by split decision.

I knew Holyfield was going to be fast and I didn't want to match his speed. I was just going to walk him down and counter. One-two-three-four-five! Catch him and counter, catch him and counter.... I took his strength and I took his legs. He was almost dead around the fourth and fifth rounds. He was almost falling out, but after that he came back. He got a second wind and his second wind was stronger than his first wind. He was running from me and I was the champion. I landed the more telling punches. He was just pitty patting and running. I didn't know how they could give him the title when I was the aggressor, but what are you going to do?

I bet you're one of the only men in history at 5'7" to fight at heavyweight.

I knew another guy who was 5'6½", but that was way back in the day. I'm not really a heavyweight. I'm a light heavyweight, but I was having problems with my weight. It was natural, genetic problems. I used to walk around at 174, 179, but then I

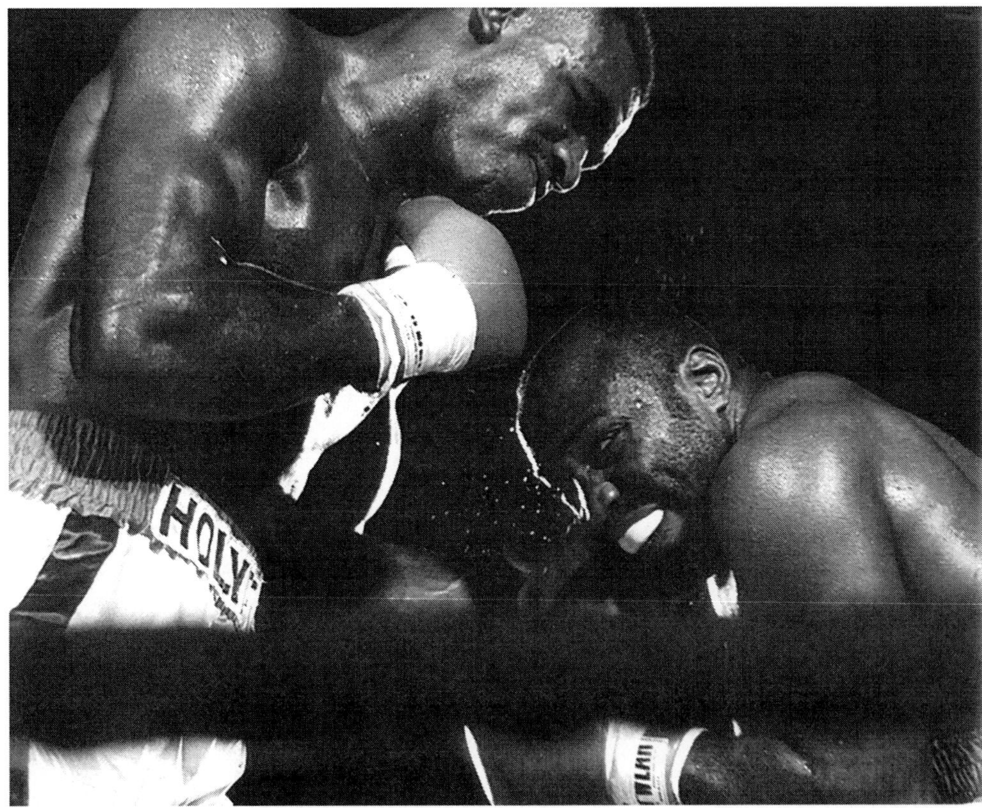

Evander Holyfield and Dwight Muhammad Qawi go to war in their 1986 encounter (Boxing Hall of Fame Las Vegas/Official Boxing Gods).

was walking around at 215, 220 and I was in shape. I would struggle and try to come down. I'd be at 202, but I was killing myself. I just got bigger and I was beating up on heavyweights in the gym, so I fought at heavyweight.

In March 1988, you lost to former world heavyweight champion George Foreman by seventh-round TKO. At one point during the fight, you staggered and looked as if you were about to go down, but then you quickly recovered and jumped on him with a flurry of punches.

I tricked him! That's from the street fighting. If I could have, I would have picked him up and thrown him down! I would have jumped on top of him and started beating on him! If you look at me in that fight, I was breathing hard. I tried to knock him out, but I punched myself out and I got tired. I only had two and a half weeks to train for that fight, but they enticed me with some money, so I took it.

You fought well beyond the fight with Foreman, even though you had nothing left to prove. Why did you continue fighting at that point?

I felt like I had missed opportunities. Even though I had become champ, I felt like I could have done it better. I wanted to come back and try it again. I got to the title in three years. People who come out of the amateurs don't make it to a title as fast as I did. Not back then, they didn't. I was just doing what I thought I was supposed to do, and suddenly, there was all the politics and the money and the craziness. That happens all the time in boxing. One thing my trainer said to me was, "Boxing makes strange bedfellows." That's what happened to me. People wanted to befriend me and do business with me. He was telling me how that was going to happen to me and he was right. I was very gullible. I listened to the wrong people and I made some big mistakes.

I had to come to terms with my life after that. Boxing was a way out. When I was nineteen, I made up my mind that I was never going back to prison and boxing helped me do that. It was a heck of a journey. With all the boxing I did, I'm still mentally intact. I'm in college now and I've got a career in counseling in front of me. I wanted to go to college all along. That was Plan A, and now I'm living the A Plan after all these years. That's the thing about it—we think our life should go one way, but God shows us another way. It's all in God's plan.

Why did you change your name from Dwight Braxton to Dwight Muhammad Qawi?

I'm a Muslim. When I changed my name, I was in touch with my excellence. That's what being a Muslim did for me. Religion helped me with that. It was in my heart. It was in my mind. The world was pulling on me. I had addictions, I had problems with my marriage.... All these things just made me weaker. Everything was fleeting. Everything was temporary, but the one thing that was real was my religion. I was so glad to be a Muslim. That's the ultimate reality.

I wish I could get a chance to live my life again, but I can't change what I did. All I can do is be grateful. That's what religion means to me. It doesn't matter if I'm champion or not. I'm proud of my name. Qawi means "all mighty and all strong," but only God is all mighty and all strong. I just possess some of those attributes. Not only strong physically, but strong in character. I'm "Abdul" Qawi. Abdul means "servant." I'm a servant of the all mighty and the all strong. That's how I live my life and that's how I fought my fight. Being a servant of the almighty and the all strong doesn't mean that you have a lot of money, or that you're better than anybody. It means that you worship God. When I die, it's going to mean more to me then than it does now.

6

Chris Byrd: Little Big Man

> "I went from being this super middleweight who wasn't going nowhere to winning the heavyweight championship of the world. God really did marvelous work."

Boxers in two different weight classes sometimes meet at a catchweight—a weight that is somewhere in between the limit that the two camps normally agree to. When negotiating catchweights, one or two pounds can be a deal breaker. But from the mid-1990s to the mid-2000s, there was a natural super middleweight willing to fight any heavyweight on the planet, sometimes giving up over fifty pounds.

Born and raised in Flint, Michigan, Chris Byrd won a silver medal at the 1992 Olympic Games in Barcelona, Catalonia, Spain as a middleweight, turning professional in January the following year in the 168-pound weight class.

Despite his Olympic accomplishments, Byrd found himself fighting in low-profile events that weren't advancing his career. With his mother and father as his trainers, Byrd jumped up three weight classes to heavyweight, facing men who had a significant size and strength advantage over him.

In April 2000, with a record of 30–1, 18 KOs, Byrd defeated WBO world heavyweight champion Vitali Klitschko, when Klitschko retired on his stool after nine rounds due to a shoulder injury. Byrd's first defense of his WBO title came in October of the same year against Wladimir Klitschko, Vitali's younger brother. Byrd lost the bout to Wladimir by unanimous decision.

In December 2002, Byrd defeated former four-time heavyweight champion Evander Holyfield via unanimous decision for the vacant IBF world heavyweight title. He defended his IBF title four times before facing former champion Wladimir Klitschko in April 2006, losing the bout via seventh-round TKO.

Throughout his career, Byrd has also faced Bert Cooper, Jimmy Thunder, Elieser Castillo, Ross Puritty, Ike Ibeabuchi, Maurice Harris, David Tua, Fres Oquendo, Andrew Golota, Jameel McCline, DaVarryl Williamson, and Alexander Povetkin, retiring in 2009 with a record of 41–5–1, 22 KOs. This interview took place over the phone in September 2011.

When did you first put on the gloves? How old were you and what were the circumstances?

I started boxing when I was five years old. My father had a gym in the basement of a school. I was just following the path of my older brothers, and my father, who was a journeyman fighter. He wanted his boys to box. And his girl, too. My sister boxed. At first, I didn't really have a crazy passion for it. I was just doing it to do it, but my father always told me, "You're gonna be good." I didn't really care. I'd go to the tournaments and just play around. My dad would take twenty of us kids to a boxing show and everybody had to weigh in. If you weighed in, you might get matched. I'd go off and play and my dad would be like, "You got matched. You gotta fight in a little bit, so go get ready." I'd be like, "Oh, okay." I'd go box, and win or lose, it didn't matter to me.

But after a while, I saw my brothers winning trophies and medals. They were traveling, and talking about their experiences, and getting free stuff. Watching them made me want to get to a higher level. When I was fourteen or fifteen, I started to get pretty good. I had international fights before I was even at an international level. Boxing was so widespread back then. That's why boxers from the past had so much talent—because we had to fight every weekend.

I learned how to fight so many different styles as I was sharpening my skills. In the professional game, you got guys who avoid certain styles. But if you're the best, you fight the best. It doesn't matter what their style is. That's what my father taught us. When we were young, you could have brought any type of fighter to the gym and we'd have fought them. We fought everybody. That's how it was my whole career.

When I was younger, we lived in a trailer park area that was a mixture of black and white poor people. We moved to the city when I was fourteen. It was the so-called hood, but my parents weren't buying into that. They were the ones that decided how we were gonna grow up. My father was a no-nonsense guy. If we brought a friend to the house and he thought he was no good, he wasn't coming back. It was just like that. That's how my father did things. There was no back talk. We knew not to mess up, because we had to face our parents. I didn't know how bad our neighborhood was, because my parents made us concentrate on boxing.

Boxing was a bigger part of our life than school was. The talk in our house was always the next tournament. When I beat Evander Holyfield and won the title, I thanked my mother for being so hard on us. I had to thank her, because look where I ended up. The ladies

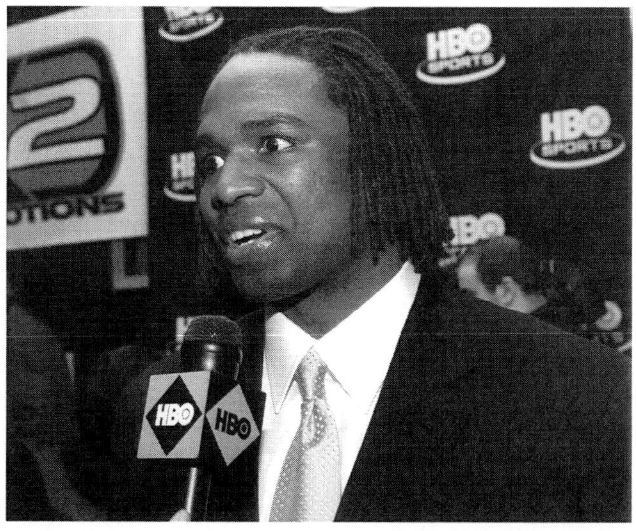

Former two-time world heavyweight champion and Olympic silver medalist Chris Byrd, 2000s (courtesy Marty Rosengarten/RingsidePhotos.com).

in my life pushed me to a whole new level. I got married when I was twenty-two years old. Tracy was my girl. I met her before all this boxing stuff. She knew me when I was broke. She loved me for me, and we love each other to this day more than we did back then. We cry together, we laugh together.... When I was boxing, she was always there ringside, standing in the corner yelling. She took care of me during the boxing and she still does to this day. That's just the kind of relationship we got.

From 1988 to 1992, I was ranked number one in the country as an amateur three out of four years, and then I made the Olympic Team. Before my final fight at the Olympics, they came up to me and said, "If you win the gold medal, you'll be the outstanding boxer in the Olympics." I was like, "Are you serious?!" I would have been the best amateur boxer in the world if I won that. Howard Davis was the outstanding boxer in the 1976 Olympics. Roy Jones won it in 1988, even though he got robbed in the finals. That's elite class and I wanted to be up there with those guys.

Oscar De La Hoya won his gold medal just two fights before me. He came into the locker room and he was celebrating. I was like, "I'm getting one of them!" But I lost. And it was so disappointing when I lost. I never cried after a fight, but I cried after that one.

Going into the third round, I knew the fight was close. After the third round, I looked over at Vernon Forrest, who was standing in my corner. He had this discouraged look on his face and he was shaking his head like I didn't get it. I was so distraught, but Vernon was my boy. He lost his first fight in the Olympics and he could have gone home like a lot of boxers did. But he stayed and pulled me all the way through it. When I was crying, he helped me put it into perspective. He said, "We trained our whole amateur career for this moment and I didn't get a medal. But you did. And you're crying." And I'm like, "Wow, you're right."

When I turned pro, my first two fights were at super middleweight. After that, I had one fight at cruiserweight and then I went right up to heavyweight. The move to heavyweight happened because something in my life had changed. We had some neighbors who were born-again Christians. My wife had a family member who died and she went to see them. They showed her the Bible and she gave herself to Jesus.

When she came home, I could see that something was different. She told me what happened and I was like, "That's not in my plan. My plan is to be champion of the world." But I started slowly going to church and thinking about the Lord. And then it all just came to me. I gave my life to Jesus Christ in 1993 and that's when my pro career *really* started. That's when I got the idea to go to heavyweight. It was just crazy. It was like the Lord said, "Son, I want you to go to heavyweight. You might not be the biggest guy out there, you might not be the richest guy, but I'm going to do great work with you."

After two fights at super middleweight, it looked like my career was going nowhere. I was a silver medalist, fighting in nightclubs. When I moved to heavyweight, that's when things started happening for me. Not everybody I was fighting was good, but they were big. I had to really study the game. I had to learn all of their habits. I watched all these heavyweights on TV from journeyman to champion, because I could end up facing one of them. I was a super middleweight fighting at heavyweight, and I hadn't felt that kind of power before. I had to be in the best condition possible to avoid that big punch.

My breakthrough fight came on the undercard of *Tuesday Night Fights*. I fought a guy named Waxxen Fikes. He fought in the '88 Olympic Trials at super heavyweight. I was 139 at that time, and there I was all these years later, fighting this big dude. It was scheduled for eight rounds and I stopped him in the fourth in such great fashion. People were like, "Look at this kid! Who's been hiding him?!" I made twelve hundred dollars when I fought on *Tuesday Night Fights*. In my next fight, I made ten grand. In the next fight, I made twenty. In the next fight, thirty. I was like, "You gotta be kidding me! How is this rolling like this?!"

My first fight on HBO was against Jimmy Thunder and I stopped him in the ninth round. At one point in my career, I was one of the most talked about heavyweights. Some of it was good, some of it was bad. A lot of guys avoided me, because I was kind of tricky. They thought I would make them look bad. I was a non-puncher, so I beat guys with finesse. Speed, elusiveness.... My career was much more than I expected it to be. It was great. God took me from scratch. I didn't start off like other Olympians. I went from fighting in nightclubs as a super middleweight, all the way to winning the title at heavyweight. It was a blessing to get to that level.

Chris Byrd's father and trainer, Joe Byrd, Sr., 2000s (courtesy Marty Rosengarten/RingsidePhotos.com).

You remained undefeated in your first twenty-six professional fights, until you faced Ike Ibeabuchi in March 1999, losing the bout by fifth-round TKO. Tell me a little about that night and where you went from there.

With Ike, I just got caught. My strategy with Ike was to make him think. That's what I did in there. If I had you thinking, you were done. I think Ike was frustrated a little bit, because at one point he smiled at me. His cornerman Curtis Cokes was smart. He said, "Hit him anywhere. It doesn't matter where. Just hit him anywhere." Sure enough, I slipped into one of those big uppercuts.

After that fight, I was so distraught. I didn't even know where I was gonna go from there. But Lou DiBella was putting the fights together on HBO at the time. He knew I was willing to fight anybody and he said,

"I'm going to keep you in mind. Be ready, because you never know when the next chance will come up."

Sure enough, Donovan "Razor" Ruddock pulled out of his fight with Vitali Klitschko and I got the call. Eight days before the fight! I was in training for a guy named Adolpho Washington. He was like 5'11". I was just sparring with my brothers and moving around, and then I get a call to fight Vitali Klitschko! I didn't know much about him, except that he was 27–0 with 27 knockouts. I went to see my lawyer to get my passport, and he popped in this tape of Vitali Klitschko beating Herbie Hide for the title. And he knocked Herbie out so bad! I was like, "Whoooooooooa! That's who I'm fighting?! Oh, my goodness!"

The next day, I was in Germany. I hadn't been overseas since the amateurs, and there I was, fighting for the WBO belt on eight days' notice. I saw Vitali Klitschko and I was like, "This guy is huge!" I was used to fighting tall guys, but not 6'7". This was just crazy. It was surreal. When we got to the center of the ring, the crowd started laughing because of the size difference. I'm like, "Are they serious?!" He was so tall and so long, and I was getting hit with punches that I wasn't used to getting hit with. My brother came up after the second round and he said, "Walk him down. Make him miss and keep going forward." I couldn't box him from the outside. I couldn't hit him, so I started making him miss and walking to him.

After a while, the crowd started chanting my name. I felt like the black Rocky. As a lefty, I throw a really good left hand to the body. I call it, "I'll gut you like a fish." I hit Ike Ibeabuchi with that shot and I hurt him with it. But with Vitali, I'd hit him with it and he wouldn't even react to it. But in the fifth round, he grunted a little bit. I was like, "Ooooooooooh! I'm getting to him!" As the fight kept going, he started to wear down. After the ninth round, my lawyer was like, "I think they're quitting." I couldn't believe it! He actually quit! He had injured his shoulder, but come on! This is boxing! You're supposed to fight! Me, personally, I don't quit for nothing. I may be small, I may not hit hard, but I fight till the end.

Your fight with Vitali Klitschko was in April 2000. In October of that year, you faced his brother Wladimir in a bout you lost via unanimous decision.

Yep. I'm not gonna gripe about it. Wladimir beat me over twelve rounds. I even went to the wrong corner at one point, because my eyes were just about swelled up. This dude came in like a brick. When he took his shirt off at the weigh in, my father looked at me and was like, "Better you than me." It was horrible. He punches like three times harder than his brother. The dude can crack.

After that, I started training again and taking smaller fights. I wasn't sure where my career was going, but the Lord blessed me by putting me in the IBF tournament. It was a four-man tournament with me, David Tua, Danell Nicholson, and Maurice Harris. The winner was supposed to get a shot at Lennox Lewis. My first fight was against Maurice Harris. To be honest, I was more worried about Maurice than I was David Tua. Even my father had concerns about it.

Maurice was a guy who nobody wanted to fight. He had a slick style, he could box, and he could punch. You don't know what day you're going to get him on. He was off and on. If you got him on a good day, the dude could beat anybody. But I

Wladimir Klitschko and Chris Byrd promote their 2006 rematch (courtesy Marty Rosengarten/RingsidePhotos.com).

fought Maurice and I beat him. David Tua knocked out Danell Nicholson, so I was fighting him next.

Everybody thought I was going to get knocked out by Tua. They were just blatantly saying it. They'd tell me, "You're getting knocked out." I'd be like, "Okay, we'll see." Going into the fight with Tua, I started watching tape. My lawyer was like, "He's got a great chin, but nobody's hitting him to the body. Check him down there." Sure enough, if you look at the eighth round, I hit him to the body. I hit him good and he was gasping big time. When I beat David Tua, I was on such a high. I felt like nobody could beat me. I was so ready for Lennox Lewis. I told my lawyer, "Let's do this! Let's make the fight! I don't care what they offer me."

At the time, Lennox was supposed to fight Mike Tyson. Lewis–Tyson was way overdue, so I could respect that. Lennox beat Tyson and I was thinking that we were about to do this. But instead of fighting me, he gave up the IBF belt. He didn't want to fight me. But I'm gonna be honest about the whole situation. I really felt that I could beat Lennox Lewis. But could I have really beaten him? This guy was 6'5", 250 pounds. He was an Olympic gold medalist and he knew how to box. I had a hard time with guys who were tall and had a good reach. I could be arrogant and say that he ducked me, but to be completely honest, my chances of winning against that style would have been slim.

When I fought for the IBF title, I ended up fighting a guy who was more my size and that's Evander Holyfield. I got one of "The Big Three"—Tyson, Lewis, and Holyfield. When I fought Evander for the title, it was so much fun! I knew I was going to beat Evander. I wish I fought the Evander who was younger. He would have thrown more punches and I would have made him miss even more! It was an easy fight and it was the only time the commentators on HBO, particularly Larry Merchant, talked good about me. I have so much respect for Evander Holyfield. When I beat him, I felt like I could face the world. I had reached the mountain top and I thought I was going to run the division.

Winning the IBF title was the best time in my life, but it was the worst time after that. Before the fight with Holyfield, I was promoted by Cedric Kushner. Don King bought him out, which meant that I had to sign with Don. Being with Don King was hard. He never paid me what was right. He'd blame it on the networks, or he'd say he didn't have enough money. I had to sue him twice. It was always a major hassle. But one thing I liked about Don is that he's lived so much history. He promoted Muhammad Ali and all these great champions, and sometimes he would tell me about it. On a personal level, I can't say anything bad about the man. I actually pray for him often. But unfortunately, the business side of it wasn't always that good.

Don King, who promoted Chris Byrd throughout his IBF title reign, 2000s (courtesy Marty Rosengarten/RingsidePhotos.com).

You defeated Evander Holyfield by unanimous decision in December 2002 for the vacant IBF title. From 2003 to 2005, you defended your title four times, with a unanimous decision over Fres Oquendo, a draw against Andrew Golota, a split decision over Jameel McCline, and a unanimous decision over DaVarryl Williamson. In April 2006, you faced Wladimir Klitschko in a rematch, losing via seventh-round TKO.

Everybody had written Wladimir off at that point. He had been knocked out by Corrie Sanders and Lamon Brewster, but I'm a realist in this sport. I knew this was going to be my hardest fight. I was glad to have the opportunity and it was the best training camp I ever had. The problem was I threw my whole game plan out the window. I decided to take it to him. When the bell rang, I just went at him. I didn't care. I'm normally the most patient and calm guy, but I just lost my head. It was stupid. I was a little man trying to fight a big man's fight.

I should have gotten knocked out sooner than I did. He battered me bad, but he'd have had to kill me to make me stop. I wasn't going to quit. After the fight, my father chewed me out for fighting that way. That fight really hurt me. It hurt me personally. I didn't handle my business like I normally do and I felt like I let everybody down.

When you look back at your career, do you feel the move to heavyweight was the best choice?

People ask me that all the time. "Why didn't you fight at super middleweight or light heavyweight? Do you think you would have done better?" I couldn't imagine not being a heavyweight. There's no way I would take it back. It was such a blast. It was such a challenge. Because I'm small, I had to perform to perfection to win fights. These guys just punched so hard. Wladimir Klitschko is a monster puncher. David Tua hit hard. Ike Ibeabuchi was punching hard. Even guys like Holyfield hit hard. I experienced all different levels of power.

Going into a fight, I was always a little concerned. My plan was to avoid the big shots and make them think. If I made them think, I had them. I really miss it. When I first started, I couldn't have fathomed fighting all these big guys and winning a title. It was crazy. I went from being this super middleweight who wasn't going nowhere to winning the heavyweight championship of the world. God really did marvelous work. He took me all the way to the top.

7

George Chuvalo: Still Standing

> "In a way, getting my nose busted was my rite of passage. I realized then that most guys probably wouldn't do this. I told myself that I think I'm tough enough."

Many historians regard the 1960s and '70s as the golden age of heavyweight boxing. Some of the fighters in the division included Muhammad Ali, Joe Frazier, and George Foreman, plus a number of tough contenders. Among this crop of heavyweights, there was one fighter who faced almost every top guy around and never went down from a punch.

Born and raised in Toronto, Ontario, George Chuvalo turned professional in April 1956, fighting four guys in the same night as part of the Jack Dempsey Heavyweight Tournament.

Having won all of his bouts in the tournament by knockout, Chuvalo went on to face several notable names in his professional career, including Alex Miteff, James J. Parker, Mike DeJohn, Zora Folley, Doug Jones, Floyd Patterson, Oscar Bonavena, Buster Mathis, Jerry Quarry, Jimmy Ellis, and Cleveland Williams.

Chuvalo's first shot at a world title came in November 1965 when he lost a unanimous decision to WBA world heavyweight champion Ernie Terrell. His second shot came in March of the following year when he lost a unanimous decision to Muhammad Ali, who was defending his WBC world heavyweight title. In May 1972, Chuvalo faced Ali a second time in a non-title affair, losing via unanimous decision.

Chuvalo was only stopped inside the distance on two occasions, when he faced future heavyweight champions Joe Frazier and George Foreman. He retired in 1978 with a record of 73–18–2, 64 KOs.

After boxing, Chuvalo was devastated by the death of three of his sons: Jesse to suicide, and Georgie Lee and Steven, both to drug overdoses. He also lost his first wife, Lynne, to suicide, after Georgie Lee passed away. This interview took place over the phone in May 2014.

When did you first put on the gloves? How old were you and what were the circumstances?

When I was seven years old, I went to a confectionery store and I saw a magazine called *The Ring*. These guys had these big muscles. They were throwing punches and it made me want to be a fighter. I ran home and I said, "Mom! Mom! Get me a set of boxing gloves!" I finally got the gloves when I was nine or ten. They were lime colored. We had a big beige bag and we took it across the street to an unpaved parking lot next to a pasta plant. We called it "The Macaroni Field." I used to buy Wheaties and they had these sporting cards in there—baseball, football, basketball, and boxing. They offered boxing tips and sometimes the tips were by Joe Louis. He would say to fake the jab to the body and throw the hook to the head, and other tricks like that.

When I was about twelve, this teenager saw me hitting the bag and he said, "George, you're pretty good with your dukes. Why don't you go to a gym?" He told me about this gym that was in the basement of St. Mary's Polish Catholic Church. I went there and I just fell in love. I loved the smell of the gym, the sound of the speed bag.... It was right to my heart. When I started boxing, I never worried about getting hurt or knocked out. I never had those concerns that some people have. I always felt that I would be okay.

When I was fifteen, I sparred this guy who was twenty-four. He busted up my nose pretty good and there was blood all over the place. He had a fight coming up and his trainer said, "He needs the work. You think you can keep working with him?" I said, "Yeah, no problem." In a way, getting my nose busted was my rite of passage. I realized then that most guys probably wouldn't do this. I told myself that I think I'm tough enough.

Your pro debut came in April 1956. You entered a tournament, knocking out four opponents in the same night. What were the circumstances of this event?

I fought in what was called the Jack Dempsey Heavyweight Tournament. The idea was to find the next heavyweight champion. There were about sixteen or twenty guys in the tournament, and they came from all over the United States and Canada. You couldn't have more than six pro fights to enter the tournament. I was eighteen and I didn't have any pro fights at the time. I fought four guys that night. It was twelve minutes and thirty-six seconds of fighting. I won the tournament and Jack Dempsey said some nice things about me after the fight. He thought I had a good future ahead of me.

Former heavyweight world title challenger George Chuvalo, 1960s (Boxing Hall of Fame Las Vegas/Official Boxing Gods).

Less than two months later, you won an eight-round unanimous decision over Johnny Arthur, who had a record of 30–7. Was it common at that time for a fighter with your limited experience to take such a big step up in competition?

No, I was the exception to the rule. You're supposed to start at four rounds and slowly work your way up to eight or ten rounds. When I fought Johnny Arthur I was as green as grass, but my manager was ninety years old and he didn't have much time left on Earth. He was in a bit of a hurry, and he figured that if I could beat Johnny Arthur that I must have a lot of promise. Johnny Arthur was a South African champion, and he was in the top ten at one time, so it was a giant step for me. I didn't knock him out, but I handled him rather easily.

As your career progressed, you compiled a record of 14–2-1, before knocking out James J. Parker in the first round for the Canadian Heavyweight Championship in September 1958.

I had sparred Jimmy before. I could handle him when I was sixteen, and I had turned twenty-one just three days before the fight. I had more seasoning, so I didn't have any problems at all. Usually, I don't remember everything about my fights, except the knockouts. Since this one ended in a first-round knockout, I remember everything about it. I went out there and I threw a jab to his body. Next time, I feinted the jab. He dropped his right hand a little bit, and I threw a hook to the head and knocked him down. That was the first of four knockdowns. After that it was like a whirlwind—up-and-down, up-and-down, up-and-down.... The fourth knockdown was the last knockdown and they counted him out at exactly the two-minute mark.

In January 1964, you lost a unanimous decision to contender Zora Folley. What do you recall about that fight?

When I fought Zora, I had an ear infection. There was a boil in my ear and a bunch of pus was coming out. The day before the fight, the doctor gave me a treatment. I don't remember the name of the drug, but it made me dizzy and I just couldn't get out of my rut. I shouldn't have fought that fight when I did, but I don't like making excuses. Zora Folley was a damn good fighter anyway.

One thing about Zora Folley is you didn't have to go looking for him. He was a boxer, but he stood in front of you. He was very clever and he was hard to hit. He didn't hit hard, but he was very smart. My next big break came against Doug Jones. He had already knocked out Zora Folley and a lot of people thought he beat Muhammad Ali. They had a ten-rounder back in March of '63 in New York, if memory serves me correctly. At the weigh-in, I heard Jones say, "Chuvalo can't fight." He was brimming with confidence, but I wore him out because I was just too big and too strong for him.

In February 1965, you lost a unanimous decision to former world heavyweight champion Floyd Patterson in what was considered the Fight of the Year.

The fight was very close. Some people thought I won, some people thought I lost. He won the last round, and apparently that's what won the fight for him. Floyd is a very likable person and he had a tremendous cheering section. He's a New York guy and we were in New York. Floyd usually comes straight forward, but he didn't do that with me and that kind of fooled me. We had a sparring partner from New York who turned out to be a spy. The lady at the front desk in our camp picked up the phone and heard him talking to a trainer in Brooklyn. He told this trainer that Floyd couldn't fight with me inside because I was too strong. With that information, they decided to move around the ring and I hadn't seen him do that before. He didn't do that with Sonny Liston and he fought Liston twice. Mind you, he froze with Sonny.

In November 1965, you lost a unanimous decision to WBA world heavyweight champion Ernie Terrell. However, most observers felt that you deserved the victory.

Everybody thought I won that fight. Even Muhammad Ali thought I won. It was a lousy fight, though. It's kind of hard to fight Terrell. He wasn't intent on fighting, he was intent on grabbing. All he did was jab and grab and hold. Ernie Terrell had the muscle behind him. Tony Accardo was his manager, but his manager of record was Bernie Glickman. Tony Accardo had a criminal record, so he couldn't *officially* be the manager. Bernie Glickman was a tough-talking guy. He came into my manager's office and told him that if I won the fight, he would end up in a cement box in Lake Ontario. The referee told me afterward that he was muscled before the fight. They told him that if I had won the fight that they would get him. I didn't talk to the judges, but I'm sure Bernie Glickman approached them, too.

In March 1966, you lost a unanimous decision to Muhammad Ali, who was defending his WBC heavyweight world title.

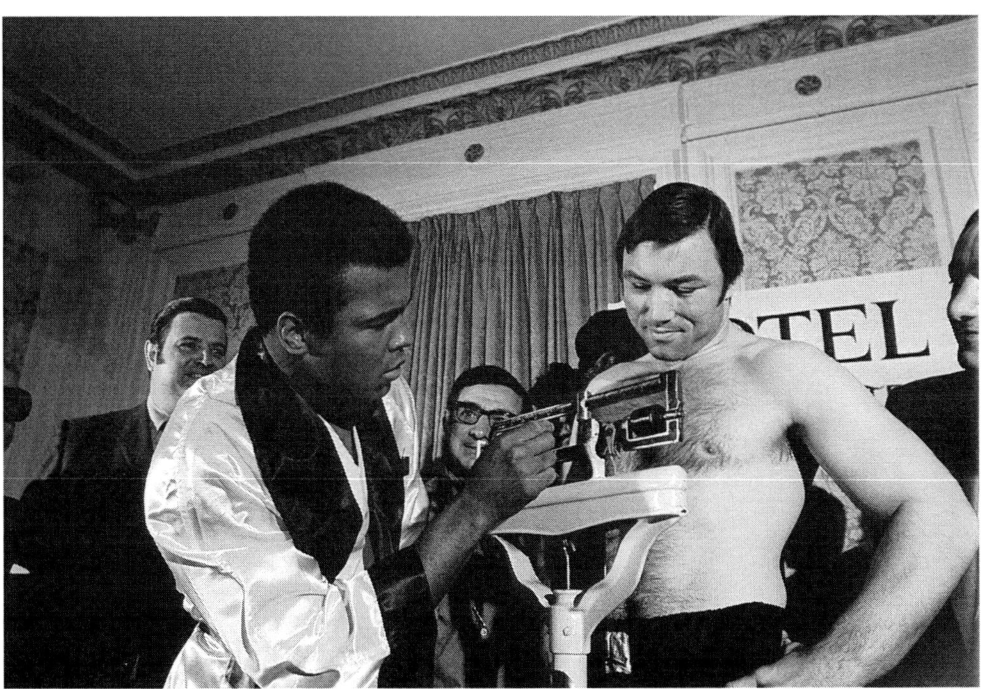

George Chuvalo stands on the scale as Muhammad Ali clowns at the weigh-in of their 1966 fight (Boxing Hall of Fame Las Vegas/Official Boxing Gods).

I took the fight with Muhammad on seventeen days' notice, because Ernie Terrell pulled out. His manager, Bernie Glickman, had been beaten up by the Black Muslims. Glickman tried to pull the same modus operandi with Herbert Muhammad, the son of Elijah Muhammad, who was the head of the Black Muslim movement in America. My manager was a pussycat compared to Herbert Muhammad. When Bernie Glickman tried the same threat that he did with me, Herbert Muhammad just snapped his fingers and the Muslims beat the living crap out of him.

I had met Ali once when I fought Mike DeJohn in Louisville. A few days before the fight, we had a press conference. Muhammad was there, and the promoter came up to me and said, "Cassius Clay is here and he has signed to fight the winner of your fight with Mike DeJohn. Will you sign to fight Clay if you win?" I said that I would, so they had us all take a picture.

Muhammad went into a pose as if he was flexing, so I grabbed one of his biceps and I decided to have a little fun with him. I said, "How're you doing, Popeye?" He looked at me and said, "Why are you calling me Popeye?" I said, "You must have some pretty big forearms, because your biceps are awfully small." He said, "Archie Moore talked that way! Sonny Liston talked that way!" I said, "Yeah, but that's not me." Not too many people got the edge on Ali speaking-wise, but I got the edge that day.

Ali saw my fight with DeJohn and I murdered DeJohn. After the fight, Ali said, "I'm not fighting Chuvalo. He fights rough and tough like a washer woman." I didn't know what he meant by that till I saw the fight twenty years later. I realized that when I had DeJohn over the ropes, it looked like I was using a washboard.

Ali was a lot quicker than anybody else I ever fought. His hands weren't faster than Floyd Patterson's, but his feet were quick. I knew he was fast, but when I saw it up close, it was kind of a shock. I tried to immobilize him by keeping him close to the ropes and away from the center of the ring. I would essentially try to have my left leg between both of his legs, and have my upper body at a forty-five degree angle, and have my head on his chest and apply pressure, so he couldn't move. If you give him the center of the ring, he's hard to trap, because he's so fast and he has such a long reach.

After the first fight, he went to the hospital with bleeding kidneys and I went out dancing with my wife. When I was dancing, I said to myself that I should have danced more in the fight!

Your 1966 fight with Muhammad Ali is what you are remembered for the most. But what fight in your career do you remember the most?

My fight with Jerry Quarry was the sweetest victory for me in a lot of ways. He was one of the better fighters around and I beat him. The judges had me behind in the fight. I didn't think I was losing, but apparently I was. I knocked him out with one second to go in the seventh round. Prior to the knockout, the referee was summoned to the corner by the doctor who advised him to stop the fight if my eye got any worse. My eye was swollen and closing, but they let me fight and I knocked him out with one second to go. If the bell had rung and I went back to my corner, the referee probably would have stopped it.

George Chuvalo sends Jerry Quarry to the canvas en route to a seventh-round knockout in 1969 (Boxing Hall of Fame Las Vegas/Official Boxing Gods).

In July 1967, you lost to Joe Frazier via fourth-round TKO. At the time, Frazier was a former Olympic gold medalist, who went on to win the WBC and WBA world heavyweight titles.

A month before the fight with Joe, I fought Archie Ray in Missoula, Montana. I hit him with a left hook to the body. When he went down, his head hit my cheek bone. As he was being counted out, my cheekbone started swelling. After the fight, I knew I was going to have trouble with my eye. I was swelling up in sparring and it never got better. I should have postponed the fight with Joe and been a little more forceful with my manager, but we were making a pretty good payday. In the third round, I got hit with a good left hook from Joe and my eye looked like a half a grapefruit. It was pretty damn big. I looked like a one-eyed Marty Feldman. You know who Marty Feldman was? He was a comic with bug eyes.

In the fourth round, Joe hit me with another left hook and my eye went through my socket. I was in extreme pain. The referee could see that I was distressed, so he stopped it. I'm lucky he did, because one more shot and I would have been blind. With most guys I fought, I never saw them again after the fight, but Joe and I became pals. One time, my phone rang and my second wife said that some guy named "Smokin" Joe was on the phone. She had no idea who he was! Joe was a real nice guy. Some guys can't believe I would be friends with somebody who did that to my eye, but that's boxing. You fight and then you're friends after.

In August 1970, you lost to George Foreman by third-round TKO. Foreman was a former Olympic gold medalist, who went on to win world titles at heavyweight in 1973, and again in 1994.

George was an Olympic gold medal winner and he had a lot of build up. A lot of good things were expected of him and it all came to fruition. I had seen George fight, and I was a little surprised when I got in there, because he started moving from the start. It was like my fight with Floyd Patterson. He was sticking and moving, and it caught me off guard. He got me to the ropes at one point, and he started throwing punches "out the window," as they say. I got hit with one good left hook and the referee stopped the fight. He said I wasn't punching back, but I thought he stopped it too early. I thought that then and I think that now. George had stamina problems in fights and he tired out quickly. I would have had a shot when he got tired, but we never got there.

In May 1972, you faced Muhammad Ali for a second time, losing a unanimous decision in a non-title affair. Over the next six and a half years, you defeated seven lesser-known opponents before hanging up the gloves. What ultimately led to your retirement?

When I hung 'em up, I was forty-one. In those days, forty-one was ancient. Nowadays, you've got Bernard Hopkins who is a forty-nine-year-old world champion. George Foreman was forty-five when he won the title again. At my age, I didn't think I could be that much of a contender anymore, so I quit on a winning note.

You faced some of the best heavyweights in the history of boxing and you never went down from a punch. After you retired from boxing, you faced a great deal of personal tragedy, with the death of three of your sons, as well as your first wife. How did you find the strength to stay on your feet?

That's a good question. All I know is if I had broke down and stopped being the patriarch of my family, a strong patriarch, a proper patriarch, I would have been doing a great disservice to the rest of my family, especially my remaining children and my grandson Jesse. My grandson Jesse and I are as tight as can be. I would never do anything to myself that would hurt him. I would never commit suicide, not that I've ever contemplated that. The thought crosses your mind sometimes when you're in deep despair, but I would never do that, mainly because I would be hurting other people.

My grandson is the one who is closest to me in my life right now. He's had to suffer the loss of his father, two uncles, and a grandmother. I wouldn't want to add to that craziness. It would take away all of his hope. It's hard to lose the people in your family, especially when you're young. I try to be as strong as I can for him. We're pretty good buddies for a grandfather and a grandson. We lift weights together, we have a nice meal after the workout, and we enjoy each other's company. He's the reason I'm still alive.

8

Caveman Lee: Runaway Child

"I didn't want to be a boxer, but I grew up *knowing* that I was going to be a boxer. It was like a nightmare come true."

Have you ever run from something that is painful or unpleasant, only to run right back because you thought you needed the very thing that caused you to leave? It's an illogical conundrum. Sometimes a person is damned if they do and damned if they don't.

Born and raised in Philadelphia, Pennsylvania, William "Caveman" Lee started his professional boxing career in February 1976 as a middleweight.

Lee was forced into boxing by his father, William Lee, Sr., who insisted that his children pursue careers in pugilism. He obeyed his father as best he could, but at times he was compelled to "run away," as the pressure and demands would get to him.

Under the management of Emanuel Steward, Lee relocated to Detroit, Michigan, and trained at the legendary Kronk Gym. While training in Detroit, Lee was involved in a few memorable bouts, including an all-action war with John LoCicero that he won by fifth-round knockout, and a challenge of Marvin Hagler's WBC and WBA world middleweight titles, which he lost via first-round TKO.

Lee's new home in Detroit gave him relief from his father, but something always pulled him back to Philadelphia. This cycle of running and returning led Lee down a dark path. He eventually found himself engaging in a life of drug abuse and bank robbery.

Lee retired in 1988 with a record of 22–4, 21 KOs. This interview took place over the phone in April 2016.

When did you first put on the gloves? How old were you and what were the circumstances?

I was indoctrinated into boxing from the start. My father bought me and my brother boxing gloves when we were little kids. You know those blow up things that have sand on the bottom, and you hit it and they bounce back up? I had Popeye and my brother had Brutus. I didn't want to be a boxer, but I grew up *knowing* that I was going to be a boxer. It was like a nightmare come true.

Boxing was the last thing on my agenda. I just wanted to be a regular guy. I played the flute when I was younger. All of us kids went to Settlement Music School in South Philly. I liked music and I wanted to try different things, but my father was a boxing fanatic. He was a dictator. He was Idi Amin in the flesh. He made us box and it broke our family up. He was harder on my brother Rick than he was on me, because I always did what I was supposed to do. Rick started running away. I started running away with him, because I wanted to make sure he was okay. My father would find us, and kick our asses, and take us back to the gym.

We went to this gym in Philly that was in the basement of Annunciation Church. It was at the corner of 12th and Diamond Street. "Skinny" Davidson was the trainer. Harold Johnson was down there. Ike White, Jimmy Young, Bobby "Boogaloo" Watts.... Those were the guys I came up with. I was sparring with grown men when I was thirteen.

I got the name "Caveman" when I was in the Boy Scouts. One of the kids, Bernard Carson, said I looked like a caveman because of my sideburns. My father heard it and he thought it was a good name for my boxing career. People call me Caveman more than they call me William. They think it's my real name.

Former middleweight world title challenger William "Caveman" Lee, 1980s (courtesy Dr. Stuart Kirschenbaum).

I went to Ben Franklin High School in North Philly. I was making bad grades and playing hooky, and I dropped out when they held me back in the tenth grade. I eventually joined the Army to get away from my father. When I got out of the Army, I was staying down in Georgia and hanging out, doing the wrong things. One day, I saw Jimmy Young fighting Ron Lyle on TV. I was always real cool with Jimmy Young. We came up together, and I was like, man, that could be me! So, I called my father and he bought me a plane ticket back to Philly.

I fought a couple of pro fights in Philly and I won them. But I was watching these other guys that I came up with and they were surpassing me. I sparred with all these guys and helped them get ready for their fights, but I wasn't making no money. In hindsight, I believe my father was getting paid by these guys and throwing me little pennies. I wanted to get away from him, so I signed a contract with Tyrone Everett's manager. He was a Jewish guy named Frank Gelb. When my father found out, he went ballistic and he got Frank Gelb to tear up the contract. But I still wanted to get away from my dad, so I went with Jimmy Young to Vegas when he fought Ken Norton.

Jimmy turned me on to his manager, really his *other* manager, which was Blinky Palermo. You heard of Blinky? He was a gangster that had done time. Jimmy Young had another manager, but Blinky was pulling all the strings. Blinky took me to a couple of restaurants in South Philly where he grew up, and he would tell me stories about back in his day when he used to have a machine gun and do drive-by shootings. He was an interesting guy, man.

Blinky introduced me to Don King when we were in New York. Don got me with his son Carl King, who became my manager. They sent me to Puerto Rico to spar with Carlos "Sugar" De Leon. I was 6–0, and living in Puerto Rico, and having a good time. Finally, they got me a fight at The Garden. I fought a guy named Don Addison. He was a light heavyweight. The day of the fight, I caught diarrhea. We were staying at a hotel in New York and they gave me some steamed prunes. It was only a couple of them, but I didn't know they were gonna give me the runs like that. Man, I was shitting all the way up to the fight! If it wasn't for that, I would have beat him. I lost a six-round split decision and it was my first loss as a pro.

After that I called my father, and he bought me a plane ticket back to Philly, and got me out of the contract with Don King. I don't know how, but he did. My father had a way of making people respect him. Growing up in Philly, the gangs tried to draft me. My father went over to the gang leader's house, and tore the house up, and smacked his mom around and everything else. My *dad* was the gang leader! I was scared of him and I would try to break away from him. You know that song "Runaway Child, Running Wild"? "Runaway child, running wild! Better go back home where you belong!" That was me. I was the Runaway Child. I always ran away from my father and then I would run right back. I figured he knew what he was doing, so I'll just do what works.

When you returned to Philadelphia, you had a record of 6–1. How did your career evolve from that point on?

I was training at Joe Frazier's Gym and my name started ringing around some of the boxing circles. There were a lot of people that wanted to manage me. One day, I got a call from Emanuel Steward. He offered me a fight at the Olympia Stadium in Detroit. I stayed in contact with Emanuel and I helped Tommy Hearns get ready for a couple of fights. Emanuel told me if I ever wanted to come back to just call him up. So, I did. I wanted to get away, so Emanuel sent me a plane ticket to Detroit.

I was basically a complete fighter when I went to Detroit, so there wasn't a whole lot Emanuel could teach me. He tried to mold me into his style, but he couldn't do it and I *wasn't* gonna do it. I was more comfortable fighting the way my father taught me. That's what worked. Emanuel would work the pads with me before a fight, but

Caveman Lee raises his hands in the air after his 1980 second-round knockout of Jamie Thomas. The referee and an unidentified man examine Thomas (photograph by Chris Cuellar, courtesy Dr. Stuart Kirschenbaum).

I was basically training myself. The problem is that I wasn't getting all the way in shape. A fighter needs somebody to push him.

After I lost to Frank Fletcher, I asked Bill Miller to train me. You know who Bill Miller is, right? He trained Dejuan Johnson and James Toney. Emanuel wouldn't pay him to work with me, so he stopped training me after one fight. But after he stopped training me, we were still friends. I used to go to his house and chill. He had this collection of jazz and classical music. It was so vast, man. Bill Miller was like one of the old-time trainers in Philly. Those trainers in Philly will get in their car and ride alongside you when you run. They made sure you were in shape. And if you weren't in shape, you weren't gonna fight. Bill Miller was one of the all-time greats. He put his all and all into the training.

One of your notable fights was a fifth-round knockout of John LoCicero in July 1981, which was regarded as one of the best fights that year.

Did you know that John LoCicero fought Tony Danza? Tony Danza was in that show *Who's the Boss?* He was a fighter before he was an actor. But I got in top condition for John LoCicero. The problem is that they cancelled it. Then they scheduled it for the following month and I had fallen out of shape. I couldn't waste no punches. I knew I wasn't gonna win on points, so I had to make sure everything I threw landed. That's what saved me.

After the fight, my dad came into my dressing room and cussed Emanuel out because of the way I fought. I told him, "It wasn't Emanuel's fault that I fought like that!" Then I told him it was *his* fault. I didn't ask to be a fighter. My dad made me box and I didn't want any of it. That fight with John LoCicero was a hard fight, man. I was shell shocked for about a year.

In March 1982, you lost to WBC and WBA world middleweight champion Marvin Hagler via first-round TKO. What stands out in your mind about that fight?

Marvin Hagler had come through Philly and beat all our fighters up. I wanted revenge. Emanuel told me I was going to fight Hagler after Mickey Goodwin fought him. You know who Mickey Goodwin is, don't you? That was my best friend, man. He was a good guy. He came from a good family and we're still in contact to this day. But Mickey hurt his hand, so Emanuel asked me if I wanted to fight him.

Let me tell you something—a boxer's heart is bigger than his brains. A boxer will fight anybody you tell him to. When you're a boxer, you need somebody who cares about you and that's going to look out for you. I didn't have that from Emanuel. He just kept me there to spar with Tommy. When I fought Hagler, I wasn't a hundred percent because of my fight with John LoCicero and I shouldn't have taken the fight.

How did your life and career unfold after the Hagler fight?

After I fought Hagler, I went back to Philly for a vacation. My cousin picked me up from the airport and he was freebasing. You know what freebasing is, don't you?

Former middleweight and light heavyweight world champion Bernard Hopkins (left) and Caveman Lee, 2007 (courtesy Bob Ryder).

He turned me on to that and I went through hell from 1982 to 2006 when I got out of prison for the third time. When my cousin turned me on to freebase, I had a lot of money from the Hagler fight and I got a big dose of that stuff. I was like Richard Pryor. I started with a big habit. I went through that money like white on rice. I got married that year, too. I had a beautiful wife named Francine and I messed that up. I went to prison for the first time in '84. I did a year and a half for bank robbery.

I got out in '86 and I started training again. I fought in downtown Detroit and I knocked the guy out. After that, I went to Italy to spar Donald Curry for his fight. Somebody dropped off the card and they asked me to fill in. But the thing is, I wasn't that guy no more. At one time, my body and my mind were one. My mind said go, my body said go. But in that last fight, my mind said go, but my body said no, so it was time to get out of the game.

I was staying in Philly at that time. And my pop, man, he had a way of talking to me and really putting me down. So, I stabbed him three times. I had to go to Philadelphia County Jail, but my father didn't press no charges. When I got out, I felt like

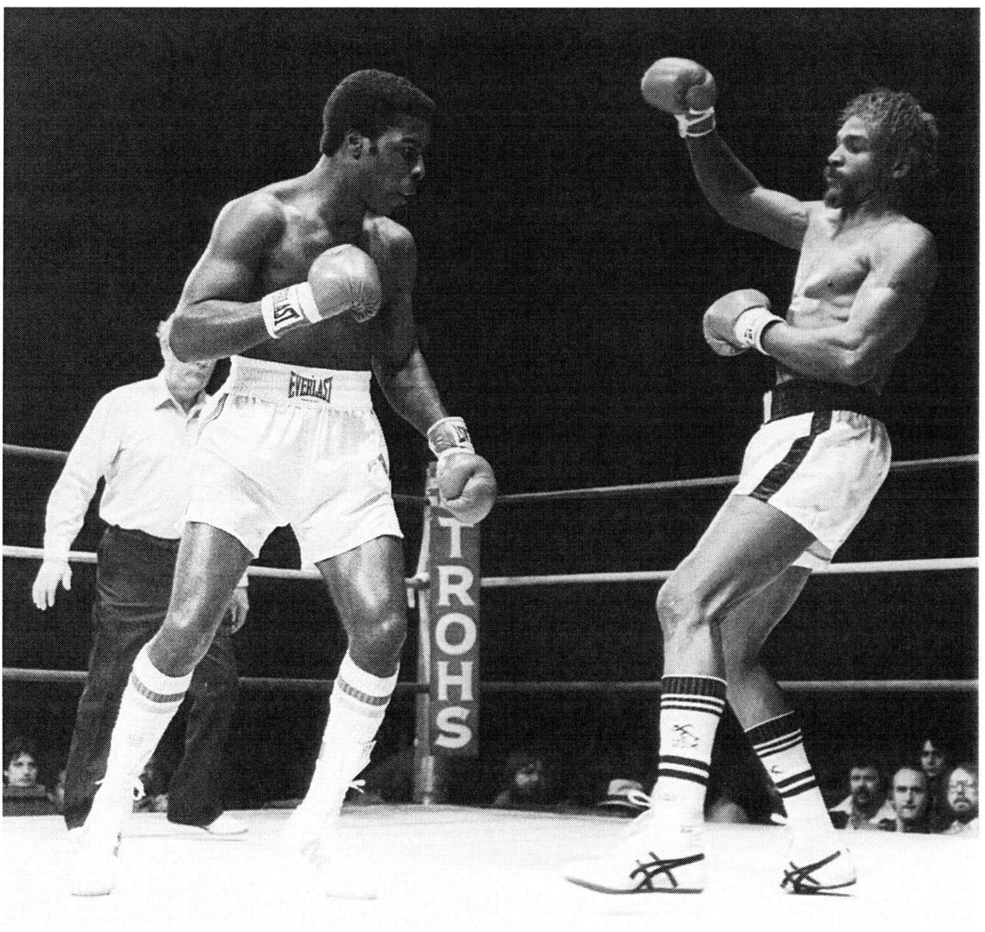

Caveman Lee has Costello King reeling en route to a 1981 third-round knockout (photograph by Chris Cuellar, courtesy Dr. Stuart Kirschenbaum).

he gave me more respect than he ever did. I think it was more fear than respect. He saw me as I saw him. I told my pop that I was going back to Detroit to try to be close to my daughter. This was the first time I left home and had his blessing.

The last time I went to prison was '93. It was bank robbery again. I did three bits, all for bank robbery. I had a gorilla on my back, but the Lord Jesus Christ delivered me from drugs. I was on the run down south. My second wife was with me, and she was smoking, too. We stayed with her friend. It was a lady named Mrs. Willie B. Marshall. She was an associate of Martin Luther King and God bless her soul—she laid hands on me, and prayed on me, and got me away from that habit.

I was gonna turn myself in, but I got caught by the police and they brought me back to Detroit. Thank God for my judges. I pleaded guilty and I told the judges that I deserved life in prison, which I did. I betrayed their trust and this was my third time. But my state judge said, "Mr. Lee, I don't know why I'm doing this, but I believe you deserve another chance. I'm giving you seven to fifteen years." My federal judge gave me twelve and let it run with my state time. I did twelve years with both state and federal, and here I am now. I'm clean. The devil had me by the balls, man.

Before my father died, I introduced him to the Lord Jesus Christ. It was on the phone when I was in prison. I introduced him to the Sinner's Prayer and it saved him. My family said he changed after that. My father forced me into boxing, but I met a lot of good people. I traveled around the world and had a good time. I don't know what I would have done in life if I had followed my own dreams. I don't even know what my dreams were. My pop gave me *his* dreams.

9

Evander Holyfield: The Warrior

> "Whatever he did to me, I did right back to him. If he hit me on the break, I hit him on the break. If he put his elbow under my neck, I had to put my elbow under *his* neck."

Boxing is a skill that is learned in the gym. But mastering the fundamentals is only part of what it takes to achieve at the elite level. In order for boxers to make it to the top, they need to have something inside them that can't be taught.

Born in Atmore, Alabama, later relocating to Atlanta, Georgia, Evander "The Real Deal" Holyfield set a goal of becoming the heavyweight champion of the world when he was eight years old.

Having established himself as one of the top amateurs in the United States, Holyfield fought as a light heavyweight on the 1984 Olympic Boxing Team. He emerged from the Olympics with a bronze medal, losing in the semi-finals via controversial disqualification.

Holyfield turned professional in November 1984. In July 1986, with a record of 11–0, Holyfield defeated WBA world cruiserweight champion Dwight Muhammad Qawi by split decision. He defended his WBA title three times before defeating IBF world cruiserweight champion Ricky Parkey via third-round TKO in May 1987.

Holyfield defended his WBA and IBF cruiserweight titles twice before defeating WBC world cruiserweight champion Carlos De Leon in April 1988 by eighth-round TKO, becoming boxing's first undisputed cruiserweight champion.

After the bout with De Leon, Holyfield relinquished his cruiserweight titles and moved up to the heavyweight division. In October 1990, Holyfield defeated WBC, WBA and IBF world heavyweight champion James "Buster" Douglas via third-round knockout, achieving status as an undisputed champion in a second weight class.

In three fights, Holyfield defended his WBA and IBF titles three times and his WBC title twice, before losing a November 1992 unanimous decision to Riddick Bowe. In November 1993, Holyfield defeated Bowe in a rematch by majority decision for Bowe's WBA and IBF world heavyweight titles.

In Holyfield's first defense of his titles, he lost an April 1994 majority decision to former world light heavyweight champion Michael Moorer. In November

1996, Holyfield won a world title at heavyweight for the third time by scoring an eleventh-round TKO over WBA world heavyweight champion Mike Tyson.

Holyfield defended his WBA title once before defeating Michael Moorer via eighth-round TKO for Moorer's IBF heavyweight title in November 1997. He defended his WBA and IBF titles once before facing WBC world heavyweight champion, Lennox Lewis, in March 1999. Holyfield's bout with Lewis resulted in a split draw, which led to a November rematch that year that Holyfield lost by unanimous decision.

In August 2000, Holyfield defeated John Ruiz via unanimous decision for the vacant WBA world heavyweight title, becoming boxing's first four-time heavyweight champion. Holyfield lost his WBA title to Ruiz by unanimous decision in a March rematch the following year.

Throughout his career, Holyfield faced several champions and well-known contenders, including James Tillis, Pinklon Thomas, Michael Dokes, Alex Stewart, George Foreman, Bert Cooper, Larry Holmes, Ray Mercer, Hasim Rahman, Chris Byrd, James Toney, Larry Donald, Fres Oquendo, Lou Savarese, Sultan Ibragimov, Nikolay Valuev, Frans Botha, and Brian Nielsen, retiring in 2011 with a record of 44–10–2, 29 KOs. This interview took place over the phone in May 2018.

When did you first put on the gloves? How old were you and what were the circumstances?

I started going to the Boys Club at the age of six. They had a boxing gym there. When I was eight, I saw somebody hitting the speed bag. I went through the gate and I saw an old man there. I said, "Hey, sir, can I hit the speed bag?" He said, "No." I said, "Why?" He said, "You have to be on the boxing team." I said, "Can I be on the boxing team?" He told me, "No." So, the next day, I asked him again and he said, "No." Then the next day I asked him and he still said, "No." On the fourth day, he saw me coming and he looked like he was going to say no, so I walked away. He turned his back on me, but I ran up there and asked him again. He said, "Yeah, come on in."

Once I got in, I wanted to hit the speed bag. He said, "No, that ain't the bag to hit. Hit the heavy bag." He told me to hit it as hard as I could. So, I hit that thing with my little fist and it skinned my knuckle. He started laughing, but I kept on hitting it, kept on hitting it.... He said, "Your hand is bleeding!" I said, "I know." And I kept on hitting it, kept on hitting it.... He said, "Oh, you're tough!" I kept hitting it and he said, "Stop! Stop!" I stopped and he said, "You're real good." I said, "Yes, sir." He said, "Do you know that you can be like Muhammad Ali?" I told him, "I'm only eight years old." He said, "You won't always be eight." I believed him, because the next week I was going to be nine.

He asked me, "What do you think about being the heavyweight champion of the world?" I said, "I've got to ask my mama." He said, "Don't you know you've got a good mama?" I thought to myself, this man don't know my mama. He said, "I'll tell you what. Go ask that good mama you've got and see what she says." I went home and said, "Mama, this white man at the Boys Club said I could be like Muhammad Ali!" She said, "What?!" I said, "Mama, I could be like Muhammad Ali!" She said,

"Do you know what they're gonna do to you?" I said, "What?" She said, "They're gonna hit you!" I was the youngest of eight, so I already got three whippings a day.

I went back to the Boys Club on Monday and I told that man, Mr. Morgan, that my mom said I could be the heavyweight champion of the world. He said to me, "Son, I ain't got that much time." Mr. Morgan was about sixty-four years old. He said, "Let me explain something to you. There's one thing called a goal and there's one thing called a fantasy. A goal is when you want to be something and you work at it. A fantasy is when you want to be something, but you *don't* work at it. Is this a goal or a fantasy?" I told him, "A goal." He said, "All right. On Friday, you have to fight."

We got to the fight and he said to me, "Here's your first instruction. You see that kid right there?" I said, "Yes, sir." He said, "As soon as that bell rings, you run out there as fast as you can and hit him on the nose. Do you understand?" I said, "Yes, sir." When I hit that kid on the nose, he started crying. They stopped the fight and they said that I won. Mr. Morgan held my hands up, and carried me around the ring, and told me that I just took my first step to being the heavyweight champion of the world. And that's how everything started.

How did you get the nickname "The Real Deal?"

"The Real Deal" started in 1983. I worked at this airport and my boss was a guy called David Booker. Back then, they talked on a CB. His name was "Papa Charlie."

Twenty-three-year-old Evander Holyfield and WBA world cruiserweight champion Dwight Muhammad Qawi, before their 1986 fight (Boxing Hall of Fame Las Vegas/Official Boxing Gods).

He said, "Man, you got to get a name." I said, "A name for what?" He said, "When you talk on the CB, you can't just be Evander Holyfield. You need a nickname." So, we came up with "The Real Deal." Real Deal Holyfield. People would say to me, "What's the deal, Holyfield?" I'd say, "Man, I'm the real deal!" When I got disqualified in the Olympics, they wanted to change my name to "Raw Deal." I said, "No, I'll just stick to 'Real Deal.'"

At the 1984 Olympic Games in Los Angeles, California, as a light heavyweight, you were disqualified in the semi-finals when you hit New Zealand's Kevin Barry while the referee called "break" in the middle of an exchange that left Barry knocked out. Most observers felt that the disqualification was unwarranted. You were favored to win the gold medal that year, but instead you were given the bronze. How did you feel about it?

Life is about how you deal with things. The first time I ever lost a decision, I was eleven years old and I started crying. My coach asked me why I was so mad. I said, "Because I lost." He told me, "You didn't lose." I said, "But they gave the trophy to *him*!" He said, "Yeah, but you didn't lose. You only lose when you quit. As long as you give it your very best, you're still a winner." If something didn't go my way, I never got discouraged. I always believed that things would turn out for the good.

I had a very good coach, who would never let me quit. And I had a very excellent mama. She would say, "Son, you got to take the bitter with the sweet." That's the reason I have a positive attitude today. In one of my last few fights, I lost a decision to this guy from Russia. Nikolay Valuev. Everybody was saying, "Man, you had to have won eleven rounds!" I should have been the five-time heavyweight champion of the world on that night. But you know what? I'm the only man who ever was the heavyweight champion of the world four times. So, I'm just thankful for the things I *did* achieve. Whether they gave me the decision or not, I always did my very best and that's it.

In July 1986, you defeated WBA world cruiserweight champion Dwight Muhammad Qawi by fifteen-round split decision. At that time, Qawi was already a two-division champion, while this was only your twelfth professional bout. Plus, you had never been past the eighth round before.

Before the fight, Qawi said, "I can't believe they would send a baby to do a man's job." Well, you know what? The baby won. That year, a guy named Tim Hallmark became my conditioning coach. This was a young guy. I was twenty-three, so he was about twenty-eight. The first thing this guy asked me was, "Do you pray?" I said, "Well, yeah." He said, "Let's pray together and ask God to help us do this thing." This guy worked me so hard and he got me in great shape. He had me doing things that boxers didn't do—the weightlifting, the stretching.... I was drinking all these different kinds of drinks. He was checking my heart rate and all this. He became a big important part of our team and we're still very close friends. If it wasn't for this guy, I don't know what would have happened. Maybe I would have won anyway, but it would have been a lot harder.

Everybody was saying, "Evander is gonna get killed." But I went the whole fifteen rounds and I became champion. I got Fighter of the Year, Fight of the Year.... Everything that you could win, I won in that one fight. I lost fifteen pounds in the fight and I had to go to the hospital. I felt so bad and I told my manager at the time, his name was Ken Sanders, I said, "I don't want to be champion no more. Here, have this belt!" He said, "Evander, I promise you, you will never fight a fighter as tough as that again." They showed the fight on TV the next day and I got a chance to see that great performance I put on—that Qawi *made* me put on. If he didn't put that much pressure on me, I wouldn't have fought like that. This guy would never stop coming.

In July 1988, you moved to heavyweight and remained undefeated, eventually facing former WBA world heavyweight champion Michael Dokes in March 1989. You defeated Dokes via tenth-round TKO, but it was a tough test.

My coach Lou Duva told me that this was probably going to be one of my easiest fights. People were saying that Dokes was on drugs and all that. I don't know if he was or not, but this guy was tough. I mean, he was *quick*! But I got him out of there and that fight showed that I was a legitimate heavyweight—that I can stand toe-to-toe with people. I'm strong for my size. I don't look strong compared to most heavyweights, but I am. That was the fight where we asked to fight Mike Tyson. We had it all planned out. After the fight, my manager Ken Sanders said, "We want to fight Mike Tyson—winner takes all!"

It's against the rules and regulations for a person to fight for nothing. For the Tyson fight, the minimum I could make was two million. Ken said, "What did you just get paid? 750?" He said, "We'll take the two million if you lose. But if you beat him, we're gonna get more!" So, Ken Sanders planted the bait. After that, we got so many bad write-ups. People were saying that Ken Sanders was gonna ruin Holyfield. But Ken knew I would win. I had sparred Tyson in the amateurs and he couldn't handle me then. He was the same guy as he was in the amateurs. It's just that he was getting more publicity because he was knocking everybody out. This was 1989, and it took people all the way to 1996 to realize that Ken Sanders knew what he was doing.

You were eventually in line for a shot at Mike Tyson, who was the undisputed heavyweight champion. But in February 1990, at the Tokyo Dome, Tyson lost to 42–1 underdog James "Buster" Douglas by tenth-round knockout in one of the biggest upsets in boxing history.

I went there with Dan Duva and Shelly Finkel, and people were saying, "How many seconds will it take for Tyson to knock out Buster Douglas?" But I had seen Buster Douglas fight before. I saw him knock a guy down with just a strong jab—BAM! Just one shot. People forget that Mike Tyson was only 5'10". He was thick. He was quick and he hit hard. But Buster Douglas looked like a defensive lineman. He was 6'4". He had big legs and he knew how to fight. He wasn't afraid of Mike Tyson and that makes all the difference.

When the fight started off, Buster Douglas was taking it to Mike, and Mike couldn't get off like he wanted to. After the fight, people were saying how Mike didn't train like he should and all that. But that's nobody's fault but the fighter. Part of being a champion is looking past all of the distractions. Don't nobody realize that except people who have *been* champions. Everybody wants to talk to you, everybody wants to know you.... It stresses you out and that's why some people don't stay champion for long. Everybody's shooting at one guy. Mike Tyson was that guy and he lost that night.

People were asking me, "Are you mad?" I said, "No." They said, "Why? You just lost fifteen million dollars." I said, "My goal is to become the heavyweight champion of the world. I never got into boxing to make fifteen million dollars." I wanted to fight Mike Tyson because he just happened to be the champion. When Buster Douglas beat him, that's who I wanted to fight. It wasn't about the money. Being the heavyweight champion was my goal when I was eight years old. Twenty years later, Evander Holyfield got to fight Buster Douglas and fulfill the goal.

In October 1990, you defeated James "Buster" Douglas via third-round knockout for the WBC, WBA and IBF world heavyweight titles. What do you recall about that experience?

Before the fight, there were about twelve reporters that came to my place. They ate my food and they wrote notes. But out of those reporters, only one of them

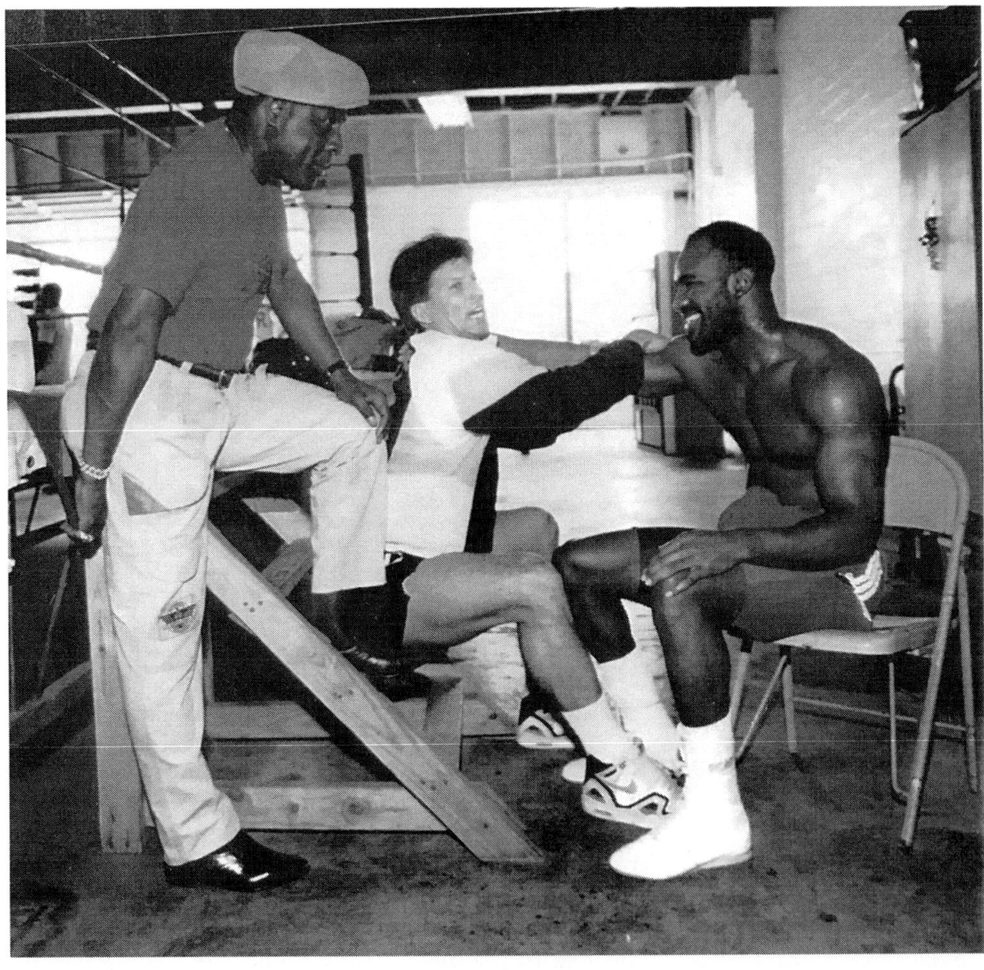

Boxing trainer George Benton, sports performance/fitness trainer Tim Hallmark, and Evander Holyfield, 1980s (courtesy Tim Hallmark/timhallmark.com).

thought I could win. On TV, they said, "Evander is a nice guy. We all agree about that. But we don't think nice guys finish first. We believe nice guys finish last." I wasn't mad about that. Everybody got their own opinion.

At the press conference, Buster Douglas felt he had to put me down to feel good about himself. He said, "Evander had all easy fights and that's why he's undefeated." I said, "When I beat you, they're gonna say the same thing." So, then he started making comments about what he was gonna do to me. He said he was faster than me and that he was stronger than me. I said, "Well, that hasn't been proven. But one thing I know that you are—you're a quitter." I reminded him of Tony Tucker. I said, "You were beating Tony Tucker and you quit. Once a quitter, always a quitter." He got *mad*! I knew that was going to stick in his head. I wasn't going to say anything about his fights, but since he started talking, I reversed it.

When we got to the fight, in that first round, he found out he wasn't as fast as he thought he was. He couldn't hit me for nothing. I was hitting him all the time. In that third round, he tried to hit me with an uppercut and I caught him with a right hand. I missed him with a left hook, but he fell anyway and he didn't get up. I got a lot of criticism for that fight. A lot of people said, "You beat a fat Buster Douglas." I said, "That ain't my business. It don't matter if he's fat, skinny, or whatever. I beat the guy who beat the guy. That's it and I don't want to hear nothing else about it."

In your next three fights, you defended your heavyweight titles against George Foreman by unanimous decision in April 1991, Bert Cooper via seventh-round TKO in November 1991, and Larry Holmes by unanimous decision in June 1992.

I didn't really want to fight George Foreman and that played on my mind a little bit. I knew people were gonna say that I beat an old man. My manager at the time was Shelly Finkel. I told Shelly that I wanted to fight Mike Tyson. Shelly said, "No. No. No. You want to fight George." I said, "No, I want to fight Mike." He said, "Evander, my job is to make you a lot of money." I said, "I'll make more money if I fight Mike." He said, "Yeah, but you'll lose twenty million if you fight Mike." I said, "How am I gonna lose twenty million?"

I was gonna make twenty million for fighting George, but I could have been making thirty million for fighting Mike. Shelly told me, "If you beat Mike, nobody's going to pay you twenty million to fight George. They're only paying you to fight George because they think George can beat you. Even though he's older, they think he can get you out of there with one shot. But if you beat Mike, they won't pay twenty million to see you fight George. I'm trying to make you *fifty* million." I said, "You know what? That makes sense!"

So, I fought George and I hit him three times to one. I tried to get him out of there, but he was able to hold his own. He fought a great fight. With the Bert Cooper fight—I had been training to fight Francesco Damiani. Damiani pulled out at the last minute, so they brought Bert Cooper in there. I don't even know how it happened, but he hit me with a good shot and got the knockdown. I recovered, but then I busted my glove, because I kept hitting him with that uppercut. They put on another glove, and then I went out there and stopped him.

Then they had me fight Larry Holmes. I didn't want to fight Larry Holmes for the same reason I didn't want to fight George Foreman. Don King was saying, "Evander only fights senior citizens! If you're not over sixty-five, he won't fight you!" What happened is Larry Holmes fought Ray Mercer, and the winner was supposed to fight me. Who in the world thought Larry Holmes would win? I didn't think he would, but Larry beat him! So, I fought Larry and he fought a very defensive fight. I wasn't able to get him out of there and Don King said, "He couldn't even knock out an old man!" But the thing is, Larry Holmes was in shape when he fought me. He wasn't in shape when he fought Tyson.

Against Bert Cooper, you displayed a warrior's spirit when you got up from a knockdown, only to become more dangerous. Throughout your career when fans have seen you hurt, you almost always took your aggression to another level. What went through your mind during those dark moments in the ring?

When I'm hurt, I go straight to what I already know. I get aggressive. I'm going toe-to-toe. When people are training, you teach them to box. Fighting is that thing that's supposed to be inside you. It's just an instinct. When it all comes down and you get hit with one of those shots that you weren't expecting, you get up and what's inside you comes out. Fighting is an emotional thing. It's not something you can teach. You can live or die in that situation, but I'm trying to live. That's what fighting really is. I was taught how to box and that's what I'm gonna do as long as I'm winning. But once you get to that point, fighting is all you got.

You had three memorable fights with Riddick Bowe in what made for one of the best trilogies in boxing history. In November 1992, you lost your heavyweight world titles to Bowe via unanimous decision. In November of the following year, you regained your WBA and IBF titles with a majority decision win. In November 1995, in a non-title affair, you lost to Bowe by eighth-round TKO.

Riddick was a good friend of mine. I used to spar him when I was cruiserweight champion. He was a light heavy. But even though he was a light heavy, he was bigger than me. My stamina was better than his. As he would wear down, I would beat the daylights out of him. But he was very skillful. He hit hard. He had a good right hand, and he had a better inside game than probably any big guy there is—his short uppercut, his left hook and overhand right....

In the first fight, I truly believe he got me off my game. He's the first fighter who did that. He said, "If you don't run, I'll knock you out." The game plan was for me to move around. George Benton said, "We're not gonna stand toe-to-toe with the big boy." So, I was moving around the first few rounds and he started hitting me with cheap shots. The referee didn't say nothing, and all of a sudden, I went to the plan in my head that he would run out of gas. I started putting pressure, putting pressure... But he didn't get tired!

My corner said, "You need to move, Evander." I said, "I can't see nothing, because my eyes are swollen up." It was easier for me to stay inside, because at least I could hit him back. I didn't want to stay on the outside and get hit with one of them long shots. So, I stayed inside and it came down to the tenth round, and he hit me on the break. If you go back and watch that round, the referee said, "Break!" I stepped back and he hit me with an uppercut. The referee was about to stop it, but he let it go on. You can see Riddick running out of gas in the last half of the round. In the next round, he hit me in the back of the head and that messed up everything. He won the fight, but I realized that I let him talk me out of my game.

Sports performance/fitness trainer Tim Hallmark puts headgear on Evander Holyfield before a 2000s sparring session (courtesy Tim Hallmark/timhallmark.com).

Before the second fight, I watched the tape and I saw that he was hitting me on the breaks. So, what I did—I made sure that I would get the last lick in every round. Whatever he did to me, I was gonna do it back. I had Emanuel Steward as my trainer. Emanuel said to me, "Don't get sucked in, in them early rounds. I want you to move around in the early rounds. In the second half of the fight, I'm gonna let you get him." He said, "If you move around early, he won't be able to catch you. But if you go in there, he's going to wear you out first and you won't be able to do what you want to do." I followed the game plan Emanuel came up with and I became heavyweight champion again.

Before the third fight, I had been training for nine weeks and a friend of mine opened a restaurant. I went there and I ate some seafood. The next day, I was feeling bad so I went to the doctor. He said, "Evander, you have hepatitis. You need to pull out of this fight." I said, "Man, I can't give up ten million dollars. I trained for nine weeks and I got three more weeks to go." He said, "You're gonna get sicker, man." I said, "I'll tell you what I'm gonna do. I'm gonna pray on it, but I got to go back to camp." I went back to camp and I couldn't even make it out of bed. For one whole week, I was sick. But all of a sudden, I started feeling a little better.

When I got to the fight, they checked me out and the doctor told me, "If he ever hits you in the stomach, it's gonna hurt so bad." I got hit in the stomach, and oh, my goodness! My energy would go up, I'd be winning, and then my energy would go down. Before the fight, this prophet told me that I would knock him down. This guy went to my church. I can't even think of his name. But he prophesized that I would knock Riddick Bowe down, and he also predicted the Tyson fight. He said, "God is saving Tyson for you. Tyson is gonna get out of jail pretty soon. When he gets out, He's gonna have him just for you."

I didn't even want to think about Tyson. I said, "What about *this* fight?" He said, "You're gonna knock him down, but you've got to stay on him." When he told me I was gonna knock Riddick down, I thought he meant that I was gonna win. So, I knocked him down and the referee said, "Box," but I had no energy. People said, "What were you doing? You had him!" I had lost all my energy, and the next round, Bowe hit me and I went down. They stopped the fight and there was nothing I could do. That fight with Bowe was November 1995. The prophet had told me that I would beat Tyson in 1996 and be heavyweight champion. So, I had been telling people that I would carry the torch in 1996. I would tell people that. And in 1996, I carried the torch and I became heavyweight champion a third time.

In November 1996, you became the second man, after Muhammad Ali, to win the heavyweight championship of the world three times when you defeated Mike Tyson for Tyson's WBA world heavyweight title by eleventh-round TKO. The encounter with Tyson was a long time coming. When did you first meet Tyson and what was your impression of him?

I first met Mike in 1982. We were at an amateur tournament in Indianapolis. He fought a guy named Al "Chico" Evans and he got knocked out. A lot of people don't know that. Mike was stopped as an amateur. The next time I seen him, we were both trying to make the Olympic Team. We were partners, because we both lost at the Olympic Trials. I tell people that the Olympic Team was so strong in '84 that me and Mike were on the losing squad! I beat Rickey Womack twice to make the team and Mike lost to Henry Tillman. Mike was an alternate for the team, in case somebody got hurt. Nobody got hurt, so he didn't get to fight. But Mike didn't quit and he became heavyweight champion of the world.

I knew Mike was gonna be good. At that time, Mike worked really hard. I've never seen anybody as focused. He was different. I watched everything Mike did. He was quick, he hit hard.... But his best weapon was that his rhythm was so unpredictable. Most people go one-two, one-two.... Mike was offbeat. You never knew where his punches were coming from and you get hit with things you don't expect. I truly believe that he changed when he stopped training with Kevin Rooney. His new trainers were teaching him the same rhythm that everybody else had, and he became more basic. He fought with a lot of energy and everything was a hard shot. He was full speed, full speed.... He had very good reflexes. He could get in and get out. But the main thing is that a guy could not be afraid of him. If he saw that you were scared, it made him ferocious.

When I fought Mike, it was real simple with me. I knew I could box and I knew I could fight. When Mike came out of prison, he didn't get hit that much. When he hit me, I knew I was gonna be able to take it. But what's gonna happen when I started hitting *him*? It's gonna be a new thing for him. That was my mentality. After that first round, he knew what it was to be hit. Whatever he did to me, I did right back to him. If he hit me on the break, I hit him on the break. If he put his elbow under my neck, I had to put my elbow under *his* neck. I had to fight the best fight that I could.

If you look at the scorecards, it looked like the fight was close. I thought I was tearing him up, but they were giving him rounds. That's why you don't leave it in the judge's hands. My thing is that I want to get you out of there. I realized that Mike was

Evander Holyfield does a plyometric drill as sports performance/fitness trainer Tim Hallmark looks on, 1990s (courtesy Tim Hallmark/timhallmark.com).

a dangerous fighter. At any time, he had that punching power that he could turn over on you. People ask me, "When did you know you had him?" I say, "When the referee waved it off." That was the only time I knew.

One of the greatest things my mama told me was, "Don't get whipped by a reputation. And never get whipped by what somebody says about you." When I fought, it would be wrong for me to say that I never had doubt. It comes across your mind, but you have to replace it with something else. I'm a Christian and I know that God is going to give me everything that's necessary to be the very best I can be. The only thing I got to do is work and apply what I know.

Ever since I was eight years old, I was focused on being the heavyweight champion of the world. My first coach told me about the difference between a goal and a fantasy. It's a fantasy when you want to be something, but you don't work at it. It's a goal when you want to be something and you *do* work at it. If you work at it and you don't quit, then the chances are that you're going to reach it.

I always tell people, "You know why I'm so good? Because my mama took all my excuses away." She always told me, "Son, if you're gonna make an excuse, you might as well not come out here. No one wins with excuses." When I got in the ring, I took Jesus with me. Whatever situation I'm in, that allows me to give it my very best each and every time. The record stands for itself. I wasn't perfect, but I did a little more than everybody else.

Trainers and Cutmen

10

Ronnie Shields: Any Given Sunday

> "In this sport, people think you're not supposed to lose. But this is a sport that was built on wins and losses, not on wins alone. Anybody can lose a fight."

Boxing is the theater of the unexpected. One fighter could appear to have all the advantages, but any man with two hands can defy the odds. No matter how many times it happens, it's a lesson that fighters never stop learning.

Born and raised in Port Arthur, Texas, Ronnie Shields was one of the best American amateur boxers of the 1970s. He turned professional in 1980, compiling a record of 26–6-1, 19 KOs as a junior welterweight, before retiring in 1988.

Having a knack for bringing out the best in fighters, Shields stayed in the game as a trainer, eventually opening Plex Boxing Gym in Stafford, Texas.

Shields is most recognized for his work with former world welterweight and junior middleweight champion Vernon Forrest, who made a statement in the boxing world with a 2002 unanimous decision victory over WBC world welterweight champion, Shane Mosley.

After two back-to-back victories over Mosley, Forrest seemed to be on his way to big things until he faced WBA world welterweight champion Ricardo Mayorga, an underdog with crude skills who defeated Forrest by third-round TKO.

Shields also trained Mike Tyson when Tyson faced WBC and IBF world heavyweight champion, Lennox Lewis, in the most anticipated heavyweight fight of the 2000s. Tyson lost the bout to Lewis via eighth-round knockout.

Having started his career as an assistant for highly regarded trainer George Benton, Shields had deep roots with former cruiserweight and heavyweight champion Evander Holyfield, whom Benton used to train. When Holyfield wanted to continue his career after a 2003 TKO defeat to James Toney, he turned to Shields who guided him to a four-fight winning streak.

In addition to the aforementioned fighters, Shields has also worked with Pernell Whitaker, David Tua, Arturo Gatti, Guillermo Rigondeaux, Juan Diaz, Kassim Ouma, Kermit Cintron, Jermall Charlo, Jermell Charlo, Erislandy Lara, Tomasz Adamek, and Artur Szpilka. This interview took place over the phone in February 2016.

What is your background in boxing and what led you to become a trainer?

I had always loved football. I used to watch the games on the weekend with my dad. When I was in middle school, I made the team. I was really, really happy about it. But then they closed our school down and I was transferred to another school. If I wanted to play football, I had to make the team again. I had some friends who were boxing at the time. I went to the gym with them and I fell in love with the sport. Right then and there, at age thirteen, I knew that's what I wanted to do.

The first day I sparred, I got beat up real bad by a friend of mine. But what that did for me is it made me want to get my friend back. I stayed in the gym, but my friend didn't. About a month later, we got in the ring again and I beat him up so bad. I really enjoyed that. I felt good. I felt like I could compete. I went on to be a three-time national Golden Gloves champion. I lost to "Sugar" Ray Leonard at the Olympic Trials. But I had traveled all around the world and beat guys that Sugar Ray and Howard Davis beat. I thought if they can turn professional and be good at it, so can I.

I did the best I could possibly do. I had a lot of injuries in my career. I used to have to go for acupuncture treatment on my elbows a lot. By the time I was twenty-eight, I was done. I started training fighters, but that was nothing new to me. When I was fifteen, I was working with fighters in the gym. I was good with the hand pads and I could always tell one guy how to beat another guy.

After my boxing career, I got a good job with Main Events. I was George

Trainer Ronnie Shields (left), Vernon Forrest, and strength and conditioning coach Charles Watson, before Forrest's 2002 challenge for Shane Mosley's WBC world welterweight title (courtesy Rick Perez).

Benton's assistant and I started working with Evander Holyfield, Pernell Whitaker, Tyrell Biggs, and a lot of those guys from the '84 Olympic Team. I was there when Evander Holyfield fought Buster Douglas and Riddick Bowe. I was with Pernell Whitaker when he fought Julio Caesar Chavez and Oscar De La Hoya. My whole career as a trainer was right in the middle of big-time boxing.

You trained Vernon Forrest, who is best known for his January 2002 unanimous decision victory over WBC world welterweight champion Shane Mosley. When did you start working with Forrest?

I met Vernon when I was working with Holyfield. Before Holyfield would come to camp, I would go down to Atlanta, and work the hand pads with him, and make sure he was in some kind of shape. Vernon was always in the gym. He liked the way I trained and he asked me if I would work with him. Eventually, he asked me if I would train him full time and things just took off. I had him right before he won the world title against Raul Frank.

Vernon had to give up that title before he fought Shane Mosley. I knew Mosley would be an easy fight for him, because I remember when they fought at the Olympic Trials. Vernon beat him back then and we watched the tape together. I said to Vernon, "You don't have to change anything. Just do what you did to him back then." This was the amateurs, but Shane hadn't changed much. He still fought the same way.

I told Vernon, "This is not going to be a hard fight for you at all." He said, "I feel the same way." I knew Vernon had his number. Vernon knew he had his number. I think deep down, *Shane* knew Vernon had his number. A lot of people were considering Shane to be the number one pound for pound guy at the time, but we were so confident. In that very first round, I told Vernon to just jump right on him and make him remember all the things he did when they fought before. That's what he did. After he beat Shane, I knew that people were going to fall in love with Vernon, because of the kind of person he was. He was one of the best human beings you could ever meet in your life.

The win over Shane Mosley was Forrest's crowning moment in his career. Was it your crowning moment as a trainer?

No. Not for me. He was the underdog and I accepted that. But I knew that Vernon was the better fighter. When you know you have the better fighter, there's nothing to brag about.

Forrest defeated Mosley a second time via unanimous in July 2002. In January 2003, he was a heavy favorite going into his fight against WBA world welterweight champion Ricardo Mayorga. However, Mayorga won the fight via third-round TKO. In a July rematch, Mayorga defeated him again by majority decision. What happened in the fights with Mayorga from your perspective?

What a lot of people don't know is that Al Haymon and I didn't want the fight with Ricardo Mayorga. Al was his advisor and we were always on the phone talking. After Shane Mosley, we had come up with a plan. We were going to move up in weight and go after Oscar De La Hoya. We felt that Vernon could beat Oscar and that

Future world junior middleweight and middleweight champion Jermall Charlo, preparing for a 2014 bout. Charlo has been one of Shields's key boxers of the 2010s and into the 2020s (courtesy Bret Newton—ThreatPhoto.com/Pound4Pound.com).

that was where the money was. Al had it all worked out so that Vernon would fight a guy to become the mandatory for Oscar De La Hoya's belt.

Vernon was in agreement, but then all of a sudden he came back and changed his mind. He wanted to clean out the welterweight division. It was Roy Jones who convinced him to do that. We were shocked. He didn't need to unify the titles. All he had to do was go up and beat Oscar. He would have been a star. Instead, he wanted to fight Mayorga. I personally didn't like the style of Mayorga. Vernon was a better fighter than Mayorga, but Mayorga was the kind of guy you couldn't take lightly. That's what happened. Vernon underestimated him.

I was so hard on Vernon in the gym everyday. We used to get into arguments because I didn't think he was training hard enough. Vernon went in there overconfident and he got knocked out. The second time around, it was a different story. He did what he was supposed to do in the gym. Believe it or not, I thought Vernon won the fight easily. He fought a smart fight, but the judges didn't give it to him. That caused a lot of friction between us. We spoke about it, and I told him I didn't think I should train him anymore. If he couldn't listen to me with the same trust he always had, he had to find somebody else. But me and Vernon were still strong. He still came to my house and we spent time together. We just didn't have a working relationship anymore.

You trained Mike Tyson for his June 2002 fight with WBC and IBF world heavyweight champion Lennox Lewis—a fight that Tyson lost by eighth-round knockout. How did you come to work with Tyson and what happened from your perspective?

I was good friends with Shelly Finkel and I had trained a lot of his guys before. He knew I was tough in the gym and that I always had the fighters' best interest in my mind. After Vernon's first fight with Shane Mosley, Shelly called me and asked me about training Mike. So, I flew out to Maui where Mike was training. When I first got there, I told Mike that all I was going to do was observe him for a couple of days. He had a couple guys there working with him and I just wanted to see what they were doing. Mike agreed with me. He said, "You know what? That's very smart of you."

I watched him train, and some things I liked, and some things I didn't. After a couple days, we went up to his room, and we sat down and talked for about four hours. It was just him and I. I told him what I expected from him and that I wasn't going to take any mess from anybody else. He was telling his guys what to do and that's not how it's supposed to be. I pointed that out to him and he said, "You're right. I'm glad you saw that." I said, "Okay. We have eight weeks. We have to get started right now."

We started working and things were clicking. We watched fights together and he did everything I asked. The problem was that Mike didn't have enough for a guy like Lennox Lewis. Mike was in his thirties, but he had the body of a fifty-year-old. He had been abusing his body and you can't go back to the gym after that. Your body will not respond to hard work. It will refuse. If it was the Mike Tyson of old, I think he would have knocked Lennox out. But Mike was an old guy at the end of his rope and I couldn't get him in top shape.

Ronnie Shields, friend Rick Perez, and cutman Joe Souza, 1990s (courtesy Rick Perez).

In October 2003, you became the head trainer of former heavyweight champion Evander Holyfield after his ninth-round TKO loss to James Toney. Your first fight together was a unanimous decision loss to Larry Donald in November the following year. At this point, the public assumed that Holyfield was finished as a fighter. Tell me about your experience working with Holyfield.

When Evander came to my gym, I noticed that something wasn't right. I asked him about it and he said, "No. I'm good." I said, "No, man. I know something isn't right. Tell me what it is." It was his left shoulder. He said he was having big problems with the shoulder, but he had to fight because he needed the money. In the fight with Larry Donald, Evander wasn't Evander. He couldn't throw a hook, or do anything he wanted to do. He lost that fight and everybody wrote him off after that.

The night after the fight, I sat down and had a long talk with him. I said, "If you don't have surgery on this shoulder, you'll never fight again." I said, "Everybody is giving up on you. Don't give up on yourself. Go get the surgery and take a year off." He agreed and he did it. When he came back to the gym, he said, "Man, my arm feels so good. I can throw hooks now, I can throw body shots...." Everything started clicking again. We started fighting and started winning.

We had a great run. Everything was going well and we went to Russia to fight Sultan Ibragimov for the world title. I felt so good going into that fight. He looked so sharp in the gym. He said it was the best he felt since he fought Mike Tyson. But after the very first round, he got old. Just like that. It took one round and he got old. He came on at the end, but he lost too many rounds and he lost a decision.

On the plane ride home, he was sitting next to me and I said, "It's over, man. You need to quit." I said, "We're always going to be friends, but you're going to have to do something different." He didn't want to believe it and he kept on fighting. But in that fight with Ibragimov, he saw the punches coming but he couldn't get out of the way. That's the sign that you need to stop. That's when you know that it's over.

You had a career as a boxer and now you're in the game as a trainer. What do you find more fulfilling?

They're both fulfilling. In my career, I had regional titles and I fought for the world title twice. The second time, I fought a Japanese guy named Hamada. After the fight, I knew I won it. I was so happy because I knew I was champion of the world. But they stole the fight from me. After that, it was over. I didn't have that feeling again. I never had the fulfillment of winning a world title as a fighter, but as a trainer, I've had a lot of guys who won world titles. That fills the void for me. Seeing other guys win is now my personal goal. It makes me happy in one sense. In another sense, you know that their career will end one day. Then you pick up somebody else and you start all over again. The goal is always the same, but it's different because it's not the same person.

Sometimes in boxing, you can have a guy train his butt off, do everything you want him to do, give you everything he has, and he still loses. You know what? There's fulfillment in that, because you know he lost to a better guy. I just had one of my fighters fight Deontay Wilder for the heavyweight championship of the world. That kid's name is Artur Szpilka. He got knocked out in the ninth round, but you

Artur Szpilka (left) was competitive in his 2016 ninth-round knockout loss to WBC world heavyweight champion Deontay Wilder (photograph by "Sugar" Ray Bailey, courtesy Pound4Pound.com).

know what? I'm proud of him. He gave me everything he had and that's all that matters.

In this sport, people think you're not supposed to lose. But this is a sport that was built on wins and losses, not on wins alone. Anybody can lose a fight. This is the part of boxing that most people don't want to discuss. In boxing today, when a guy loses a fight, people say that's it for him. They think that's all he is. This way of thinking really hurts the sport. Everybody wants to protect their "0," but that's not what it's about. It's about the best fighting the best.

11

Virgil Hunter: From the Root to the Fruit

> "I said that if I ever trained another fighter, it would be a kid. And a kid showed up."

When a farmer plants a seed for a tree, in faith, he waters it. If the seed is treated right, he knows that the tree will produce something good. The same can be said for a young fighter, who is given the proper guidance.

Born and raised in Berkeley, California, Virgil Hunter started as a boxing trainer by working with teenagers out of juvenile hall, while he was a probation officer.

In the mid–1990s, Hunter met Andre Ward, then a nine-year-old boy who was eager to learn the sport. Under Hunter's guidance, Ward became one of the top amateur boxers in the world, winning a gold medal as a light heavyweight in the 2004 Olympic Games.

Still with Hunter in his corner, Andre "Son of God" Ward turned professional in 2004 as a super middleweight.

Ward remained undefeated throughout his professional career, retiring in 2017 with a record of 32–0, 16 KOs. He captured world titles at super middleweight and light heavyweight, defeating a number of top fighters, including Mikkel Kessler, Arthur Abraham, Carl Froch, Chad Dawson, and Sergey Kovalev.

In addition to Ward, Hunter has worked with other notable boxers, including Amir Khan, Alfredo Angulo, Andre Berto, Brandon Gonzales, Karim Mayfield, Mike Dallas, Jr., Andre Dirrell, Chazz Witherspoon, Demetrius Andrade, Abner Mares, Daniel Jacobs, and Mario Barrios. This interview took place at the Morongo Casino in Carbazon, California, in July 2011.

What is your background in boxing and what led you to become a trainer?

My grandfather was a fighter and my father was a military champion. All of my uncles boxed. It was just a given in my family. As far as my experience is concerned, it never exceeded the amateurs. Back in those days, you had what you would call a lot of unsanctioned fights. I excelled in unsanctioned fights. To be exact, I had about seventeen or eighteen of them, and then some amateur fights on top of that.

I started at a young age with the Boys Club. I didn't go as far as some of the other kids, but I had a knowledge of the sport because I was always at the gym. I knew I could develop champions. I had an eye for it. And I had a feel for it. Training fighters is something my grandfather encouraged me to do. He felt that it was something I should pursue, based on conversations we had, and based on my working with some of the kids in our neighborhood. He felt that I would be good at it because I have a patience for it.

I'm a retired probation officer. I initially trained kids out of juvenile hall, but they never stuck with it. You're talking about kids who were sixteen or seventeen. I had a couple of them who were undefeated. Just when they would get good, before they could move into the national tournaments and stuff, they either went back to jail or they would get in trouble. If it wasn't one thing, it was always another.

So, I quit doing it. But I made myself one promise. I said that if I ever did it again, I would have a young kid that came from a solid family background. Not a situation where you get a kid who you've been working with for two years, and one day he's got to move out of state, because his mother can't pay the rent or they have to live with another relative. I learned real quick that you can spend a lot of time and effort in boxing, and one little simple situation like that can throw it all out the window. I promised myself that if I ever did it again, it would be a young kid with a solid foundation. And I got that opportunity.

Super middleweight Andre Ward, trainer Virgil Hunter, and promoter Dan Goossen after Ward's 2006 sixth-round TKO of Andy Kolle (courtesy Marty Rosengarten/RingsidePhotos.com).

Tell me about the first time you met Andre Ward. What was your impression of him and how did your relationship with him evolve from there?

I happened to be at the gym that day, working out. After I finished, I sat on the ring apron. I looked over and I saw this little kid hitting the heavy bag. I thought that little kid was hitting the heavy bag pretty good. He didn't know what he was doing, but he was hitting it pretty good. By the time I thought that, he turned around and looked at me. I nodded my head at him and he went back to hitting the bag. About twenty seconds later, he stopped and looked at me again, so I nodded my head again.

It just so happens that his father had brought him to the gym. His father used to box. He brought him to the gym, because he was telling him about his boxing days and he wanted him to give it a try. They left, and about a week later, I went back to the gym and they were there. His father came up to me and asked me if I knew of any good trainers for his son. I said, "There are a lot of trainers. What are you looking for?" He said, "Naturally, as a parent, I want him to learn how to hit and not be hit." I said, "Well, you're looking at *that* trainer." He said, "Will you give him a try?" I said, "I'll work with him for two weeks and then you can decide if you want me to keep working with him." After two days, they decided.

I started teaching him the fundamentals of boxing. Of course, you never know if they're going to stay with it or if they're going to lose interest. At the time, he was playing little league baseball. I went to a few of his games. He was a pretty good pitcher, but for some reason he wanted to come to the gym every day. Right then, he showed unusual commitment for a nine-year-old kid. He never wanted to stop doing the drills. He just wanted to do it over and over and over again.

Andre was a student and he loved what he was doing. He had passion for it. And he had a vision for it. Because he had a vision, I was able to map out step by step the goals of the future. That's how we did it. I used to tell him stories about real fighters who got up in the morning and ran, so he wanted to do that. I used to pick him up at five in the morning. Every morning, he would be in the window with a little cap on. I'd take him running, and he would go back home and go to school. He was in elementary school at the time. In the evening, his dad would bring him to the gym.

Once I started putting him in the ring, his first sparring partner was Glenn Donaire, Nonito's older brother. Glenn was four or five years older, but he was small. He was Filipino. Glenn would run him all over the ring. Andre would run and duck and dodge, and was scared to throw a punch. I would just watch him. His father came to me one day and said, "I don't think he's got it." I said, "No, leave him alone. He's learning how to survive." He said, "He ain't throwing punches." I said, "I actually like what I see. Just wait."

This went on for about three weeks. A couple of times Glenn would hit him real hard and I said, "That's enough!" I'd stop it and pull him out of the ring. I'd spar him again a couple of days later and, BAM! He hit him again. Glenn didn't slack up just because he was a nine-year-old kid. He would actually hit him and I would stop it every time. One day, he hit him again and I said, "That's it!" Andre said, "No, I'm all right." That's what I was waiting on. I was waiting on him to tell me that he was okay.

When he told me that, I said, "Okay, now I'm going to teach you how to hit *him*." I said, "Every time you move and you stop, he stops in front of you because he knows you're not going to throw nothing. He stops in front of you and he actually *looks* at where he wants to hit you." I said, "He's standing right there. So, every time he stops in front of you, slam your jab in his face and move again." Lo and behold, the next day, that's what started happening. As soon as Glenn would stop, BAM! He would hit him with the jab and go.

Once he realized that he could hit him with the jab, I said, "You could hit him with the right hand, too. Left-right as soon as he stops." He started frustrating him. Within six weeks, it wasn't even a match. He closed the gap that quick. That's when I knew I had something special. I seasoned him about nine months before I put him in his first amateur fight. Because once we started rolling, we were going to roll.

Tell me about Ward's first amateur fight and how his amateur career progressed.

He lost his first fight. Of course, we thought he won it. The kid he fought already had fifteen fights. I just put him in there. He had a rematch with the kid, and he beat the kid crazy, and the kid never fought again. In Andre's seventh fight, I put him in there with a kid with forty-four fights and he won. They wanted a rematch and the kid edged him in the fight. Andre played with his friends all day and he had his friends with him at the fight. He was fatigued and he lost a close decision. So, that was a good lesson for him. We fought the kid a third time and he really handled him in the rubber match.

Andre used to play football and I always encouraged that. I thought it was good for him. I didn't want him to get burned out on boxing. All the important tournaments were after football season. By this time, he couldn't get any show fights around California anymore. Nobody would fight him, so he got all of his fights at the tournaments. The Silver Gloves nationals were in February and we did that two years in a row. He was fifteen when he won his first Junior Olympic title and that's when he knew he wanted to box. That's where it was for him.

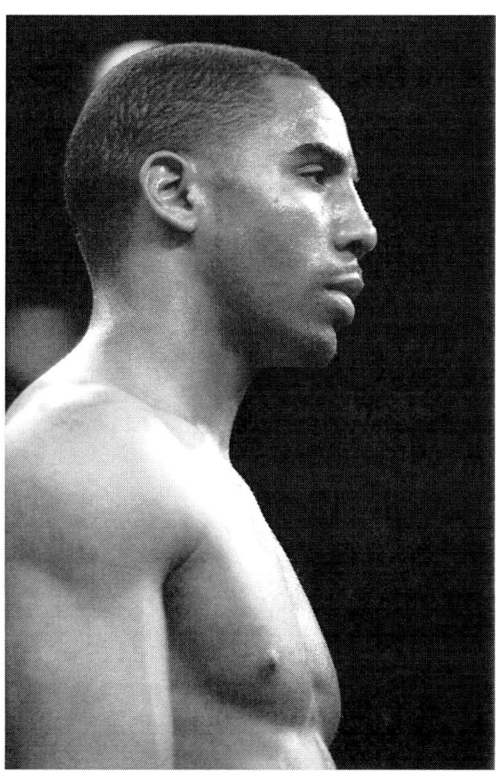

Former two-division world champion and Olympic gold medalist Andre Ward, 2006 (courtesy Marty Rosengarten/RingsidePhotos.com).

Teenagers are known to run wild and get into trouble. As Ward grew into his teen years, how did you make certain that he remained focused and disciplined?

It goes back to what I said earlier when I said that if I ever did it again, I would find a young kid. By the time all the temptations came along, he had something to balance that. He had periods of rebellion just like any other kid, but boxing would always help him toe the line. He wouldn't cross the line; he would *toe* the line because he knew he had a future. A lot of times, teenagers don't have anything solid that they want to do, so they are susceptible to a lot of other things. If you have something solid that you want to do, you'll still do the things that teenagers do, but you'll toe the line.

When Ward was just a boy, you had a premonition that he would one day win a gold medal at the Olympics. Tell me about that.

I have a spiritual background. I'm a praying man and I believe that God has been with me my whole life. I believe that he blessed me with visionary skills. The gold medal was something I predicted to my friends and anybody who would listen. By the time he was twelve years old, I predicted the year that he would do it. I actually wrote it down in a diary. When he saw that diary years later, it blew his mind. Earlier on, I ran across a book called *The Book of Five Rings* by Miyamoto Musashi. It's a book of strategy. Of course, the Olympic symbol is five rings. I felt that this was confirmation that he would make the Olympic team and that he would win the gold medal.

The Olympic journey started when he was twelve years old. We would count down the years. Eight more years, seven more years, six more years.... We went to the '96 Trials when guys like Antonio Tarver, Floyd Mayweather, Zab Judah, and David Reid were amateurs. He got their autographs. Al Mitchell was their coach. I told Al that this kid was going to win a gold medal one day. Al Mitchell gave him a pen. Lo and behold, Andre reminded him of that years later. He still had the pen.

In November 2009, Ward won his first world title when he defeated WBA world super middleweight champion Mikkel Kessler via eleventh-round technical decision.

I knew Andre was going to fight Mikkel Kessler the first time I ever saw Mikkel Kessler fight. That was when he fought Librado Andrade. I knew that day was coming. I didn't know when, but I knew it was coming. I'm a Kessler fan. When I saw Kessler fight, I told Andre that if anybody can write the book on fundamentals and technique, this guy can. I followed him and paid attention to him. I studied him

Andre Ward goes to work en route to his 2009 eleventh-round technical decision over WBA world super middleweight champion Mikkel Kessler (photograph by Ray Flores, courtesy Pound4Pound.com).

and knew what he had going for him. I knew that he didn't have the versatility or the ability to adapt. It had to be his way, or it was going to be a problem.

When Andre won the title, I might have shown a few seconds of congratulations, but then I went home and went to bed. It was just another day at the office. I didn't go to any party. I didn't even really feel anything. It was expected. When something is expected, you're not surprised.

We won the title about five years after he turned professional. Earlier on, we were accused of bringing Andre along too slow. Of course, he had some injuries that set him back. But Andre was a world class amateur. In the amateurs, you have to beat the computer. Once a fighter turns professional, you can't just talk him out of that style. You have to wait for it. You have to drill it. Repetition, repetition… I always thought that Andre could win a title, simply from youth and energy. But every fight after that would be tough in the sense that he would still be using youth and energy to win. Just like Juan Diaz. He won the title early because he had youth. He won a lot of fights with youth and energy, and that can wear a fighter down.

With Andre, I wanted to wait on his maturity. Because once he got the title, he would be able to keep it. That is the goal and I think this Super Six Tournament came at the right time. So far, we haven't taken any damage as far as rough and tough fights. That's why I wanted him to mature into a fighter who has the ability to make things easy. Not to take anything away from his opponents. It's just a simple fact that he has that ability. But the downfall of that ability is that he doesn't get the credit he deserves. Like the Mikkel Kessler fight. He didn't get the credit, because he made it look easy.

I like bringing kids along, but I'll never go back to doing that again. I'm fifty-seven years old. But I think that by being able to go back to the beginning, from the root to the fruit so to speak, I think that sets me apart as a trainer. Some coaches get a lot of credit for firing the weapon, but they don't know how to *make* the weapon. I know how to make the weapon *and* fire the weapon, along with Barry Hunter, Naazim Richardson, and other guys who have labored from the root.

In 1994, I had no idea that any of this was coming about. I was just doing my thing. I said that if I ever trained another fighter, it would be a kid. And a kid showed up. This kid didn't show up for nothing. God brought this kid into my life at a time when I needed him as much as he needed me. The time will come, and it might be on my death bed, when I'll be able to reflect about what we did. God will allow me to get the full effect of it, where I have a smile on my face and I know that I did a good job.

What do the words "from the root to the fruit" mean to you?

You ever plant anything in a garden before? A farmer tends to the soil, because he needs the soil in the proper condition. Then he plants a seed. Once he plants the seed, even though he can't see the seed, in faith, he waters it. If he waters it, he expects to see that seed come up. The best plum tree, the best orange tree—it started at the root before it got to the fruit.

You see a lot of fruit trees where you're not going to eat the oranges off of it, because there's something wrong with the roots and it's not producing sweet fruit. You judge a tree by the fruit it bears. When I say "from the root to the fruit," it means he was grounded. When the seed was planted, it was watered right. Because it was watered right, I expected to see it come up the way it was supposed to come up. When it started coming up, you just knew the roots were in there right. Because you knew the roots were in there right, when that tree started bearing fruit, you knew it was going to be good fruit.

12

Roger Bloodworth: Different Seasons

> "I think you have to understand that with whatever it is that you do, you only have a certain time to do it. When that time is done, you're done. I had a good run in boxing."

In an ancient, philosophical book called the *Tao Te Ching*, one of the phrases reads, "There is a time for being ahead, a time for being behind; a time for being in motion, a time for being at rest." Life is a cycle that is lived from a variety of perspectives. Whether young or old, at the top or on the bottom, there is a time for all of it.

Born and raised in Granite City, Illinois, Roger Bloodworth first got involved with boxing in the 1970s when he took his son to the gym and began helping out with the other kids, gradually becoming a trainer.

While at the 1988 Olympic Trials, Bloodworth crossed paths with New Jersey–based trainer/manager Lou Duva, who took an interest in a couple of Bloodworth's boxers. Bloodworth and Duva developed a strong rapport, which led Duva to offer Bloodworth a job with his family's promotional company, Main Events.

As an assistant trainer for Main Events, Bloodworth worked with several high-profile boxers, notably Pernell Whitaker and Evander Holyfield. Bloodworth eventually became a head trainer, himself, and began training other fighters on his own.

Throughout his career, Bloodworth worked with a host of amateur boxers in the East St. Louis and St. Louis area, including Eddie Hopson, Nick Kakouris, Kevin Bozada, TJ Davis, Ray Lathan, William Guthrey, Ray Kube, Jr., Danny Mendoza, Carl Daniels, Lavell Fingers, Terrell Fingers, and his son Derek Bloodworth.

In the professional ranks, Bloodworth worked with several marquee fighters, including Andrew Golota, Joel Casamayor, Tomasz Adamek, David Tua, Meldrick Taylor, Raul Marquez, Robbie Peden, John John Molina, Fernando Vargas, and Robert Garcia. This interview took place over the phone in September 2018.

What is your background in boxing and what led you to become a trainer?

I got involved with boxing because of my son. When he was six or seven, he tried Taekwondo. I did Taekwondo, too. I also did wrestling and jiu-jitsu. He liked Taekwondo okay, but when he was nine, he saw the movie *Rocky*. After he saw the *Rocky* movie, he asked me, "Dad, do you think I can box?" I said, "Are you asking me for permission to box, or are you asking me if I think you have the *ability* to box?" He said he was talking about having the ability to box. I said, "Well, I don't know. How about we look around and see what's out there?"

I ran into a man by the name of Mercy Mendoza, who ran a boxing club in Granite City called the Mexican Honorary Commission Gym. I told him about my son and he said, "Bring him on down." So, I brought him to the gym, and for the first few months, my son wouldn't let me come anymore. He was having a hard time with it. In those days, kids started boxing at five or six years old. By the time they were my son's age, some of them had ten, fifteen, twenty fights. He was sparring with kids who had a lot more experience than him and he wasn't looking too good. But he stuck with it and Mercy did a good job with him. One day, my son said, "Okay, you can come back again." I said, "Are you still having problems?" He said, "Yeah, but I can handle it."

I started going to the gym and helping Mercy with the kids. I wanted to learn the sport, so I started sparring. I had to correct the things that I was doing wrong and that helped me teach some of the other fighters. Back then, there were a lot of boxing gyms. We had clubs all over East St. Louis. And of course, on the other side of the river, you had all the St. Louis clubs, both in the city and in the county. There were a lot of fights back then, sometimes two or three times a week.

As I started getting really involved as a trainer, Mercy ran into a situation where he had to quit training and close his club. I had been working with some amateurs who were pretty hard core—Danny Mendoza, my son, TJ Davis.... So, I took the kids I had over to Ray Kube's South Broadway Athletic Club on the South Side of St. Louis. When we went to South Broadway, at first, we were just doing our own thing. But I ran into some of the top amateurs in St. Louis at the time, like Nick Kakouris,

Professional boxing trainer Roger Bloodworth, 1990s (courtesy Roger Bloodworth).

Kevin Bozada, and Ray Kube, Jr, and I started working with them, too. After a while, we left South Broadway and went out to Jim Howell's gym in North County. He had some really good fighters out there and I learned a lot from them.

In 1988, I took four kids to the Olympic Trials. There were some other St. Louis fighters there, too, like Carl Daniels, and Lavell and Terrell Fingers from Kenny Loehr's gym. I was the only St. Louis coach there, so I helped them out. We did really well at the Trials. While I was there, I ran into Lou Duva. I had met him once before. He was interested in Eddie Hopson, who I was working with, and also Nick Kakouris. Eddie was still in high school, so I made a deal with Lou that Eddie was allowed to finish school while he was fighting. He actually turned pro while he was still in high school.

At that time, I was working at McDonnell Douglas. They were getting ready to lay off a lot of people and Lou had offered me a job with Main Events. I talked it over with my wife and I decided to tell McDonnell Douglas that I would be leaving. Two weeks later, they laid off about five thousand people.

When I started working for Main Events, they had some very good fighters—Evander Holyfield, Pernell Whitaker, Meldrick Taylor, John John Molina.... While I was there, I worked with George Benton, who was the head trainer. Ronnie Shields and I were the assistants. George Benton was a defensive type of trainer and he was very good at what he did. He would not just work with you; he would *teach* you. He wanted things to be the way he wanted, and he would take his time and show you how he wanted it. I learned a lot from the other trainers and I also learned from the fighters.

One fighter who taught me a lot was Pernell Whitaker. Pernell was the kind of guy who, until he really knew you, he kind of left you alone. But I liked him a lot and we got along good. The more time I spent around Pernell, the more I learned about boxing. That boy could fight. He's one of the best I've ever seen. People talk about these young guys who are coming up now like Vasyl Lomachenko, who is a damn good fighter. But I'm telling you, he'd have his problems with Pernell. He just amazed me with what he was able to do. I've never met another fighter who had as much ability as he did. Evander Holyfield was also very special. Those two are the best I've ever met and they taught me a lot.

I spent quite a few years at Main Events and worked with guys like Andrew Golota, David Tua, Fernando Vargas, and so on. After a while, I started working with guys on my own, like Joel Casamayor, Robbie Peden, and Tomasz Adamek. I had Casamyor when he first came to this country. We were together for about twelve fights, but there was a conflict and I wasn't able to keep working with him. He went on to become a champion, and after he lost the championship, he wanted to come back to me. I was with him later in his career when he beat Diego Corrales in their third fight. And I was with Robbie Peden both times he knocked out Nate Campbell.

In that first fight, Robbie hit Nate with a half uppercut and knocked him out cold. I don't even think Nate knew that he got knocked out. I was still with Robbie when Tomasz Adamek's manager Ziggy called me and asked if I would work with him. We ended up working together for a number of years and had a good little run.

I've been very lucky in boxing. I've worked with a lot of really good fighters, and I've been in the right place at the right time a few different times.

Andrew Golota was a heavyweight contender from the mid 1990s to the mid 2000s, who is best known for twice losing to former two-time heavyweight champion Riddick Bowe, via disqualification. Both times, he repeatedly hit Bowe with low blows, while he was ahead on the scorecards. What do you recall about the time you spent working with Golota?

I first met Andrew when he came to camp. He was a big white kid with a European style. His English was almost nonexistent. But he was a pretty bright guy and he learned enough English to understand what we were trying to tell him. We went to work and he eventually got to the point where he was going to fight Riddick Bowe. Nobody thought Andrew had a chance. They had no idea how good he was. Andrew was beating Bowe in that first fight, but there are some things that there's just no explanation for. I guess he got frustrated that Bowe wouldn't go down, because he kept hitting him low. He got disqualified, and of course, there was a big riot after because the two camps got into it.

After that first fight, Main Events was talking about letting him go. I told Lou, "If you do that, you're making a big mistake. This guy can fight. If we can keep him from going low, he'll beat this guy." So, they brought him back to camp and we explained the situation to him. He understood what we were telling him and we went back to work. Andrew gave Bowe an even bigger beating the second time. I felt that fight should have been stopped. But Bowe stayed in there, and as we know, Andrew hit him low again.

The night Andrew fought Lennox Lewis, he seemed to not really be there. I can't really explain it, but while I was wrapping his hands, I knew something was wrong. When we got into the ring, he was looking around like the whole thing was very strange to him. He got knocked out in the first round, and when we were standing in the corner after the fight, he said, "What happened?" I said, "You got hit." He said, "I had no peripheral vision."

We went back to the locker room, and when he was putting on his pants, he had a convulsion and went down. One of his friends stuffed a wallet in his mouth to keep him from biting his tongue. I had no idea what was going on. I kept yelling his name and he finally came around. An ambulance took him to the local hospital. They examined him and couldn't find anything wrong with him. The commission also had him examined and they couldn't find anything wrong with him either.

Against Michael Grant, from where I was at, things were going fine. He had Michael down in the first round and he was doing what he was supposed to be doing. But in the tenth round, I saw the referee stopping the fight. I didn't know what happened. Somebody said, "Andrew quit." I said, "What?! Why did he quit?!" I guess he got frustrated. I have no idea. You would have to ask him. But he quit in that fight and I was totally shocked.

In 1998, at the age of twenty-one, Fernando Vargas became the youngest man to ever win a world title at junior middleweight. You were with Vargas throughout his early years as a professional. What stands out in your mind about the time you spent with him?

Former world junior middleweight champion Fernando Vargas wraps his own hands, 2007 (courtesy Bret Newton—ThreatPhoto.com/Pound4Pound.com).

Fernando came to camp before he turned pro and he didn't have anybody with him. I spoke a little Spanish, so I talked to him a little bit and helped him with things. Fernando was a very loyal guy. He told me that he had a trainer back in Oxnard, and I said, "Yeah, but you don't have a trainer here. If you're going to be in camp, you need somebody helping you." So, I started working with him, but I didn't have any intentions of becoming his trainer. I just liked him and thought he was a good guy. When he was set to have his first professional fight in Oxnard, he asked me if I would be going with him. I said, "I don't know. That's up to you and your trainer."

They invited me out and he won his pro debut. His trainer was Eduardo Garcia, who was like a father figure to him. Eduardo's son Robert was like his brother. I became friends with the Garcias and spent some years with them. I was with Robert when he won his championship fight. He and his dad were going through a tough period together, so Eduardo asked me if I would work the corner. After the fight, they mended things and he went back with his dad. I had a good relationship with them. They're very good people and Robert is doing terrific now as a trainer.

Fernando had a big heart. That's the way he was brought up and that's the way he was. You could say that he was too ahead of his time. He won the championship when he was young, so he had a lot of really tough fights. But Fernando was a good fighter. He got the win over Winky Wright, he picked Ike Quartey apart.... He was only twenty-two when he fought Felix Trinidad.

Felix was a great fighter, but he was one of those guys who would find a way to beat you no matter what. I told Fernando before the fight that if you happen to drop him, he's gonna hit you low. That's what he does and that's what he did. It was a tough fight. It was tough for both of them. Before Fernando's fight with De La Hoya, he said that he wanted to bring Robert in as his assistant trainer and that he was going to let me go. I said, "You gotta do what you gotta do." There were no hard feelings. He gave De La Hoya a good fight, but the fight with Felix Trinidad was his finest hour. It was his finest and also his toughest.

From the mid 1990s, all the way to the early 2010s, David Tua was a notable heavyweight contender, who was known for his devastating punching power. At what point did you begin working with Tua and what is your assessment of his career?

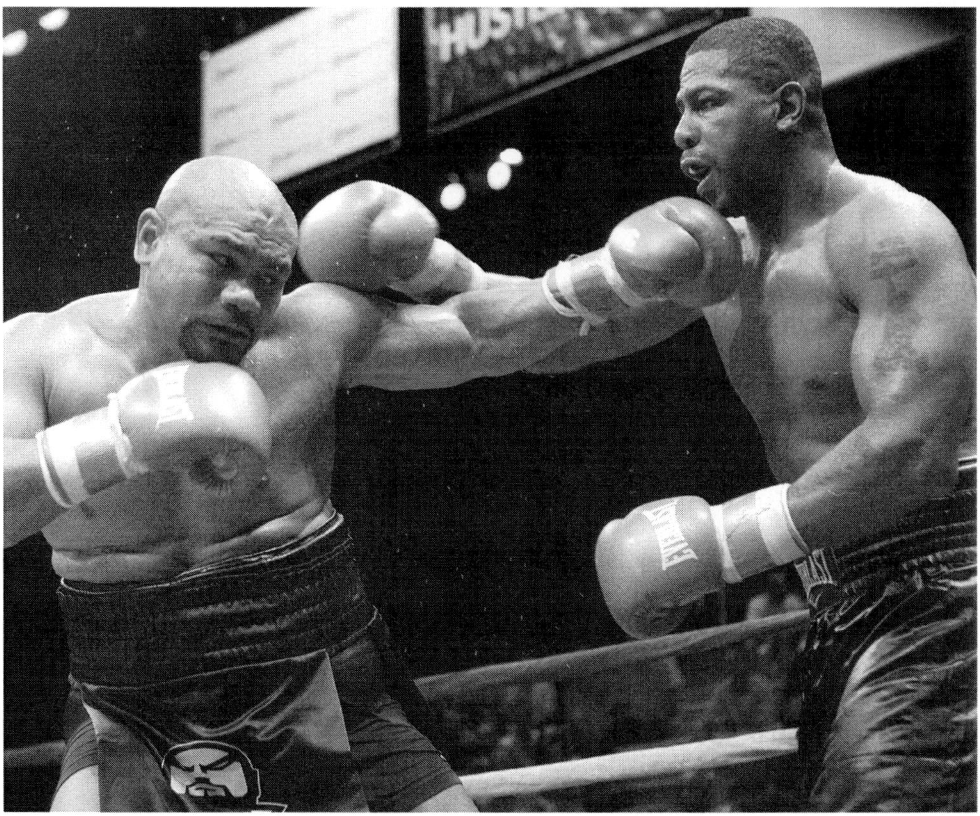

Former heavyweight world title challenger David Tua (left) struggles against Monte Barrett in their 2010 encounter, which resulted in a majority draw (courtesy Marty Rosengarten/ RingsidePhotos.com).

David Tua first came to camp in the early '90s when we were working with Evander Holyfield. He was kind of a smaller heavyweight, maybe 190, 195. But he was very strong. George Benton really liked him, so Lou decided to sign him. In his first pro fight, he hit this kid with a left hook and I heard something go, BOW! I thought, what the hell was that? He hit the kid so hard that he broke his ankle. It was unbelievable. I think Tua was one of the best heavyweights who never won a championship. He almost set the record for the most first-round knockouts ever. He had real punching power. As he grew older, he went from the 190s, all the way to above 250.

I think he went through some hard times before he got his shot at Lennox Lewis. When he lost to Lewis, I don't think he intended to keep fighting. But sometimes we do things because we need the money and because we are who we are. I think he did it for both reasons. Later in his career, he spent some time out of the ring and wanted to make a comeback.

I ran into Tua when I was in Australia and he asked me if I would work with him. The fight I remember the most was Shane Cameron, who had been calling him out. Before that fight, there was a press conference. This kid was talking bad about Tua and how he didn't like him. "Sugar" Ray Leonard was there and he asked Tua,

"Do you dislike this guy?" Tua said, "No. I'm a Christian. I actually love him. And come Saturday night, I'm going to hit him with all the love I got in my body!" That's exactly what he did. He hit that kid so hard. The guy somehow beat the count. I didn't think they were going to let him continue, but they sent him out for the second round and Tua finished him off.

I spent some years with Tua. You always think your boy has a chance of making it to the top. I did think he could be a champion, but he just ran out of time. It happens to all fighters and that's what happened to Tua. You can't be in this sport forever.

In the mid to late 2000s, Tomasz Adamek won world titles at light heavyweight and cruiserweight. He eventually moved up to heavyweight where he challenged WBC world heavyweight champion Vitali Klitschko in September 2011, losing the bout by tenth-round TKO.

When I started working with Adamek, he was already a two-time world champion. I remember watching him fight Paul Briggs when he was at light heavyweight. They went to war with each other and I was impressed with what he had. He was just a natural born fighter. Mentally, he was very strong. When he moved to heavyweight, he had to learn to box a little bit, because everybody was bigger than him.

In our first camp together, we were getting ready for Chris Arreola. He did a real good job in that fight. He out-boxed Arreola and he went on to beat some good heavyweights. With Vitali Klitschko, he was in with a guy who was just too big for

Former world light heavyweight and cruiserweight champion Tomasz Adamek (right) tests the waters at heavyweight against Chris Arreola, winning a 2010 majority decision (courtesy Bret Newton—ThreatPhoto.com/Pound4Pound.com).

him. It's a hard situation when your fighter is 6'2", 215 pounds, and he's too small. Vitali was huge. If you saw the fight, then you know why it went the way it went.

One of the statements I made after the fight is that there should be a heavyweight division and a super heavyweight division. Somebody said, "Well, there's a cruiserweight division." I said, "Yeah, but a cruiserweight is not a heavyweight." A guy who's 220 pounds is too big for cruiserweight and too small for a guy that's 250. That's always been my position, especially after that fight. I would say that super heavyweight should be anything over 230.

I was with Adamek when he had his last fight in Poland. After the fight, I was having problems with my hips and I got to the point where I couldn't do it anymore. You can't be an old man in this game. I think you have to understand that with whatever it is that you do, you only have a certain time to do it. When that time is done, you're done. I had a good run in boxing. Today, I'm just a fan.

To be in boxing as long as I was, I guess you have to be good. If you're not good, you're not there and it's just that simple. But there were some who were better than me. I know that and I don't mind saying it. I was a fortunate person, who happened to be in the right place at the right time. That's the bottom line. I was working a job and it got to a point where I had a choice to make. I chose boxing and then I became very lucky.

13

Jack Loew: Grooming the Pride of Youngstown

"I don't care what people say, because I know that Kelly Pavlik and Jack Loew made a good team. Not too many people can do what we did."

Over the years, certain fighters from Youngstown, Ohio, have gained worldwide recognition because of their success in the ring. In the 1980s, former WBA world lightweight champion Ray "Boom Boom" Mancini created a great deal of pride and excitement for local fans. But it wasn't until over twenty years later when another fighter from Youngstown made his mark.

Born and raised in Youngstown, Ohio, Jack Loew has been a key figure for keeping boxing alive in his hometown—opening the Southside Boxing Club, organizing local events, and training young boxers. One of these boxers was a nine-year-old boy named Kelly Pavlik, who went on to become one of the top amateurs of his time.

In June 2000, Kelly "The Ghost" Pavlik turned professional with Loew in his corner, building a record of 31–0, 28 KOs before facing WBC and WBO world middleweight champion, Jermain Taylor, in September 2007. Pavlik defeated Taylor via seventh-round TKO, and went on to win a unanimous decision over Taylor in a rematch the following year.

After the rematch with Taylor, Pavlik defended his middleweight titles three times, before losing to Sergio Martinez by unanimous decision in April 2010. In October 2008, Pavlik lost a unanimous decision to former middleweight champion Bernard Hopkins in a non-title affair, fought at 170 pounds.

At the tail end of his career, Pavlik boxed under the guidance of trainer Robert Garcia, facing modest competition before retiring in 2012 with a record of 40–2, 34 KOs.

In addition to Kelly Pavlik, Jack Loew has worked with Ken Sigurani, Billy Lyell, Craig Kikta, Darnell Boone, Willie Nelson, Dannie Williams, and Harry Joe Yorgey. This interview took place over the phone in August 2011.

What is your background in boxing and what led you to become a trainer?

In the amateurs, I boxed for a while in the novice division and I fought one year in the open division. That's when I was in high school playing football, so it was kind of a part-time thing for me. Coming from the streets of Youngstown, I always liked to fight. Unfortunately, it wasn't always inside the ring.

I did a lot of fighting and I started helping one of our older trainers, Eddie Sullivan, train some fighters. That's who I had my amateur fights with. Ed trained Ray Mancini among others. I started working with Eddie, but he was getting older and older, and eventually he closed his gym. I wanted to keep going, so I opened up an old storefront building back in '88 and that's when it started.

Youngstown is a blue collar city, but the crime rate is big. We've been fourth in the country in murders. It's a suppressed area. The work has diminished because of all the steel mills, so it's definitely a rough city. It's also a big boxing city. Boxing was very big back in the '60s and '70s and early '80s. At the Golden Gloves, you would see four or five or six thousand people at every event. Pro boxing was always big, too, but it kind of died a little bit after Ray Mancini stepped down.

Ray was the last big thing around here. That's right around when I started to train fighters and start things up again. We started doing the right thing with the Golden Gloves, and then of course, the pros started following. Right now, boxing is extremely large here. Even our little club shows draw three or four thousand people.

I used to work at a Teamster warehouse as a union rep. I worked there for seventeen, eighteen years. I opened the gym just because I love boxing. I love working with kids and teaching them things. I used to coach football, too. For me, it was just a hobby. But once Kelly Pavlik turned sixteen, seventeen years old, he started getting national attention. I realized that there could be a future here, but I couldn't have envisioned what would eventually happen and how far we would go.

It's always a dream when your first fighter is signed by a promotional company like Top Rank. That's when we knew we were on our way. In the amateur days, I would need to take time off from work, so I could take Kelly to the tournaments. I used to tell my boss, "We've got a world champion here." I really believed that this kid was something special and he was.

Tell me about the early years when you were training Kelly Pavlik and how things progressed.

Kelly was nine years old when he first came to the gym. Gangly white kid. More heart and balls than talent. He wanted to spar every day he came in. He used to leave the gym with a lot of bloody noses, but he didn't give a shit. He was always coming back and ready to go the next day. He used to do karate, but he quit karate and came to boxing. In karate, they wouldn't let him have the kind of contact he wanted. They made him pull his punches.

Kelly's first fight was in a tournament. I was taking these kids up there and he begged me to take him along. I wasn't even going to take him, but he wanted to do it so bad. All the kids on the team had uniforms, so I threw him a red shirt and said, "Come on, you can come with us." We went to Steeleville, Ohio, and I put him against a kid who had twenty-four fights. This kid had just won the Ohio State Fair and Kelly just kicked the shit out of him. That was his first amateur fight and he didn't even have that much training at the time. He was just a tough kid.

Kelly was a hell of a baseball player, too. They had him in one of the toughest

Trainer Jack Loew and middleweight champion Kelly Pavlik at a 2009 press conference (courtesy Marty Rosengarten/RingsidePhotos.com).

positions as a catcher. In football, he was a running back and a linebacker. He was always on the aggressive side of it. I encouraged him to play all the sports he could. I never held him back from baseball and football. He was always playing sports, always playing competitively, and always playing on the upper level. If he was twelve years old, they would put him on the thirteen- or fourteen-year-old baseball team. If he was ninety-five pounds in football, they had him play at one-fifteen.

When he was sixteen years old, he would spar with one of my pros, who used to handle him easy. One day, Kelly turned the corner and put an ass-whipping on him. That was the difference in Kelly's whole career. That one day. That's when boxing really took over. Around this time, he started developing that right hand and he was stopping people in tournaments. Finally, I said to him, "Hey, it's time to make a decision about what you want to do. Boxing, baseball, or football. What's it going to be?" Fortunately, he chose boxing.

Pavlik turned pro in June 2000 with a third-round TKO victory over Eric Benito 't Zand. Tell me about the first few years of Pavlik's professional career.

His manager Cameron Duncan had an eye for talent and he liked what Kelly was doing in the amateurs. They got him on TV in his first fight and he knocked the guy out. They were all knockouts on the way up. He went 14–0 with fourteen knockouts. He was knocking them out early and that's what everybody likes to see. People love the brutality of boxing. They'll pay to watch someone like Mike Tyson for thirty seconds. Kelly brought that kind of excitement.

Early in Kelly's career, I was still working as a Teamster. The company I worked for grew from one hundred twenty people to almost fourteen hundred people overnight. Since I was one of the original guys, I got a lot of vacation time. Instead of spending it with my family, I geared all my vacations toward Kelly and boxing. On the weekends, I was sealing driveways as a way to make a few extra dollars.

In 2002, the company I worked for closed. They came in at break time one day and said, "Okay, we're out. We're done." At that point, I started devoting more time to the asphalt business and working with Kelly and focusing on that world title we were after.

In May 2007, Pavlik defeated Edison Miranda via seventh-round TKO, in an eliminator for Jermain Taylor's middleweight titles. Going into the fight, many viewed Miranda as the future of the middleweight division.

Coming from the neighborhoods where we came from, there was always the bully around the block. There was always the bully on the playground. Those are the types of kids where when you're playing kickball, they like to throw the ball hard at

Kelly Pavlik rocks Edison Miranda with a right hand, en route to a 2007 seventh-round TKO victory. Referee Steve Smoger looks on (courtesy Marty Rosengarten/RingsidePhotos.com).

all the little kids. Guys like myself never worried about bullies. When they would throw the ball at me, I threw the ball right back at them. Those are the types of kids I love to fight.

Miranda fit the bill perfect. He was the bully. Everybody told Kelly to box and move and be careful. I told Kelly to back this fucking kid up and bully the bully. After the weigh-ins, we were at the press conference. Miranda made a move towards Kelly and tried to intimidate him like a jerk. All Kelly did was wink his eye and blow him a kiss. You should have seen the look on Miranda's face. He was like, "Holy shit! I can't get under this kid's skin!"

When we went to the middle of the ring to hear the referee's instructions, he wouldn't make eye contact. Before the bell rang, he was standing in his corner looking at the canvas. He just wouldn't look at us. Now, before all that happened at the podium, he was continuously trying to get in Kelly's face. I think that little wink from Kelly took the heart right out of him and I think we laid the blueprint on how to beat Edison Miranda. Everybody started beating him after that.

In September 2007, Pavlik defeated Jermain Taylor via seventh-round TKO for Taylor's WBC and WBO middleweight titles. In the second round, Pavlik was knocked down and hurt, but he went on to turn things around and get the victory.

Right before the fight when we were in the locker room, I was nervous as hell. It was the most nerve-wracking thing in the world knowing that nobody thought we deserved to be there. We got no attention going into the fight and everybody thought we were coming there to lay down and let Jermain Taylor win.

In that second round when Kelly went down, it wasn't so much that I was disappointed in what happened. It was just like, godammit! These people are going to say we told you so and I'm going to be sealing driveways for the rest of my life! I saw Kelly get up. I knew he was hurt, but every second that went by, I knew he was getting stronger. In the last thirty seconds of that second round, Kelly was actually firing back. When he came to the corner, my first question was, "Are you okay?" He was fine. It was just an equilibrium shot. He said, "My head is clear. It's just my legs aren't there yet."

Everybody in the corner was hollering, "Box! Box!" I said, "No, man! You go across this fucking ring and jump in Jermain's ass! If you're clear and if you're okay, you've got to go across this ring and take charge right now!" That's what he did. In the fifth and sixth rounds, Kelly was missing with that big right hand by an inch here, a half inch there. We were just missing. All I said to Kelly was, "Throw that right hand to his chest. Right at the neck. Don't chase that head. He's a slick kid." He did what I said. He doubled with the jab and caught him with the right hand. Once he hit him, I knew then that we hurt him and that it was over.

Pavlik's victory over Jermain Taylor really shook things up in your hometown of Youngstown, Ohio. What was life like in the weeks and months following the fight?

It was crazy. This town hasn't had anything like that since "Boom Boom" Mancini. Ray was a great friend of mine. We went to school together, boxed together, played football together.... It had been over twenty years since Ray was at the top and along came Kelly and he just took the town by storm. Parades, golfing at the nicest golf courses.... I would walk into a restaurant and people would be buying me beers. I was like, so this is how the other half of the world lives. It was great.

I've never had this kind of success in this sport or anything else, but I've always been a popular person around town. I put on a lot of great amateur events, I played football here, and I've been here my whole life. Youngstown is not that big. As far as the fame goes, I stayed pretty humble. I didn't do anything extravagant. My wife and I bought a new house, but that's what you do when you get a good job. I didn't let anything get to my head, but Kelly, on the other hand—I think he struggled with the popularity. I think he struggled with the demands on him.

Kelly Pavlik surrounded by the media, 2000s (courtesy Marty Rosengarten/RingsidePhotos.com).

Kelly would go to a hospital to see a kid who was on his deathbed and he was supposed to go in there and cheer him up. He did a lot of stuff like that and I think it was hard on him. He's thinking to himself, this kid is dying and he wants to see me? It made him sad, but he couldn't go in there with a sad face. He was supposed to cheer the kid up. I would see him afterwards and he tried to keep that tough face, but I could see that he wanted to break down. I could see the hurt on his face. I'd try to talk to him, but he wouldn't let it out. I think that took a big toll on him.

Pavlik held the middleweight championship until April 2010 when he was defeated by Sergio Martinez via unanimous decision. A few months after he lost his titles, it was revealed that he checked into an alcohol rehabilitation program.

He went to rehab twice. The first time, he was in there for thirty days. He was supposed to do sixty, but they offered us the Sergio Martinez fight. I was against the Martinez fight at the time. I just didn't think we should have been fighting anybody right then and there, but Kelly left rehab early and came out to train for the fight. Things didn't go well in training camp. I was hoping that we would make it through and come out victoriously, but we didn't. Kelly didn't handle the loss very well and things started getting worse, so he checked into rehab for the second time.

In the past, Kelly had always been able to control his drinking. I treated it as a kid who was going out after his fight and having some beers. When I was younger, I was able to go out till five o'clock in the morning, get a shower, sleep for a half an hour, get up and go to work, and maybe go back out again that night. We're all able to do crazy things when we're younger, but it sometimes catches up to us. It caught up to Kelly. He just wasn't able to lead his life outside of boxing and come back to the gym and be the same old Kelly Pavlik.

The toughest part about this sport is the ups and downs. When you're at the top, life is different. Everybody loves you. But when you fall off, the outside world treats you different. You're no longer special. When Kelly loses to a Bernard Hopkins or a Sergio Martinez, it's because he either had a bad night or he lost to a better man. That doesn't make him any less of a person.

Boxing is a very, very mental sport. You as the coach have to play psychologist, father.... You try to talk them through it and get them past everything and it's hard. Let me tell you, Kelly is a great, great kid. I've been around him since he was nine years old. People have said some bad things about him and I just hope they forgive and forget some of the things he's done. Alcoholism is a sickness. This kid doesn't want to live like this. It's a sickness. Nobody else is going to suffer because of it except for Kelly and his family.

I've been there for Kelly every day—busting my ass, running at the park, at the gym.... I show a lot of passion for what I do, whether it's sealing fucking driveways or working with nine-year-old kids. I love this kid so dearly, but I can't control what he does when he leaves this door all the time. It's impossible. If I didn't think I was doing a good job, I would have walked away. I don't care what people say, because I know that Kelly Pavlik and Jack Loew made a good team. Not too many people can do what we did.

I knew that the day would come when there was going to be life after Kelly Pavlik. Do I think it should have come this soon? Absolutely not. But no matter what Kelly's story is, he's still done a lot of good for this town and he's done a lot in boxing. He didn't win a vacant title. Nothing was handed to him. Kelly was *the* middleweight champion of the world and nobody can take that away from him.

14

Winston Shaw: A Place Called Gamble

> "Fame and fortune is great, but the biggest reward is working with the kids. If I can keep a kid off the street and point him in the right direction, I think I have accomplished my goal."

Boxing trainers are highlighted when their fighters reach an elite level in the professional ranks. Rarely are trainers acknowledged when they take kids from scratch and teach them the fundamentals. Training youths is a thankless job, but it's the foundation that leads to achievement on bigger stages.

Born and raised in St. Louis, Missouri, Winston "Buddy" Shaw began training amateur boxers in the 1970s. Having competed as an amateur himself, Shaw became involved as a trainer because he was a helpful father, assisting other coaches who were working with his sons. He committed himself to the gym every day, eventually finding himself running a boxing program of his own.

In the late '80s, Shaw's work with his amateurs was recognized on the national level. He was hired as a coach for the USA Team, where he worked with, and against, some of the sport's future champions.

One of Shaw's protégés, a welterweight by the name of Tony Robinson, signed a managerial contract with Detroit-based trainer/manager Emanuel Steward. Robinson began training at Steward's Kronk Gym, only to be seduced by the streets of his old neighborhood, where he was involved in an incident that led to his imprisonment.

Shaw has worked the corner of a few top professionals in St. Louis, including former world welterweight and junior middleweight champion, Cory Spinks, and former bantamweight world title challenger, Arthur Johnson. However, Shaw has preferred to stay at the amateur level of the sport and work with children, mainly as a way to help them with their personal lives and develop them as young men. This interview took place at the Wohl Recreation Center in St. Louis, Missouri, in January 2015.

What is your background in boxing and what led you to become a trainer?

I fought in my first Golden Gloves when I was twelve or thirteen. One-hundred-twenty-six pounds, sub novice. We had to fight twice that night. It started at 5:30 in the evening and went till midnight. The Golden Gloves were real big then. We filled Kiel Auditorium to the rafters. That's when amateur boxing was amateur boxing. There were people there from all over the Midwest.

When I first started, it was just a bunch of us kids in the neighborhood. We would put some old clothes in a duffle bag and use it as a punching bag. After a while, I started boxing at Soulard Center. We trained in an empty swimming pool. That's where we ran, too. There were no bags. We basically just sparred. Gradually, I picked up on the sport and fell in love with it. I wasn't quite athletic enough to excel at baseball, football, or basketball. With boxing, there's a place for you even if you aren't particularly athletic.

I did it until I was twenty-one or twenty-two. After I stopped participating, I worked as a judge and a referee on the amateur level. I continued with that till I started a family. When my sons came along, I started them in boxing, which gave me a way to spend a lot of time with them. I actually took the kids to a gentleman who ran the City Parks and Recreation program by the name of Sam Westbrook. We called him "The Godfather." I really admired him a lot. With all the time I spent in boxing, my only regret was that I never boxed for him. I told him that if he would train my kids, I would help him with all the other kids. I wasn't trying to be a coach. I was just a father helping out.

After a while, Sam asked me to start a boxing program at the DeSoto Center at 20th and Cass. I told him I would, but I said that I didn't know anything about coaching or training. He said, "You have the number one ingredient. You're here every night." From that point on, I've been coaching.

I was working midnights in the warehouse for Schnucks grocery stores. I would get off work at seven, go home and get a few hours of sleep, then meet up with Sam around one and pick his brain about boxing. What he told me is that I should handle the kids the same way I would handle my own sons. That's basically the way I've always looked at it. Sam was my inspiration for coaching, but I never thought I would have done it for as long as I did. I figured when my kids were done boxing that I would be done, too. But I got hooked.

I did a year and a half at the Desoto Center. After that, they moved me to the Gamble Center. Then to Wohl's, then Cochran, then back to Gamble. Most of the kids who come to Gamble come from single-parent families, usually the mother. What I find more than anything else, they're looking for love or for someone to care for them. Once you give them a little compassion, even the toughest and baddest kid will show you a different side to them. That's what it's always been about for me. It hasn't been all about boxing. It's about showing young men a different side of life.

As an amateur coach, you have traveled to a lot of the national and international tournaments. Who are some of the kids you watched coming up who later went on to become champions?

I saw Mike Tyson in Green Bay, Wisconsin, at the national Junior Olympics. He was fourteen, fifteen, knocking out other kids. He could punch. Oh my God, could he punch! Just spectacular! Most officials in the amateurs didn't like how he would roll under so low. One time, this referee was about to jump in and call him for a foul,

Trainer Winston "Buddy" Shaw (center) with a group of his amateur boxers, 2007 (courtesy Winston Shaw).

and Tyson knocked the kid out. It was unbelievable! The referee was standing in limbo, trying to figure out what to do next.

I saw Roy Jones, Jr., at the Junior Olympics in Saginaw, Michigan. He beat our guy Terron Millett in the finals at 125 pounds. Good God, was he terrific! After the fight, I was sitting next to him in the stands. There was a fight going on that was just an all-out street brawl. I remember he said to somebody, "Man, that's crazy to just stand there and bang like that." That really impressed me how he recognized that—that it's foolish to bang when you can box.

Floyd Mayweather, Jr., had a lot of flash. Good speed, good boxing.... I figured he could be a world champion some day, but never to the magnitude that he is today. I saw Andre Ward and Virgil Hunter at the tournaments every year. I don't think Andre ever lost on his way through the amateur ranks. If I am correct, Andre was Virgil's only boxer, so he could spend a lot of personal time with him. Most amateur boxing is team oriented, but when you train one on one with a guy, you can work on the little stuff.

One year, I was a coach for the USA Team at a tournament in London. I was working with a kid named Michael Brittingham from Philadelphia. Everybody at that tournament was talking about this kid, Naseem Hamed. They called him "The Little Ali." He had a loud mouth and he talked a lot, just like when he was a pro.

Michael had to fight him and he was a little concerned. I told him, "This guy might have beaten a lot of kids, but he's never faced *you*." I told Michael to not let Hamed get set and do what he wants to do. Take him out of his comfort zone. If you take him out of his comfort zone, he's an ordinary fighter. Michael was able to prevail with sound fundamentals and a lot of pressure.

You trained an amateur boxer by the name of Tony Robinson, who was eventually trained and managed by Emanuel Steward in the pro ranks. After compiling a professional record of 7–0, Robinson went to jail on a drug-related charge.

I started training him as a ten-year-old youngster. We actually started right here at the Wohl Center. His mom had him in a lot of sports to keep him off the streets. He started boxing one summer and he showed me a lot. That winter, he came back and decided that he wanted to really focus on boxing. Muhammad Ali was his idol. In his first fight, he was boxing real well in the first round, but then he went to the ropes and he started doing the rope-a-dope. He had never heard me raise my voice before, but when he got back to the corner, I scolded him. After that, he went back out and did what he was supposed to do.

He was like a son to me. I took him everywhere. He was a standout talent and he outgrew most of the kids around here. In '87, he came out of the junior division at sixteen years old and he was ranked number two in the nation. In 1988, he was seventeen and I was getting him ready for the Olympic Trials. We had a lot of time to prepare and he had been spending so much time in the gym, so I gave him two weeks off. He was just a baby. I wanted to give him a break and let him rest. When he came back, he wasn't the same. He lost his focus and he never got it back. He had all these distractions—girls, the street... I would set up sparring sessions for him and sometimes he would show up and sometimes he wouldn't.

Former amateur boxer Richard Scott stands nearby as a young boy is weighed in for a 1970s amateur bout. Sam Westbrook, who was Winston Shaw's mentor, checks the scale (courtesy Winston Shaw).

We went to the Trials in Concord, California, and he lost in his second fight. I thought he would have been perfect for the Olympics in '92, but he didn't want to continue in the amateurs. Emanuel Steward had been courting him a little bit—approaching us at the tournaments and asking about him. We signed with Emanuel and he moved to Detroit. Two weeks before every fight, I would go up and see where he was. Emanuel would always make sure I was there in the corner. He went 7–0 with Emanuel. Then one Christmas, he came home and he never went back. The streets just got him. He went to jail and he spent all of his youth behind bars.

You prepared Arthur Johnson for an August 2000 fight against IBF world bantamweight champion Tim Austin, a fight that Austin won by unanimous decision. You and Angelo Dundee were in Johnson's corner for that fight. What do you recall about that experience?

This was my third fight with Arthur. He fell out with his other coach, so he came to me because he knew me from the amateurs. Arthur was easy to work with. Very disciplined. You didn't have to question his running. Always on time. I was familiar with Timmy Austin from the amateurs. He came from a good gym in Cincinnati. I knew his coaches, so I knew what to expect. Angelo was Arthur's manager. I trained Arthur, but when we got to the fight, I knew Angelo would be the cornerman.

In the fight, I kind of disagreed with what Angelo was telling him. I knew from

Former welterweight Tony Robinson out-boxes Chuck Peralta for a 1988 unanimous decision victory (courtesy Winston Shaw).

the amateurs that Timmy was a converted southpaw. I wanted Arthur to move to his right, and move away from Timmy's right hand, but Angelo had him moving to his left. It didn't work out, but I loved working with Angelo. He was a heck of a guy and he had so many stories. At his gym in Miami, the gym was on the second floor. He said that when he would get to the bottom of the steps, he always knew when Muhammad Ali was hitting the heavy bag, because his punches had a certain melody to them. Nobody else punched like that.

In March 2008, you worked the corner for IBF world junior middleweight champion Cory Spinks when he fought Verno Phillips. Spinks had a falling out with his longtime trainer Kevin Cunningham before the fight, and he lost his title via split decision.

I got a call late on a Sunday night from Mike Spinks. I knew Mike as an amateur here. I've been in boxing all my life! It was two weeks away from the fight. Evidently, Cory was having problems with his trainer and they needed somebody to work the fight. I had spent a little time around Cory when he was an amateur. My kids were terrified of him. He could box. *Man*, could he box! Oh, my God! Personally, I thought if he learned to sit down just enough to earn the proper respect, he would have been a much better fighter. He wasn't really taught to sit down. Boxing got him there, so boxing was going to keep him there.

Michael Spinks (left), Cory Spinks, Winston Shaw, and Leon Spinks after the weigh-in of Cory's 2008 fight with Verno Phillips. Leon, Michael, and Cory Spinks all won world titles as professionals (courtesy Winston Shaw).

When I was with Cory, he was overweight. We were trying to get the weight off, so he didn't lose the title on the scales. We accomplished that. He started out fighting the right fight, but he wasn't in the best physical shape and it cost him. He should have been able to out-box Verno easily. A football coach named Vince Lombardi had an old saying, "Fatigue makes cowards of us all." It's true. When you get tired, you do things that you never thought you would do. Cory got tired.

In the professional ranks, trainers have an opportunity to make a good payday and gain notoriety if their fighters win a world title. What is the incentive when you train a kid who is only fighting for a trophy?

Fame and fortune is great, but the biggest reward is working with the kids. If I can keep a kid off the street and point him in the right direction, I think I have accomplished my goal. But boxing is something that has kept me out of trouble as well. When I stopped boxing, I found myself getting on the wrong track. Once I got back into boxing as a coach, it steered me back to reality. It reminded me what life is really about. The kids have helped me as much as I've helped them.

15

Ray Rodgers: Golden Gloves Education

> "For every five boxers that stay, ninety-five of them go. You hear people say how boxing builds character. I always say that boxing doesn't *build* character, it reveals it."

The Golden Gloves is an annual tournament in the United States where amateur boxers match-up to determine the best boxer in each weight class. It's a crowning achievement for dedicated youths, who have shown commitment to their craft. But in the long run, trainers and mentors often hope that the lessons kids learn from boxing will help them as young men when they leave the sport.

Born in Shawnee, Oklahoma, later relocating to various cities in mid–Oklahoma, and eventually settling in Conway, Arkansas, Ray Rodgers has been involved in boxing as an amateur boxer, a trainer, and a regulator of the amateur level in a number of capacities.

Rodgers became something of an ambassador of amateur boxing in the United States, which led to his becoming president of the National Golden Gloves in 2005. He stepped down as president in 2015, but remained as the immediate past president.

On the professional side of the sport, Rodgers has worked strictly as a cutman. He was the cutman for former undisputed middleweight champion Jermain Taylor, who fought professionally from 2001 to 2014. Rodgers was also the cutman for former WBO world heavyweight champion Tommy Morrison, who fought from 1988 to 2008.

In addition, Rodgers has worked as a cutman for Wayne McCullough, Hector Camacho, Sr., David Diaz, Iran Barkley, Phillip Jackson, Tony Smith, and Lamar Murphy. This interview took place over the phone in October 2016.

How did boxing first become a part of your life and what led you to become president of the National Golden Gloves?

I started boxing in 1947 as a ten-year-old, and I've been at it ever since. When I was in the fifth grade, they sent a note around that said you could try boxing if you get written permission from your parents. At that time, boxing was a letter sport in virtually every school. In Oklahoma, it was very, very prevalent. For me, it was a way to get out of school and travel. All the other kids were sitting there in the classroom listening to Ms. Counts recite the alphabet. I was having more fun than them!

The first bout I ever had, the kid gave me a real shellacking. I had to wear a sock cap for a week, because I had knots all over my head. These were the days before headgear and shirts. If you lost your mouthpiece, they didn't pick it up and let you wash it off. They just kicked it out of the ring, and your trainer could put it back in your mouth between rounds. It was a different time.

I grew up at the end of the Depression. I saw kids come to school barefooted. Somewhere, I probably have a school picture of me with a pair of overalls on and no shirt. There was nothing shameful about it. That's just the way it was. The kids today are spoiled. They live in a fantasy world of video games and interactive computers. If you have a new kid come in the gym and he finds out he's gonna break a sweat, you may not see him again. For every five boxers that stay, ninety-five of them go. You hear people say how boxing builds character. I always say that boxing doesn't *build* character, it reveals it.

I boxed from the fifth grade, all the way through college. When I was fifteen, I started coaching as well. In 1953, I took three little boys to the Junior Golden Gloves. We got there and they told me, "We can't let you enter those boys. You're not old enough to coach." I said, "Show me the rule book where it says that." They had a little huddle and they couldn't find anything wrong, so they said, "Okay, but we're gonna watch you." Well, my boys did pretty well in that tournament and I kept on coaching through my whole amateur career. In the old days, you had some guys that played professional baseball and also managed a team. That was similar to me. I was a coaching boxer. I would box, take my wraps off, and go work the other kids' corner. It's just something I always did.

Cutman and former National Golden Gloves President Ray Rodgers (right), and former Arkansas LBC President James Humphreys, 1985 (courtesy Ray Rodgers).

In 1960, I graduated from Arkansas State Teachers College, which is now the University of Central Arkansas. I got a degree in industrial management and I moved to Little Rock to conquer the world. I was in the construction business. I worked for one company for about twenty years, had my own company for about twenty-two years.... In 2008, I finally decided to lay it down. Over the last fifty, sixty years, I've had a number of gyms in the Little Rock area. I still own a Golden Gloves Gym in what's called a junior deputy sports complex. We have an education center in conjunction with our Golden Gloves Gym where we do tutoring—The Golden Gloves Education Center. It's right next door to my Golden Gloves Gym.

I came up boxing and coaching in the Golden Gloves locally, and have been involved in it ever since. In 1975, the man who ran the State Golden Gloves in Arkansas called me one Saturday afternoon and said, "Ray, I'm going to move to Miami, Florida. Do you want to take over the Golden Gloves?" Now, that's a prized possession in Arkansas. I told him, "You bet, I will!" I took it over, and in 1990, the guy that ran the Regional Golden Gloves in Jackson, Tennessee, told me he was gonna quit and asked if I would take *that* over. We had Louisiana, Mississippi, Arkansas, and West Tennessee, over past Nashville.

I take the kids from the Regionals to the Nationals every year. I ran for the board of directors of the Nationals and was elected. I was put up for vice president and got that. Then they wanted me to run for president, so I ran for president and was elected in 2005. I could have stayed forever if I wanted to, but there's a lot of stress in that job—people calling you at all hours of the day and night, whining about this and that....

After ten years, I gave it up. I'm the immediate past president, so I have all the perks. I just don't have the headaches. I'm also president of the National Silver Gloves, I've been on the board of directors for USA Boxing, I'm head of the Golden Gloves Coaches Committee, I was vice chairman of the USA Boxing safety committee.... My whole life has revolved around amateur boxing.

Having observed the amateur side of the sport for a number of years, who are some accomplished professionals that stand out in your mind from when they were younger?

In the early '60s, I was good friends with Joe Martin, who ran the Golden Gloves in Louisville, Kentucky. He trained a kid named Cassius Clay, who had star stamped all over him. Brash, braggadocious, noisy.... But a real boxing talent. I got to see Ray Leonard, Tommy Hearns, and Aaron Pryor, who just passed away yesterday. All those kids came up through the Golden Gloves.

Mike Tyson could punch like a son of a gun. If I recall, he was gonna box a kid in the finals of the National Junior Olympics and the kid didn't even show up. I guess you gotta give him credit for being a smart guy. He was still the runner up, but he didn't get beat to death. I remember when Oscar De La Hoya won the Silver Gloves, the Golden Gloves, and the USA Boxing Tournament all in the course of a year. He was only sixteen years old at the time. I don't know how long he had been boxing, but he was a total and a complete boxer at that age. When I say a "complete boxer," that's the highest compliment I can give. Offense, defense, footwork, agility....

The first time I saw Roy Jones, he was just a boy, boxing in a tournament in Biloxi, Mississippi. They were calling him "Little Sugar," after Ray Leonard. Floyd Mayweather won the National Golden Gloves his first time right here in Little Rock in 1993. Like all the others, he had star stamped all over him. I've seen a lot of them come and go. Some good, some bad, some indifferent.

What led you to work as a cutman in the professional ranks?

I came up in the days before headgear and we had a lot of cuts. If you were a trainer, you either learned how to stop a cut, or your kids didn't survive. So, I picked it up in the amateurs and perfected it. Local professionals knew I was good with cuts and they would ask me to be in their corner. Word got around and I started working pretty regularly.

Billy Bock (left), former Miss Arkansas Sally Miller, and Ray Rodgers, 1958 (courtesy Ray Rodgers).

One night, I worked a show in Memphis at the Mid-South Coliseum. I was the house cutman. If there was a coach that didn't have a cutman, I worked their corner. At the end of the night, I went in to get paid. The guy that was running it said, "Ray, I'm real busy. I'll mail you your check." I said, "Well, I'm not that busy. I'll just wait." I think he was Italian and I suspected that he might be part of the Southern Mafia. So, I sat outside his door and he finally gave me my check. I figured it would bounce as high as a rubber ball, so I immediately took it to the bank at daylight and cashed it. I probably beat everybody else by getting my check early, 'cause it didn't bounce.

There was another interesting story that confirmed my faith in mankind. I had a fight with Wayne McCullough in Atlantic City and Robert McCracken was on the card. They said, "Ray, this guy doesn't have a cutman. Would you work with him?" I said, "Well, sure." After the fight, McCracken said, "How much do I owe you?" I told him five hundred dollars and he asked me if he could mail me a check. Now, he's goin' back to London, so I figured I'd never hear from him again. But guess what? Within a week of the fight, he mailed me a cashier's check from the Bank of England for what was the equivalent of five hundred dollars. I was with Jermain Taylor when he fought Carl Froch and Robert McCracken was in Froch's corner. I reminded him of that when I saw him and we had a jolly ol' visit.

What led you to work as cutman for former middleweight champion Jermain Taylor and what stands out about the time you spent with him?

When Jermain was fourteen years old, he was in the Junior Golden Gloves. He told me, "Ray, when I turn pro, I want you to work as my cutman." I hear that all the time, but sure enough, the day he signed a promotional contract, they called me. Jermain had thirty-eight pro bouts and I was in his corner for each and every one.

Now, you need to understand, I don't get involved in a fighter's business affairs. I got one job and that's a cutman. But if I had been Jermain Taylor's manager, you might say that I would have done some things different. Jermain's first trainer was Pat Burns and he got him to 25–0. But after Jermain beat Bernard Hopkins twice, they brought in Emanuel Steward to replace him. May his soul rest in peace, but hiring Emanuel Steward was one of the worst things they did. He brought nothing to the table. I'm not diminishing his achievements as a trainer or saying anything negative about him, but he brought nothing.

They paid Emanuel a lot of money and I think that's why he took the job. I don't think he was really interested in Jermain's career. When we were fighting Winky Wright, Emanuel took the end-swell out of my hand and started jamming it into a knot under Jermain's eye. He was probably frustrated with Jermain because he wasn't doing what he wanted him to do, but you don't take your frustration out on the fighter and interfere with the cutman. I've worked with all kinds of trainers and I never had anybody do that before or since.

Future world middleweight champion Jermain Taylor (left), Ray Rodgers, and future heavyweight contender Dominick Guinn, at the 1999 National Golden Gloves tournament in Syracuse, New York (courtesy Ray Rodgers).

I had remembered Kelly Pavlik from the National Golden Gloves, but I don't think anybody realized what a tough kid he was. We lost to him twice in one year. In that first fight, Jermain went into the amateur mode and he spent all his energy trying to knock Pavlik out. He was just throwing one shot after another and he ran out of gas. In Foxwoods against Carl Froch, he ran out of gas *again*. He was ahead on two cards and they stopped it with just a few seconds left. When he fought in that tournament, it was like they were leading him into the bear's den. I thought we might be wading into deep water and it turned out that we were.

An old trainer told me one time that you don't get to the top by fighting contenders. You need to give a fighter different looks. You need a short guy, and a fat guy, and a guy with long arms.... What you don't want to give him is a Goliath. For Jermain, it was Goliath, after Goliath, after Goliath. After he got knocked out in Germany, he went to the boxing doctors in Las Vegas. They did all these neurological tests and he came out clean as a whistle. I was a little reluctant when he fought again, but he asked me to be in his corner, so I caved in.

After he won another championship, he started getting into trouble. People figured it might have been the blows to the head that caused him to act that way, but that wasn't it. He had got into drugs and alcohol real bad. The devil had him by the coattails and dragged him through the quagmire of sin and iniquity. You could probably recite a bunch of cases like that in professional boxing. It's a very common story and that's the shame of it.

Tell me about the time you spent as cutman for former heavyweight champion Tommy Morrison.

I was with Tommy from '88, all the way to '96. I remember when he fought Pinklon Thomas in Kansas City. Tommy pummeled him pretty good in the first round. The referee said, "Pinklon, I'm gonna give you one more round." Pinklon said, "No, you're not!" When Tommy fought Ray Mercer, he was beating Mercer like he had broke into a church. Then all of a sudden, Tommy had no more energy and it ended pretty badly. Tommy was on the ropes and the referee was tapping on Mercer's shoulder like he wanted to break in at a dance. He should have jumped in immediately and protected that kid.

I was there when he fought George Foreman. Tommy fought the only fight he could—boxing and moving. He couldn't stand there and trade blows with George, because even in George's old age, he still had a very heavy hand. The minute the fight was over, George went back to his corner and put on a pair of sunglasses. Tommy had peppered him pretty good with that left jab of his. Years later, George had a book signing here in Little Rock. I bought George's book and told him that I was Tommy Morrison's cutman that night. He said, "Boy, I sure could have used you in *my* corner!"

Tommy's loss to Michael Bentt was the upset of the year and maybe the biggest shock of my career. My eyes got about as big as silver dollars. John Brown looked at me, and held out his paw, and said, "Can you imagine seven million dollars just disappearing out of a hand like that?" If Tommy had won the fight, they had a tentative agreement to fight Mike Tyson. At that fight, Tommy had four different girls, one on every side of the ring, unbeknownst to each other. If the truth be known, I think he had been out with one of them the night before.

Against Lennox Lewis, Tommy just got manhandled. Lennox is a big boy. I mean a *big* boy! Tommy was a massive puncher, but he wasn't that big. Maybe just over six feet. Lennox was 6'5". You know you're in trouble when a boxer can touch gloves with you without coming out of his corner.

In '96, we were in Las Vegas set to box a guy by the name of "Stormy" Weathers. I was in the room getting my bag ready, making sure everything's in the right pocket and so forth. And I got a phone call from his manager, Tony Holden. He said, "Ray, I need to talk to you." I said, "Okay, go ahead." He said, "No, I need to see you in person." Five or ten minutes later, I got a knock on the door and it was Tommy Virget, who was Tommy's trainer at the time, and Tony Holden. They were both white as a sheet. I said, "What's the matter, guys?" They said that Tommy tested positive. I said, "What kind of drug was it?" They said, "It wasn't drugs. It was HIV." I said, "Oh, no!" I couldn't believe it. I said, "Where's Tommy right now? I want to talk to him." They said he was already on his way back to Tulsa.

When Tommy died, Tony Holden called and asked if I would speak at his funeral. I had just had an operation on my knee and I was immobile, so I wrote up a testament. There was a little poem I used to recite for Tommy. It went, "I saw a little man upon a stair, a little man who wasn't there. He wasn't there again today. Gee, I wish he'd go away." Tommy always liked that. He wanted me to recite that every time I saw him. He'd say, "How did that go again, Ray?" Me and Tommy were as close as nine is to ten. We never had a problem and you can't say that about everybody. We really enjoyed each other's company.

Ray Rodgers around the time when he first put on the gloves, Tecumseh, Oklahoma, 1947 (courtesy Ray Rodgers).

You have been involved in amateur boxing as a fighter, a trainer, and in a number of other capacities. In professional boxing, your only involvement has been as a cutman. Why is that?

I've seen too many fighters led astray by people who are unscrupulous. That's not an indictment of everybody in professional boxing. But there are certain people who will prostitute these kids, get 'em a few fights, build 'em up, and get 'em beat to death. Next thing you know, they're walking around with a sock cap on talking to themselves. That's my big problem with it.

I was in Iran Barkley's corner in Germany when he fought Henry Maske. If you look at the fight, Iran took such a beating. They stopped it in the ninth round and it took a doctor sixty-two stitches to sew him up. After that, he called me and asked if I could help him with another fight. I said, "No, I can't make it." I didn't tell him why, but I just felt that he didn't need to take any more punishment. You gotta have a human aspect in this sport and sometimes you don't see that.

If a kid comes to me in the gym and says he wants to be a professional, I say, "Well, you're in the wrong gym. You better go across town." In the pros, I'm just a cutman. I don't make any moral judgments against somebody who asks me to be in their corner. I just do my job and then I get gone. The main thrust in my involvement in boxing is to help the youth of America, and give them a sense of purpose and direction. It has been a great endeavor for me and I love this sport with every fiber of my being. It's something I've always done since 1947 and I don't intend to quit. I got a gym downtown, I work with kids, and that's what I'm gonna do from now till beyond.

16

Don Turner: The Gym at Clark & Central

"Boxing is like morality. It's a lifestyle. If you do everything right, you'll be okay. If you cheat, you're going to get hurt."

As time goes by, athletes often get better from one generation to the next, because of improved training methods and scientific discoveries. What worked a number of years ago may now be considered archaic. However, there are some who insist that the old school way is the only way.

Born in Norristown, Pennsylvania, and raised in Cincinnati, Ohio, Don Turner grew up in the 1940s and '50s, watching fighters like Joe Louis, Ezzard Charles, and "Sugar" Ray Robinson.

Turner boxed professionally as a middleweight from 1959 to 1969, compiling a record of 7–9-1, before learning the finer points of being a trainer.

Throughout his career as a trainer, Turner has worked with several notable fighters, including Larry Holmes, Aaron Pryor, Mike McCallum, Livingstone Bramble, Christophe Tiozzo, Larry Stanton, and John David Jackson.

Turner is best known for training former world cruiserweight and heavyweight champion, Evander Holyfield, from the mid-1990s to mid-2000s. He was in the corner for Holyfield's November 1996 eleventh-round TKO over WBA world heavyweight champion, Mike Tyson, as well as Holyfield's June 1997 rematch with Tyson, when Tyson was disqualified for biting Holyfield's ear.

In addition to Holyfield, Turner has worked with a number of other heavyweights, including Vitali and Wladimir Klitschko, Henry Akinwande, Hasim Rahman, Clifford Etienne, and Michael Grant. This interview took place over the phone in June 2013.

What is your background in boxing and what led you to become a trainer?

It all began for me in 1949 when I was ten years old. I used to watch Ezzard Charles work out. They opened up a gym at Clark and Central, and we would go up there. When you're born and raised in the slums, there's not much to do. With Ezzard Charles being a fighter, that was a big thing in Cincinnati. We used to listen to him on the radio.

When I was in elementary school, we used to play around with what we called body punching. It was a big deal in my neighborhood to have good hands. At age eleven, I started going to the gym to train. Jimmy Brown was the first guy who wrapped my hands and told me what to eat. I only had five amateur fights, but I spent a lot of time in the gym and picked up on things. I turned pro in 1959. In 1969, I retired.

From there I went into an apprenticeship with Sid Martin. He was an older guy. I'm from the old school where you're taught that you're supposed to learn from the best. After four years, I went out and started training fighters on my own. When I started training, I knew about cuts and everything there was to know about it.

Boxing is a serious business, man. If anybody took it serious and treated it as such, this would be a hell of a game. You can't name me ten complete fighters in the game today. Floyd Mayweather, Jr., is a complete fighter. So are Bernard Hopkins and Andre Ward. Before that was James Toney. James Toney could stand in front of you and he didn't care how hard you punched. You couldn't hit him solid.

Why do you think old time fighters knew how to fight? It's because they had teachers to teach them things. Today, you've got fathers training sons, just because they're their sons. You've got young kids training other kids. You've got guys that come in and work the pads, and they call themselves trainers. The pads is bullshit. You're not supposed to cross your body when you throw punches. Your opponent only has one head. Why would you train a guy to hit a guy with one head on the right, and one head on the left, with a foot in between? It don't make sense, man.

There're a few good trainers in the game today—Floyd Mayweather, Sr., Roger Mayweather, Nacho Beristain, Miguel Diaz.... Do you know who Bobby McQuillar was? He was the Godfather of all teachers. How about Harry Amberly? He's the guy they hired to teach Joe Louis footwork. These are the kind of people I've been around, man. Old school!

Throughout my career, I trained Larry Holmes, Larry Stanton, Aaron Pryor, Mike McCallum, John David Jackson, Livingstone Bramble.... I didn't come on the scene big until I worked with Evander Holyfield. When I was training Holyfield, I had the Klitschko brothers, Hasim Rahman, Michael Grant, and Henry Akinwande at the same time. I had all heavyweights. I had two heavyweights win the title in the same year—Holyfield over Tyson, and Akinwande over Jeremy Williams. That's when it was big, man. I won Trainer of the Year in '96.

In 2000, I had Clifford Etienne. I was with him when he gave Lamon Brewster his first loss. He beat Cliff Couser, Lawrence Clay-Bey... He was hot. When we were in camp, there was a restaurant I used to go to. The guy who owned the bar said, "You train Etienne, right?" I said, "Yeah." He said, "How is he gonna be a boxer if he's at my bar every night?" Before the Oquendo fight, he was sneaking out and getting drunk every night. Oquendo must have knocked him down about five times.

A lot of these guys today don't have a work ethic conducive to being a fighter. Boxing is like morality. It's a lifestyle. If you do everything right, you'll be okay. If you cheat, you're going to get hurt. You see guys doing roadwork, and they've got earphones on, and they do three miles in thirty minutes. Man, you can *walk* three miles in thirty minutes. If you can't do a six-minute mile, why did you get up and run? You gotta get your heart rate up. You can't get it up running slow. You don't fight at a slow pace, so you shouldn't run at a slow pace. The fighters of old got up

Trainer Don Turner and former world cruiserweight and heavyweight champion Evander Holyfield, 2000s (courtesy Don Turner).

in the morning and put combat boots on. Army boots, brother. Later on, these new trainers came along and told them to wear sneakers. It's ridiculous, man.

One thing I know, if I don't know nothing else, I know about boxing. I've had people today say they want to interview me for a trainer position. I say, "Listen, man, I'm un-interviewable. If my record don't speak for itself, you don't need me." I'm not interested in a salary. I'm interested in training a champion. I will not take your money if you give me a guy who can't fight. Today, everybody wants to make the fighter happy. Well, I'm nobody's butt brother. If I have to go along to get along, then we ain't gonna get along. That's the way I am. Some people don't like me because I'm brash, but I tell the truth.

You spent some time working with Aaron Pryor, who won the WBA world junior welterweight title in August 1980. What stands out in your mind about the time you spent with Pryor?

Jimmy Brown, the guy who trained Ezzard Charles—he had Aaron Pryor and I went down to help him. I was with him all the way until his second defense of his title. What a fighter, man! He was the epitome of a professional. You didn't have to beg him to train. You had to *stop* him from training. He used to knock sparring partners out. These guys thought they could just take his money, and he'd hit them on the chin and down they'd go. You can't play with your sparring partner, man.

You're not gonna play with your opponent. Some of these sparring partners try to come in and befriend the fighter. Not Aaron Pryor. What a fighter!

We had a good relationship until I leaned on him. If I feel I'm right about something, you can't change my mind. Not with no bullshit. I'm not gonna compromise right from wrong at no time. I don't need to compromise my integrity to make you feel good. A guy pays me for my leadership and expertise. Just because he's paying me doesn't mean he can tell me what to do.

You trained former heavyweight champion Larry Holmes in the early '90s, when Holmes no longer held a title and was fighting at an advanced age. What stands out in your mind about the time you spent with Holmes?

My job with Larry was to remind him of what he was capable of doing and let him know what he couldn't do no more. That's the way you handle a fighter's career. You can't train a forty-year-old guy the same way you train a twenty-year-old. You have to make adjustments. You know why Larry Holmes was so good? He was disciplined. If his sparring partner wasn't it shape, Larry would beat him up. He'd say, "How are you going to get me in shape, if *you* ain't in shape?" Larry had the best jab of any heavyweight. He used to stand in front of the mirror and practice for hours with that jab.

I knew Larry since he was a kid. I knew him when he was shining shoes and washing cars. He used to come to the gym, and get beat up by Randy Neumann and all those guys. He got knocked out by Nick Wells in the amateurs. He was a top four guy at light heavyweight, but he couldn't beat Nick Wells. I didn't think much of Larry till he fought Ken Norton. He showed a lot of guts in the Norton fight. He had to win the last couple of rounds to win the fight and he did. The will to win is insurmountable, man. I think Larry might be the best heavyweight that ever lived.

Former world heavyweight champion Larry Holmes, 1970s (courtesy Jackie Kallen).

You began training Evander Holyfield when he defended his WBA and IBF world heavyweight titles against Michael Moorer in April 1994, a fight that Holyfield lost by majority decision. The highlight of the time you spent with Holyfield was his eleventh-round TKO victory over Mike Tyson in November 1996 for Tyson's WBA heavyweight title. You remained with Holyfield until he lost to James Toney via ninth-round TKO in October 2003.

Holyfield knew of me because I

was with Larry Holmes when he fought him. Larry was old and he gave Holyfield problems. They called me up and I went down there to meet them. I told Holyfield what a great fighter he was, but that nobody showed him how to fight at the right distance. If you got a guy who's 6'1", you fight him at a different distance than a guy who's 6'5". I stood up and showed him what I was talking about. He said, "I've been fighting fifteen years and nobody's told me that." After he lost to Michael Moorer, everybody thought I was gonna get fired, but guess what? He gave me a $100,000 bonus, because I stopped the cut.

When I had Holyfield, people thought he was washed up. What I saw was a fighter in transition, who was getting older. Instead of overpowering everybody, he had to use his skill. Holyfield was a real intelligent guy. Nobody thought he was going to beat Tyson, but that was an easy fight. I've seen all of Tyson's fights and I spotted a flaw early on when he fought Mitch Green. If you take baby steps, you throw him off. He has to reset. Just as soon as he sets, you step to the side. Step and touch him, step and touch him... That was the best fight that Holyfield ever fought in his life. Everything worked perfect.

Before the fight, one of Tyson's guys came up to me and told me that I was going to have to throw in the towel. He said, "We don't want to see Holyfield get hurt." I said, "Let me explain something to you, man. First of all, you don't know nothing about boxing. I've been going to the gym since 1949." He said, "I don't care how long you've been going to the gym for. Don't let Holyfield get hurt. Throw the towel in." I said, "I want you to do me a favor. Tomorrow after Tyson gets knocked out, I want you to come here and apologize in front of the same people you're talking to." And he did.

In the second fight, Tyson didn't want to fight, so he bit the guy. Tyson had been having psychological problems his whole life. Any time you got a guy with psychological problems, they're easy to beat. People were intimidated by Tyson, but Holyfield wasn't. With Tyson, that was the best camp we had. I had his attention the whole time, but Holyfield wasn't the same fighter after that. He didn't want it as bad no more. When he beat Tyson, it weakened the animal psyche. The human psyche is weaker than the animal psyche. Cats in the wild have to fight for every meal. Humans get their meal in the conference room.

I tried to keep Holyfield focused, but one day he said to me, "I've been fighting long enough to know what's good for me." There was nothing I could do. Every time I turned around, there was somebody in his ear. Holyfield fought past his prime and I knew that. The only reason I was all right with the James Toney fight is because Toney wasn't a big puncher. When I stopped the fight with Toney, the whole corner thought I shouldn't have done that. I said, "I don't give a damn what you guys say. I'm stopping the fight." At the time, Holyfield said I did the right thing. He was all right with it, but the next morning, he said that if I didn't have confidence in him, then I shouldn't work with him no more. That was it. I was okay with that, because I felt I did the right thing.

You grew up watching heavyweight champions like Ezzard Charles, Joe Louis, and Rocky Marciano. How would you compare Holyfield's career to the greatest heavyweights in history?

Evander Holyfield, promoter Dan Goossen, and former multi-division champion James Toney at a press conference leading up to the 2003 fight between Holyfield and Toney (courtesy Bret Newton—ThreatPhoto.com/Pound4Pound.com).

I'll put it to you like this, man—on any heavyweight's best night, they could have beaten any heavyweight. That goes back to Jack Dempsey, and Jack Johnson, and all of them. When Holyfield beat Tyson, he could have beaten any heavyweight that night. That was a night like Louis and Schmeling. He couldn't be denied.

You trained Michael Grant, a 6'7" 250-pound heavyweight who remained undefeated in his first thirty-one fights, until he lost to WBC and IBF world heavyweight champion Lennox Lewis by second-round knockout in April 2000.

When I started working with Michael Grant, Ray Mercer needed a sparring partner for Lennox Lewis. I told Michael, "You ain't no sparring partner. You're gonna work with Ray Mercer for *nothing*. All you're gonna get is room and board. No money, but you're gonna learn how to fight." He was in camp with Ray Mercer for thirty days and he didn't lose a round.

If Michael Grant was mean, nobody would have beat him. Grant was the strongest fighter I ever worked with. He could knock out a thousand sit-ups like it was nothing. He could run three miles in eighteen minutes in the snow. He was a hell of an athlete, but he was a mama's boy. He didn't have a strong mind. He should have beat Lennox Lewis, but he punked out at the last minute.

For every fight, I would give him a little pep talk. While I was wrapping his hands before the fight, I tried to talk to him and he said, "Man, I don't want to hear that shit." Right then, I knew it was over. Thirty-one fights together and now he doesn't want to listen to me. Five minutes before we got in the ring, he was looking for a telephone so he could give his friend a ticket. Can you believe that? Here's a guy about to fight in Madison Square Garden for the heavyweight championship and he's looking for a telephone. He had the ability to beat Lennox Lewis, but he just didn't want it.

Sports performance/fitness trainer Tim Hallmark (left), Don Turner, and boxing trainer Tommy Brooks, 1990s (courtesy Tim Hallmark/timhallmark.com).

How does the sport of boxing today compare to when you began following the game in 1949?

Boxing is the only sport that hasn't gotten better over the years. All the other sports—hockey, football, basketball, baseball, golf, tennis—they've gotten better. You used to have real fighters in the top ten. When Ray Robinson had his last fight, you know who he lost to? Joey Archer. He was the number-one contender for the middleweight title. He lost a ten-round decision. Today, everybody wants their fighters to fight stiffs. They don't hone their skills on good competition. In any other sport, if you don't make it through the minor leagues, you don't graduate. They don't have a professional team beat a college team, and call it a win. Am I correct?

Henry Armstrong defended his title five times in twenty-one days. Today, they might defend their title five times in five years. It's a different era and a different mindset. Guys that come to the gym have been in front of the computer all day. They spend one hour in the gym and eight hours in front of the computer. I got two computers and I don't even know how to turn them on. I don't know how to text either. Picking up the phone and calling is easy. Why would you text, if you can just pick up the phone and call?

Kids used to walk two or three miles to school. Today, they take the bus. When I was coming up, kids didn't eat candy and soda like they do today. Why do you think people have all these sicknesses, man? I was in the doctor's office today and I had a one o'clock appointment. The doctor came in at two o'clock and left after ten minutes. My insurance company is gonna pay five hundred dollars for that. It's greed, man. People is greedy. I never was greedy. Success never changed me, because I was grounded. I learned it from my grandfather.

The realities of life are very simple, man. I'm not a religious person, but I do know that life is about helping people. If I can help a person, why shouldn't I? I knew how it was when I was coming up. People helped me and they didn't ask for nothing in return. My mentors was guys who didn't care about money. They could do without. They were proud. I used to see bums on the street and I'd give them a twenty dollar bill. People would be like, "Why did you give him a twenty dollar bill?" Because a dollar ain't gonna feed him. That's why. It ain't gonna make me no richer and no poorer.

When I started making a whole lot of money, I bought me five Brioni suits. That's $4,500 a suit. Guess what? I've never worn any of them three times in twenty years. I bought a Cartier watch. Sold it. I thought that's what I wanted, but I don't need that shit, man. I'm just as satisfied to go fishing with you and talk boxing all day.

I've seen a whole lot since I've been coming up. I've seen the riots, I've seen Hoover.... I've seen all that nonsense. I'm surprised I've lived as long as I have, because I've never taken shit from nobody. I was born poor, raised on welfare, and been on my own since 1955. I met my wife in front of Studio 54 in August of 1962. It's been fifty-one years since the first day I've seen her. That's how long I've been with her. My daughter will be fifty. My son will be forty-nine.

Nothing really changes. Five hundred years ago, you had to eat, you had to drink, you had to shit. That ain't changed. Am I right or wrong? Evolution is just a passage of time. My fate will be the same fate as the Pharaohs. I'm gonna die. When you're born, the process of dying starts. That's the truth about the whole situation. From the womb to the tomb is a short trip, my friend. All in between, you're gonna be sad sometimes and you're gonna be happy sometimes. But the final fate that we're living is dying.

Promoters and Managers

17

Lou DiBella: After Dark

"Most world champions can walk down Times Square and nobody knows who they are. Boxing is about fights. When there's a great fight, people know about it and fighters become stars because of that."

HBO was once the king of televised boxing. In 2018, the network announced that it was getting out of the business, because the sport had become more available for viewing on other networks and digital platforms. But during its forty-five-year run, HBO featured some of the best fighters and broadcast some of the most memorable bouts of that time.

Born and raised in Brooklyn, New York, Lou DiBella graduated from Harvard Law School with the intentions of pursuing a career in either sports or music. In 1989, he went to work for HBO Sports as their attorney.

One of the first projects DiBella worked on was world lightweight champion Pernell Whitaker's long-term contract with HBO. The very first fight DiBella wrote the contracts for was the legendary upset that occurred in February 1990, when heavyweight champion Mike Tyson was knocked out by 42–1 underdog James "Buster" Douglas.

Because of DiBella's passion for boxing and knowledge of the game, he eventually became Senior Vice President of HBO Sports, which put him in a position where he was buying the fights and doing the matchmaking.

While at HBO, DiBella created *Boxing After Dark,* a series that was something of a platform to HBO's *World Championship Boxing. Boxing After Dark* featured competitive matches between up-and-coming prospects who were hungry to reach the championship level.

In 2000, DiBella left HBO and formed DiBella Entertainment, a promotional company located in New York City.

Since the founding of his company, DiBella has represented a number of well-known champions and high profile contenders, including Sergio Martinez, Jermain Taylor, Bernard Hopkins, Paul Malignaggi, Micky Ward, Andre Berto, Ricardo Williams, Glen Johnson, Ike Quartey, Andy Lee, Edwin Rodriguez, Heather Hardy, Alicia Napoleon, Amanda Serrano, Tevin Farmer, and Deontay Wilder. This interview took place over the phone in December 2018.

What is your background in boxing and what led you to become a promoter?

Boxing became a part of my life, because of my grandfathers who were Italian immigrants. When they came here, soccer wasn't getting any U.S. playtime at all, so both of them became boxing and baseball fans. My dad was a football and baseball fan, but he also watched boxing. So, I don't really remember my life when boxing wasn't a part of it. I wasn't even ten years old when I saw Emile Griffith vs. Nino Benvenuti. I also watched Nino Benvenuti vs. Dick Tiger. I was a big Benvenuti fan, because of my grandparents' Italian heritage.

Around this time, I discovered Muhammad Ali, who became my hero and my idol. I used to listen to his fights on a transistor radio under my pillow. Growing up, the things that excited me were sports and music. Those were the areas I wanted to pursue. I was always a pretty good student in school. I was good at taking standardized tests, and I took the business boards and the law boards when I was graduating from college, because I couldn't find any job other than a radio gig for low pay in Tallahassee, Florida. I got a near perfect score on the law boards and I wound up getting into Harvard Law School. I figured if I go to Harvard Law School and graduate from there, it would be a much easier road to a career in sports or music.

When I got out of law school, I interviewed with various agencies and companies, and they all told me the same thing. They said to go get some experience at a big firm and then come back in a few years. So, I ended up at a firm called Sullivan & Cromwell, which is a very big firm on Wall Street. I never wanted to be a lawyer and it wasn't my permanent home, but I learned a lot there. The people there knew I eventually wanted to do sports and entertainment, and they gave me an opportunity to work on some things that really helped prepare me.

Professional boxing promoter Lou DiBella, after receiving Ring 10's Steve Acunto Lifetime Dedication Award in 2014 (courtesy Claudia Bocanegra).

When I was ready to move on from there, I interviewed for a number of jobs in music, but nothing really turned me on. I ended up interviewing for the job as the lawyer for the New York Yankees. I made it through the whole interview process, and I was set to have my final interview with George Steinbrenner, who was the owner of the Yankees. But right before I left my apartment for the interview, I got a call from Steinbrenner's secretary. She said, "My boss didn't realize that you're still in your twenties. He thinks you're too young for the job." She felt really bad and she said, "I don't know if you're interested, but another guy who might be getting the job had been interviewing to be general counsel for HBO Sports. Maybe that's something you could pursue?"

As soon as the secretary told me that, the bells went off in my head. I was a huge boxing fan and I knew what HBO meant to boxing. So, instead of heading for the Bronx to meet with George Steinbrenner, I headed to 42nd Street near Times Square, which is where the HBO building was. I was already wearing my suit and I had my resume in my pocket. Back then, security in the HBO building wasn't so tight. I talked my way past security and convinced a secretary to let me into the office of HBO's chief lawyer. He told me that they were about to hire somebody else. Being a little bit cocky, I said, "Whoever you're going to hire is the wrong guy." I said, "Their resume is not going to be any better than mine, and there's no way they know as much about boxing as I do."

I think he was so impressed with my bravado that he agreed to get me up to Seth Abraham's office. He was the president of HBO Sports. I went up there and I talked to Seth for about an hour and some change. We talked about boxing, as well as our mutual love for baseball. That was Friday afternoon. On Monday, I got a call offering me the job. I took a huge pay cut at first, but my career skyrocketed pretty quickly.

There were some really good people at HBO at that time, but they weren't boxing people per se. So, even though I was attending all these meetings as the lawyer, I had a lot to say about the matchups and stuff like that. I was an *insane* boxing fan. I knew who the fighters from Thailand and Japan were. I hung out at the gyms and knew who the up-and-coming amateurs were. Nobody at HBO had that kind of passion for the sport. Naturally, because of that, my role evolved. It didn't take long before I was promoted to being the primary guy who was buying and making the fights for HBO. By the mid '90s, I was listed as one of the most powerful people in boxing.

During this time, I founded *Boxing After Dark*, which is something I'm very proud of. I believe that boxing is about matchmaking. People want to see fights where the outcome is in doubt and the action is electric. With *Boxing After Dark*, we delivered that with regularity. What differentiates me from other people who put fights together is that I don't believe that boxing is star-driven. Most world champions can walk down Times Square and nobody knows who they are. Boxing is about fights. When there's a great fight, people know about it and fighters become stars because of that. Let's face it—Arturo Gatti became a big star because of all the great fights he was in. There are endless fighters that became stars because they were involved in fights that people remember.

Boxing After Dark was about building up-and-coming fighters by matching them against other up-and-coming fighters and giving the public the kind of quality fights that they wanted. People tuned in, not because of the names, but because they knew they were gonna get a good night of boxing. There were so many good fights on *Boxing After Dark* that you can't even name them all—Marco Antonio Barrera–Kennedy McKinney; Orlando Canizales–Junior Jones; Kostya Tszyu–Vince Phillips; Arturo Gatti–Wilson Rodriguez; Arturo Gatti–Angel Manfredy; Arturo Gatti–Ivan Robinson; Derrick Jefferson–Maurice Harris....

These fights came month after month after month, and we didn't have to spend crazy money to put them together. The ratings were extraordinary, and it got to the point where *Boxing After Dark*'s success was approaching the success of *World Championship Boxing*. In a weird way, *Boxing After Dark* almost became too successful. It was supposed to be a platform for *World Championship Boxing*, but it became such a big stage of its own that HBO wanted to cut the legs out of it. They started deemphasizing it and blurring the lines between *World Championship* and *Boxing After Dark*. But that was after I left HBO.

In 2000, I went to a bunch of meetings that were also attended by a man who is now chairman of Time Warner. I didn't appreciate the way he talked to me or treated me, so I basically told him that I wanted out. I wasn't fired, but I worked out an agreement with HBO where I would leave. That's when I started DiBella Entertainment.

At first, I didn't set out to be a promoter. I wanted to be a packager who hired promoters, similar to the model that Al Haymon has. But some of the promoters at the time jumped up and down because of what I was doing. They went to the state commissions, and one of the commissions said that I needed to operate as a promoter. Once that happened, I became a promoter and I've been operating that way ever since.

It wasn't such an easy road at first. I had some HBO dates early on for the fighters I was going to be working with. But let's just say that the people who were at HBO after I left weren't going to do me any favors. And I had to be exclusive to HBO for a few years, so I couldn't really branch out. I was lucky to have signed some great champions, and to have had some great runs with some great fighters, who helped me sustain those early years.

If you look at the business side of boxing, you'll see that the success rate is very low. Look how many people have come and gone. It's hard to withstand the ups and downs that come with the territory. Boxing is the most unforgiving sport—for the athlete, for the manager, for the promoter.... One bad night can change your entire life. If you're a promoter or a manager who is investing a lot of money, and the ratio of fighters you work with who become champions is over twenty percent, you're doing very well. Being a boxing promoter is almost a form of degenerate gambling. I'm now close to twenty years with DiBella Entertainment. We've lasted in this business the whole time and I think that's something to be proud of.

In the early 2000s, you were an advisor to Bernard Hopkins, now a former world middleweight and light heavyweight champion, who is the oldest man in history to win a world title. How did you become involved with Hopkins and what stands out in your mind about the time you spent working with him?

Lou DiBella and former undisputed world middleweight champion Jermain Taylor, 2000s (courtesy Marty Rosengarten/RingsidePhotos.com).

There was a one-year period where it was clear that I was going to be leaving HBO. Part of my exit package was that I was going to have dates from HBO that I would be able to program. I identified Bernard Hopkins as someone who I wanted to work with. HBO didn't believe in Bernard Hopkins, but I did. I got Bernard onto HBO, and helped him get into that four-man middleweight tournament that Don King was doing in 2001. I made the Trinidad fight for him. And as soon as he beat Trinidad, he said that I had, in effect, taken a bribe of some kind when I was at HBO.

No one has ever lied about me like that in my life. He tried to ruin my reputation. I sued him for libel and won a million bucks. When Jermain Taylor beat Bernard the first time, it was the most emotional moment of my career. I jumped so high, I could have dunked a basketball. The second time was emotional, too, because it was Lou DiBella 3, and Bernard Hopkins 0. I beat him in court and Jermain beat him twice in the ring.

At the weigh-in for the first Jermain Taylor–Bernard Hopkins fight, I was standing behind them during the staredown. Bernard looked at me, and he knew my brother had committed suicide, and he said to me, "Why don't you kill yourself like your brother did?" Jermain heard that and he went at him to throw a punch. That was a really meaningful moment in the lead-up to that fight. But Bernard and I have since buried the hatchet. If I see him now, I'll shake his hand. There's no more anger or hatred. I'm past it.

You were the promoter of former 2000 Olympic bronze medalist Jermain Taylor throughout his whole career. In July 2005, Taylor won a split decision over undisputed world middleweight champion Bernard Hopkins. He won a title at middleweight again in October 2014 with a unanimous decision over IBF world middleweight champion Sam Soliman. Taylor lost the middleweight championship the first time in September 2009 to Kelly Pavlik via seventh-round TKO. He had a rough go of it beyond that point, losing a decision to Pavlik in a rematch, and losing inside the distance to Carl Froch and Arthur Abraham before going into semi-retirement. Taylor came back after the losses, but he was later arrested for domestic battery and was engaging in behavior that was unlike the classy way he presented himself earlier in his career.

To this day, Jermain is one of the saddest stories I've ever been associated with. I'm not going to get into the whole CTE discussion, though I have no doubt that Jermain has it. But Jermain's problems weren't just by virtue of getting knocked out. When I first met him, he had a beautiful girlfriend who became his wife. She was a WNBA player. She was gorgeous, she was smart, she was sweet.... He had wonderful kids. And at some point, he went off the rails. But he didn't go off the rails because he got knocked out. He started to go off the rails *before* the knockouts.

He had always been a very nice and humble kid, and he had never been a drinker. But after he started becoming successful, he was drinking and abusing drugs, and cheating on his wife, and buying Ferraris and Maseratis. And then he got knocked out a few times. After his fight with Arthur Abraham, he wanted to go on to the next round of fights of the Super Six, but I forced him to pull out. I resigned as his promoter, saying that I was concerned about his health and safety.

Before he came back, he was cleared by the biggest neurological institutions in the world. He won a world championship, and immediately thereafter, his life crumbled. But I don't have any regrets about getting involved with him the second time. Part of my reason for working with him again was to protect him. When he fought for the title again, he didn't fight Peter Quillin, or Danny Jacobs, or "Triple G." You know what I mean? He was protected.

Lou DiBella and former junior welterweight contender Micky Ward, 2000s (courtesy Marty Rosengarten/ RingsidePhotos.com).

You promoted junior welterweight contender Micky Ward toward the end of his career, when he had three memorable fights with Arturo Gatti, who was then a former junior lightweight champion. The fights with Gatti took place from 2002–03, with Ward winning the first bout by majority decision, and Gatti taking the last two via unanimous decision. When you became involved with Ward, he had several losses on his record and he wasn't a likely candidate to do anything significant. What compelled you to work with him?

Before the first Gatti fight, Micky had lost a technical decision to Jesse James Leija. After that, he thought his career was over. I told him, "No, come with me, and I'll get you the Gatti fights, and we'll make some money." I pretty much knew that Micky and Arturo would have a trilogy. Micky Ward was the Irish alter-ego of Arturo Gatti and I knew that these fights needed to happen. It turned out to be one of the best trilogies in boxing and I'm proud to have been a part of it.

I never had a written agreement with Micky. It was always a handshake. After the first Gatti fight, which Micky won, people made a run to get him away from me. They told him, "We can do it without DiBella and you'll get more money." Micky said, "I fought on ESPN for years and I never made any real money. Now all of a sudden, I'm in great shape because of Lou. The last thing I'm gonna do is walk away from him." When someone is loyal to you like that, you never forget it.

After Micky retired, they were planning on making a movie about him called *The Fighter*. And these unscrupulous production people got Micky to sign over his life rights for a thousand dollars in cash. When I found out, I went after them and filed a lawsuit. That's how Micky was able to get a deal that was fair to him. When *The Fighter* was made, Micky made a lot of money and did a lot of personal appearances. It was a great way to follow up his career.

You promoted Sergio Martinez, who won the WBC and WBO world middleweight titles from Kelly Pavlik by unanimous decision in April 2010 and remained a champion until his June 2014 loss to Miguel Cotto, when he couldn't continue after ten rounds.

Sergio's advisor, Sampson Lewkowicz, sent DVDs to Top Rank and a number of other promoters, including me. Sergio was already in his thirties, and he had lost to Antonio Margarito in a fight that he got paid nine hundred dollars for. Nobody knew who he was. The other promoters never responded, but I looked at the DVD and I said, "Holy shit! Where the fuck has this guy been?!" His athletic ability was bizarre. His speed, his movement... He was a beautiful fighter to watch in the ring. I paid him forty thousand for a four-round fight, as part of signing him, and he went on to be a dominant middleweight champion.

I don't think he would have ever lost to Miguel Cotto, until that moment in his career. Sergio had a bad knee when he first came over here. He got into boxing because he injured himself when he was a bicycle racer/soccer player. In a lot of his fights, he fought at less than a hundred percent. When he fought Cotto, he got caught early after being out of the ring for over a year. He never fully recovered and I think his body had had enough at that point. But I will say that not only is Sergio a tremendous talent and one of the best fighters I've ever worked with, he's also an honorable and decent guy, and remains a dear friend of mine.

It seems that a lot of the choices you make as a promoter are influenced by how you feel about the fighters as people.

Former world middleweight champion Sergio Martinez, 2000s (courtesy Marty Rosengarten/RingsidePhotos.com).

Very much so. And the older I get, the truer that is. I have a lot of affection for fighters. Fighters by definition are underdogs. I like underdogs. Through boxing, I've met some of the worst pieces of shit I've ever known in my life. But there's a flip side to it—I've also met angels. I've met people whose hearts are so overwhelmingly in the right place, who love the sport, and who want to help kids who have no place to go.

When I started at HBO, I wasn't even thirty years old. When I left HBO, I wasn't even forty. Then I woke up one day and I was in my fifties. At this point in my life, I don't feel like I have a lot to prove. With the success that I've had in boxing, I'm more secure than any member of my family has ever been. I didn't come from a poor family, but I'm in a place where I have choices that my parents and grandparents didn't have. If someone is unpleasant, or if I think there's going to be a conflict or misunderstanding, I'd rather avoid those situations. I want to work with people I respect and care about, who feel the same way about me.

18

Pat Lynch: Legendary Nights

> "It's the stuff that you can make a movie of. Just incredible! People still talk about it today. If you want to watch boxing, these are the fights to watch."

Throughout the early 1990s to the mid–2000s, former IBF world junior lightweight champion and WBC world junior welterweight champion Arturo Gatti became one of the most appreciated fighters in the history of the sport. He was known as a blood and guts warrior. Win or lose, he always gave it his all, putting on display his tremendous heart and crowd-pleasing style.

Born in New York City and raised in Union City, New Jersey, Pat Lynch was a businessman who just happened to be a boxing fan. He dabbled with the sport as an investor, then eventually as a manager. Lynch began managing Arturo Gatti in 1991, remaining with Gatti throughout Gatti's Hall of Fame career.

Gatti is best known for his trilogy with Micky Ward, which took place from May 2002 to June 2003. Even though these three fights had no title at stake, Arturo Gatti and Micky Ward were at the center of the boxing world because of the sheer excitement they brought when they faced each other.

Gatti won two out of the three fights against Ward, fighting on for four more years, before retiring in July 2007 with a record of 40–9, 31 KOs. Lynch remained close with Gatti after his retirement, all the way to Gatti's July 2009 death.

While vacationing in Brazil, Gatti was found in a hotel room with a leather strap around his neck. Brazilian authorities first determined that the death was a homicide, later declaring it was suicide. Lynch hired private investigators to look into the matter, finding strong evidence suggesting that Gatti was murdered. This interview took place over the phone in March 2016.

What is your background in boxing and what led you to start managing fighters?

Boxing was always my favorite sport. My dad boxed in the Navy, and if there was a fight on *Wide World of Sports,* that was on the TV before anything else. I didn't think I would get into boxing as a career. I own a ticket agency in New Jersey. Back in 1988, I got involved with a management company called Triple Threat—Ray Mercer, Al Cole, and Charles Murray. When the Olympians were turning pro, Bob Arum signed all the fighters and split the group in half. Half were staying in Vegas, while half were coming to Jersey. Marc Roberts was the manager and he was looking for a few guys to invest in that side of it. I was one of the four original investors. But what started out as just an investment turned into another business for me altogether.

When Matthew Hilton was fighting Doug DeWitt for a title, they were looking for a gym to use. We had just purchased a gym at that time and I offered the gym for their use. When Matthew started sparring, his chief sparring partner was Joe Gatti. At that point, I signed Joe to a managerial contract. I was still involved with Triple Threat, but I had started doing a few things on my own. I turned Joe pro in 1990. He told me he had a younger brother up in Canada named Arturo, who he wanted to bring down.

I really took a liking to Arturo. He was very respectful and easy to bring around my family. We became very close and I was more than happy to help him with his career. I signed Arturo and turned him pro on June 10, 1991. It was a walkout bout on a Main Events card. Joe Gatti was the main event. The idea was to have Arturo fight after Joe, so Joe could fight his fight and not worry about his brother. He could watch his brother after his fight. Arturo looked fabulous that night and he stopped his opponent in the third round.

His second fight was at the Blue Horizon in Philadelphia on a Russell Peltz card. That's a tough place to fight, because the balcony is hanging right there in the ring. It's a real fight fan's place. He fought Luis Melendez and knocked him out in nineteen seconds. At that time, I believe he broke the Pennsylvania state record for the fastest knockout. In his third fight, he fought Richard De Jesus in Newark, New Jersey. We had opponents fall out, so we settled on De Jesus at the last minute.

Before the fight, Russell Peltz came up to me and said, "I just want to give you a heads up. Gatti is in really tough. I know that's not what you wanted, but this guy De Jesus can really fight." Panic started to set in and I went up to Arturo's room to have a talk with him. I said, "Listen, this guy is a little tougher than we thought." He stopped me before I could say anything else and he said, "If I can't beat Richard De Jesus, I'll never be a world champion. Don't even worry about it."

I watched the replay of the De Jesus fight and even Teddy Atlas said, "I think the Gatti people took a real risk in fighting De Jesus." With that, Arturo blows the kid out in thirty-two seconds and possibly ruined his career. Blood was shooting out of his nose. It looked really bad. After the fight, we were walking up the stairs to the dressing room and I saw somebody fly past me jumping two stairs at a time. It was Dino and Lou Duva. They came rushing in and wanted to sign Arturo. We had a conversation with them and we ended up signing with Main Events. He was with them his entire career.

In November 1992, Gatti lost his first fight as a professional by split decision against King Solomon. This was just his seventh pro fight. What do you recall about that fight and how you reacted as a team?

King Solomon was a slick boxer and it was a very close fight. I don't want to make any judgments, but it was not a smart idea on our part to fight this Philadelphia guy in his own backyard. Marvis Frazier was working King Solomon's corner and they ruled a slip a knockdown. That being said, that loss turned out to be one

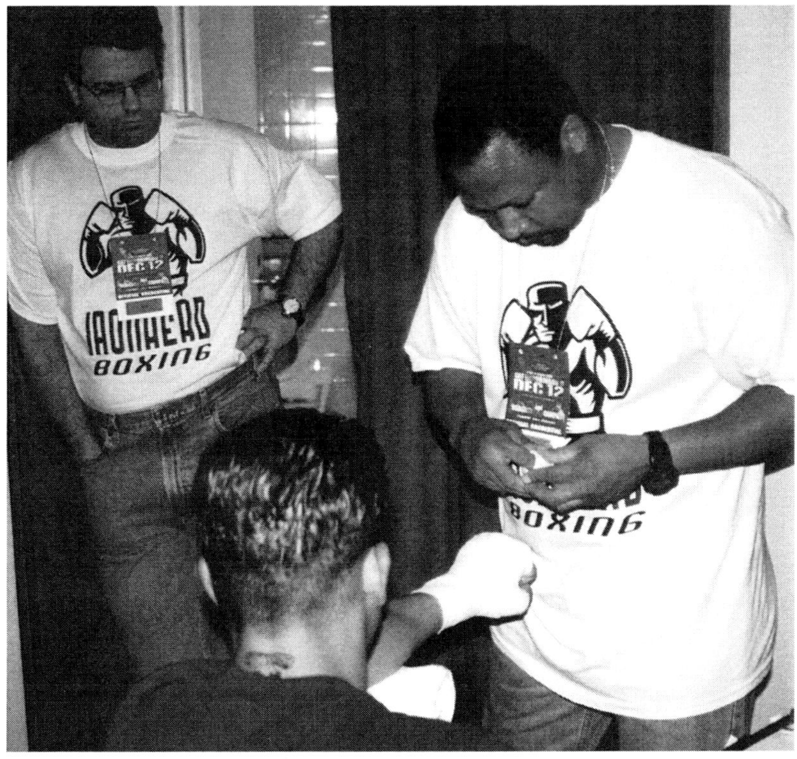

Manager Pat Lynch (left) looks on as trainer Ronnie Shields wraps former two-division world champion Arturo Gatti's hands before a 1990s bout (courtesy Rick Perez).

of the better things. Arturo was devastated and I had a long talk with him. After his first few wins, a lot of people were coming around, so we reevaluated things and got rid of a lot of distractions.

He got back to winning and he kept winning all the way to his title fight with Tracy Harris Patterson. We were the co-feature on an Oscar De La Hoya card. The place was rockin'. Lou Duva suggested a strength and conditioning coach before the fight, so the great Bob Wareing became a part of our team. He was Pernell Whitaker's strength and conditioning coach. He was tremendous. Arturo had never trained that hard in his life. He dropped Tracy early and won a decision. It was a phenomenal performance.

Gatti started his career off as an intelligent boxer who lived by the code of hitting and not getting hit. At some point, he became a "blood and guts warrior" who was willing to trade punches with his opponents. How did this shift come about?

I think that as he would get into more exchanges, he heard the crowd and he might have started to play for the crowd. He loved to rumble. He enjoyed that more than he did boxing. He wasn't crazy about the patience that came with hitting and not getting hit. He would just rather brawl. He knew he could get you out of there with either hand, as he did with Gabriel Ruelas. One punch could change the whole fight and he did that in a few different fights.

The fight with Angel Manfredy bothered him more than any fight in his career. I even mentioned that when I spoke at the Boxing Hall of Fame when he was inducted. The fight was stopped on a cut and I think rightfully so. But if he didn't get cut, I think he would have run Manfredy out of the ring. He was so mad and I told him, "Arturo, you were cut to the bone." You could actually see the bone. He said, "That's right. It couldn't go any deeper. That's why they shouldn't have stopped it." That was the type of kid he was.

After the fight with Angel Manfredy, in August 1998 Gatti faced Ivan Robinson in what turned out to be the Fight of the Year. He lost to Robinson via split decision. He then faced Robinson in a rematch in December of that year, losing a unanimous decision. At that point, Gatti had lost three fights in a row.

I give Ivan a lot of credit. He was always a great boxer and he did his homework on Arturo. But it goes to show you what a crowd pleaser Arturo was and how he was so well loved. He could lose three fights in a row and HBO would still want him back. They knew what kind of heart he had. It took a lot to beat him. He was never ever going to give up in a fight, to the point where it was sometimes scary.

In March 2001, Gatti lost to former multi-division world champion Oscar De La Hoya by fifth-round TKO. The common perception was that Gatti's career was winding down, when in actuality, it marked a new beginning.

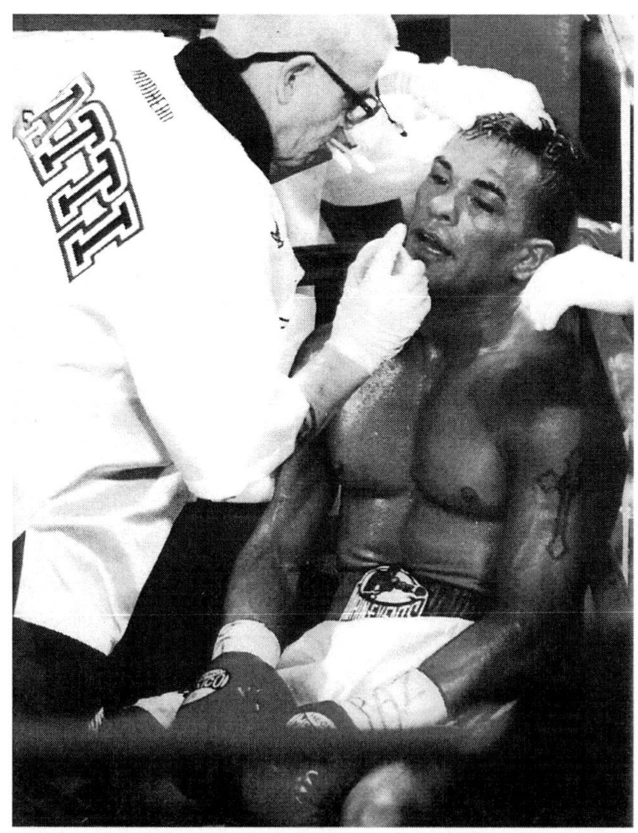

Arturo Gatti sits on his stool between rounds as cutman Joe Souza goes to work, 1990s (courtesy Rick Perez).

In the minds of HBO, I believe they saw the De La Hoya fight as a going away present for Arturo. He was a big underdog and it was a nice payday. But Arturo didn't take it as a payday. He believed he could win and he took it very, very seriously. Oscar was just too big. When Arturo landed that left hook and Oscar walked through it, I knew we were in for a long night.

After the fight, Arturo was really contemplating his future. He went down to the House of Pain gym in Florida to work out, but he wasn't sure if he wanted to fight again. When he was there, he ran into Buddy McGirt. Buddy started talking to him and working with him. And he called me and said, "I found a new trainer." I said, "I thought you were going to take your time." He said, "No, this is the guy. He's going to bring me back to my old way. He's great. We're a perfect fit."

So, I told HBO that Arturo was back in the gym and wanted to fight. They put us against Terron Millett on the undercard of Vernon Forrest and Shane Mosley. He knocked Millett out and he looked great. HBO was obviously happy, so they gave us another spot.

In May 2002, Gatti faced Micky Ward in the first of three fights, which are regarded as some of the best fights in the history of the sport. Gatti lost the first fight by majority decision. The rematch took place in November of that year, with Gatti winning a unanimous decision. The rubber match took place in June the following year with Gatti winning a unanimous decision once again.

When I told Arturo that HBO was offering us Micky Ward, he said, "No problem." He had a good training camp, but we never could have expected what happened. After the fight, Arturo said, "I've always said to myself that the toughest fight of my life would be if I fought somebody just like me. Guess what? I just fought somebody just like me."

In that ninth round, I was just sinking into my seat, and covering my face, and peaking through my fingers. Forget it! I was so relieved when it was over. Afterwards, I was in the Mohegan Sun walking back to my room with my wife. I ran into Bob Canobbio with CompuBox and he looked at me with this blank stare. He said, "I've got one word. Brutality." Then he just kept going.

That was done and over, and all of a sudden they're talking about a rematch. I thought, oh my God! We have to go through this again? Jesus Christ! Arturo really wanted it, so the negotiations started and they got it done. Never had I been a part of an event where the hair just stands up on the back of your neck. The electricity in that building was unreal. Micky's attitude was if he trained a little harder, he'd stop him this time. Arturo's attitude was if he trained a little harder, he'd box his ears off.

They went in there, and Arturo caught Micky behind his ear, and threw his equilibrium off. He shattered his eardrum and Micky fought the whole fight like that. When Arturo had him hurt, he went in for the kill. He started to hit him and he caught Micky with a left hook that woke him up. That punch actually helped Micky recover! There are so many memories of those three fights. Arturo was the one who insisted on the third fight. He said, "He gave me a chance with the second fight. He deserves a shot back at me. I want him to make as much money as he can."

When we were negotiating with Lou DiBella, there was a snag in the negotiations and we were going to move on. Arturo asked me what was going on. I told him and he said, "I'm not fighting anybody but Micky Ward. Call them up and make this fight happen." It was unbelievable. In the third fight, Arturo was boxing him and Ward dropped him. Arturo broke his hand and had to fight through that. It's the stuff that you can make a movie of. Just incredible! People still talk about it today. If you want to watch boxing, these are the fights to watch. They made history together.

After the trilogy with Micky Ward, Gatti won the vacant WBC junior welterweight title with a January 2004 unanimous decision over Gianluca Branco. He defended his title twice before losing to former two-division world champion Floyd Mayweather, Jr., via sixth-round TKO in June 2005. Gatti fought on after the Mayweather fight, eventually retiring in July 2007 when he was defeated by Alfonso Gomez by seventh-round TKO.

Against Floyd Mayweather, Arturo was just outclassed. Floyd was the best fighter in the world and he had too much speed for him. After the fight, I think Arturo still wanted to fight, but I don't think he had the same spark as before. He was really winding down at that point.

He beat Damgaard, and we had an opportunity to win another title against Carlos Baldomir, but Baldomir was just too big. Plus, Arturo wasn't the same fighter anymore. The fight with Alfonzo Gomez was against Buddy McGirt's wishes. It was against *all* of our wishes. Nobody wanted it, but he begged us for the fight. He said, "Look, even if I win and I don't look good, I'll retire." I wish to this day that I could take that fight back. Alfonso Gomez is a good fighter, but the real Arturo Gatti would be too much for him.

At this point, Micky Ward was retired and had started training fighters. He became a part of our team and he would walk Arturo into the ring before his fights. When Buddy McGirt pulled out after the Baldomir fight, Arturo needed a new trainer and he asked me if I thought Micky would train him. I said, "Call him and see." He called him up, and Micky trained him for his last fight, and it's just a great, great story. They're just two phenomenal human beings.

Former world junior lightweight and junior welterweight champion Arturo Gatti, 2000s (courtesy Marty Rosengarten/ RingsidePhotos.com).

On July 11, 2009, Gatti was found dead in a hotel room in Ipojuca, Pernambuco, Brazil, while vacationing with his Brazilian wife. It appeared that Gatti was hung by a leather strap. Brazilian authorities initially ruled the death a homicide, then later determined it was suicide. What is your assessment of the situation?

In Arturo's adult life, I don't think anybody knew him better than me. We were close from the time he was an eighteen-year-old kid, all the way to his death. I don't know what happened that night, but I can tell you that Arturo Gatti did not commit suicide. It would have been virtually impossible for him to hang himself the way they said he did.

I hired private investigators and

they felt he was murdered. We held a press conference and presented scientific evidence that shows this. I took it as far as I could possibly take it, but the incident didn't happen in our country or in Canada. It was done in a foreign country where we don't have much say. I don't think we'll ever know what happened that night unless the person responsible finds God and decides to tell the truth. But I know in my heart that it wasn't suicide.

I think about Arturo everyday. I think about all the laughs we had, and I miss a great friend and great person. This whole journey was something I never expected to be involved in. I look back and I wish I appreciated it more when it was happening. When you look at what was accomplished, it's really an amazing thing. I don't know if we'll ever see another person like him, that's for sure. Not like Arturo.

19

Kathy Duva: Ice World

> "We were this little, local promotional company and we had just put on the biggest fight of all time. A week later, we were back in Ice World, promoting a regular club show. That's how life has been ever since—from one extreme to the next."

In the late 1970s and early '80s, promoters Bob Arum and Don King essentially had control of televised boxing. If another promoter wanted to sell a fight to the networks, they had to go through Arum or King. Other promoters eventually broke through the barriers, but only one other name from that era has stood the test of time.

Born and raised in Totowa, New Jersey, Kathy Duva is the CEO of Main Events, a promotional company that was founded in 1978 by her late husband Dan Duva.

The Duva name is well known in boxing, particularly because of Dan's father, Lou, who was the face of the organization. With Dan as the promoter and Lou as a trainer/manager, this father-son duo got its start putting on local fights.

In 1981, Main Events was hired to promote the mega-fight between world welterweight champions "Sugar" Ray Leonard and Thomas Hearns. This opened a lot of doors for the Duvas, giving them opportunities to promote other fights on worldwide stages.

The Duvas promoted several fighters from the 1984 U.S. Olympic Boxing Team, including Evander Holyfield, Pernell Whitaker, Meldrick Taylor, Mark Breland and Tyrell Biggs.

In addition, Main Events has either promoted or worked with a number of other high-profile boxers, including Arturo Gatti, Lennox Lewis, Vernon Forrest, Livingstone Bramble, Vinny Pazienza, Kermit Cintron, Zab Judah, David Tua, Johnny Bumphus, Andrew Golota, Vivian Harris, Pinklon Thomas, Bobby Czyz, John John Molina, Tomasz Adamek, Ike Quartey, Juan Diaz, Rocky Juarez, Mike McCallum, Fernando Vargas, Jesse James Leija, Rocky Lockridge and Sergey Kovalev.

In 1996, Dan Duva died of brain cancer. Kathy Duva took charge of the company and has kept the family name in mainstream boxing. This interview took place over the phone in March 2018.

What is your background in boxing and what led you to become a promoter?

I was an only child, and my father and I were both huge sports fans. I would walk through the living room and my father would say, "Come on. Let's watch the game." One of the sports we watched was boxing. Back then, fights were on Saturday and Sunday afternoons. There were three channels and every one of them showed boxing.

I started dating my late husband Dan Duva when I was nineteen. Early into the relationship, we were going to the fights. At that time, his father Lou was managing fighters and doing little promotions in the area. If you were in their household, boxing was really all they talked about. As Dan and I continued to date, I started working as a newspaper reporter. I became a publicist for a local college, and that evolved into writing press releases for my soon-to-be father-in-law. He was paying someone one hundred dollars to write the releases for his boxing events, and I told him that I would do it for nothing.

Prior to that, when we were still in college, Lou would put on shows and my husband and I would set up concession stands. We would sell hotdogs and beer, and we'd probably make more money than Lou did. When it was over, we'd get together at the kitchen table and talk about the next promotion.

While Dan was in law school, he told me that he wanted to be a boxing promoter and compete with guys like Bob Arum and Don King. He wanted to be the biggest promoter in boxing. I made the mistake of laughing. I said, "Make sure you finish school, so you can get a job!" Dan finished law school in '77. He got a job as a lawyer, and it didn't take him long to come to the conclusion that he didn't want to do that anymore. In 1978, he formed Main Events. In '79, we got married.

Lou Duva had been in the fight business his whole life. He started out when he was a teenager, carrying the bucket for his older brother who was a fighter. At one point, Lou became a fighter himself. He would say, "You can tell by my face that I wasn't very good." When Lou was in the Army, he promoted fights on the base. When I met Dan, he was promoting fights at local armories and high school gyms. He wasn't quite the celebrity that he became, but people in the subculture of the boxing world all knew who he was.

He was a Teamsters Local President full time and was doing boxing part time. He would leave at seven in the morning and be home at midnight, and it was a very stressful, very exhausting life. Around this time, Lou had a heart attack. Dan, who was a natural businessman, saw what his father was doing and said, "I know what needs to be done here. I know how to run a business and I want to enable my father to be successful." So, he proceeded to put the company together and the promotions started to make money.

We did our fights at a place called Ice World. It was a local ice rink that opened up in northern New Jersey. Any time Lou saw a building that could hold more that five hundred people, it would get him thinking. Ice World was perfect for what he wanted to do. It became a real historic venue for the few years we were there. The local fight scene just gravitated toward it.

With Dan as the promoter and Lou as the guy managing the fighters, Main Events continued promoting fights on the local level, and did very well at that.

Through a mutual friend, they met Shelly Finkel, who was looking to get into the boxing business. They formed an alliance, which opened a lot of doors for us. Through Shelly's contacts, we were able to promote the Leonard–Hearns fight. Because of that, we were able to get television deals, and we were suddenly able to compete with mainstream boxing promoters.

In the early '80s, when you went to the networks and tried to sell them a fight, they would say, "Go see King or Arum and make a deal with one of them." They wouldn't deal with local promoters, but the time came when we finally broke through. In '84, we signed a bunch of really talented fighters from the Olympic Team—Holyfield, Breland, Taylor, Whitaker, Biggs.... That same year, four of our fighters won world titles—Rocky Lockridge, Livingstone Bramble, Mike McCallum, and Johnny Bumphus. Lou was on the cover of *Ring* magazine with the four of them.

Dan loved that his father was the face of the organization. He was always very comfortable in the background, where he could handle the business aspects of the company. The working relationship between Dan and his father worked very well.

In 1996, my husband passed away. Before he died, he set up a board of directors so his family and I could work together. While the idea was to keep the business moving forward, Dan told me that he didn't think the company would last more than two years. He said, "Just run it as far as it will go, and then go on and do whatever you're going to do for the rest of your life." I tried working with my in-laws, and found out that inheriting your husband's business is not necessarily a good thing. Dan was the glue that held everything together. With him gone, we were all just lost.

Professional boxing promoter Kathy Duva and former world light heavyweight champion Sergey Kovalev, at a 2016 press conference (photograph by William Trillo, courtesy Pound4Pound.com).

I enrolled in law school, thinking I would go out and get a job. I was forty-two at the time and I had three children. My focus was on my family, and I just figured that whatever happens to the business would happen. I was walking away. But it's like that line from *The Godfather*—"Just when I thought I was out, they pulled me back in."

Dan's brother Dino ran into some problems with his personal business, so I came back when I finished law school with the intentions of being a temporary caretaker. The relationship with the family kind of imploded at that point. My in-laws left, and I came in to tell the staff that we would be closing down in a few months.

We still had some fights coming up, so we had to get through that. But one by one, the staff came into my office and said that they wanted to stay. I said, "You want to work for me?" They were all still on board with the idea of me taking charge. They just wanted to keep their jobs. This was not something I had planned on, but I said, "Okay, let's see what happens."

While I was in law school, Shelly had brought in Gary Shaw to run the company. Gary and I didn't get along very well, so we eventually hired a new guy to run things. This was about mid–2002, around the same time as the Lewis–Tyson fight. I was out of school, my kids were a little older, and I was able to focus more on the business. That's when I took full responsibility.

The first fight I negotiated was the Gatti–Ward rematch. I had just been in a car accident a few days before and my right eye was swollen shut. It was kind of ironic, because it was like I knew how Gatti felt. That's when I started and I've been in that position ever since.

We were doing well at first, but we ran into some hardships. In 2006, Arturo Gatti and Fernando Vargas both lost, which was a blow to the company. Then in 2008, the whole world was going through an economic crisis, and we thought we had reached the end. I honestly thought it was over. I was letting people go and ready to shut things down, but then Tomasz Adamek walked through the door. His manager wanted me to promote his fight with Steve Cunningham. Adamek was Cunningham's mandatory, and I thought he was up against it. But much to my surprise, Tomasz won the fight and that kicked off a whole other run.

When Sergey Kovalev was brought to us in 2012, we put him in a fight to see how he looked. He destroyed his opponent, and again, it breathed new life into the company. At this moment, Sergey is still the man in his division. We're also developing a few other young fighters and the future looks bright.

Main Events promoted the September 1981 mega-fight between WBC world welterweight champion "Sugar" Ray Leonard and Thomas Hearns, who held the WBA world welterweight title. Leonard won the bout by fourteenth-round TKO. How is it that Main Events became involved with this fight?

Dan was hired to promote the fight by Mike Trainer, who represented Ray Leonard. Mike Trainer was mad at King and Arum, so he decided to prove that any moron can promote a big fight. Dan was far from a moron, but he was only twenty-nine years old. He said that by the time this was over, he was going to have learned everything there was to know about promoting boxing.

He hired six consultants to work for us, and they taught him about venues, insurance, ticket sales, publicity, television.... They taught him about every aspect of promoting big fights. Until then, we had known nothing except how to promote on the local level. The fight generated forty million dollars, which was a record for that time.

Afterwards, I was walking through the airport, and saw magazines and newspapers with the fight on the cover. The whole world was aware of what we did. We had to keep pinching ourselves. We were this little, local promotional company and we had just put on the biggest fight of all time. A week later, we were back in Ice World, promoting a regular club show. That's how life has been ever since—from one extreme to the next.

Main Events signed several of the future champions who emerged from the 1984 U.S. Olympic Boxing Team. What stands out in your mind about that time?

Evander Holyfield is the one who really stands out in my mind, more than anyone. He had been disqualified for hitting Kevin Barry on the break and it was a horrible robbery. The referee hadn't warned him; he just disqualified him right away. As a way to make amends, the Olympic committee gave Evander a bronze medal. People who are disqualified aren't supposed to be given medals, but they gave Evander the medal anyway.

At the awards ceremony, they gave Kevin Barry a silver medal, and he took the medal off his neck and tried to give it to Evander. It was one of the worst robberies ever, and everybody's heart just went out to him. During the finals, we were sitting

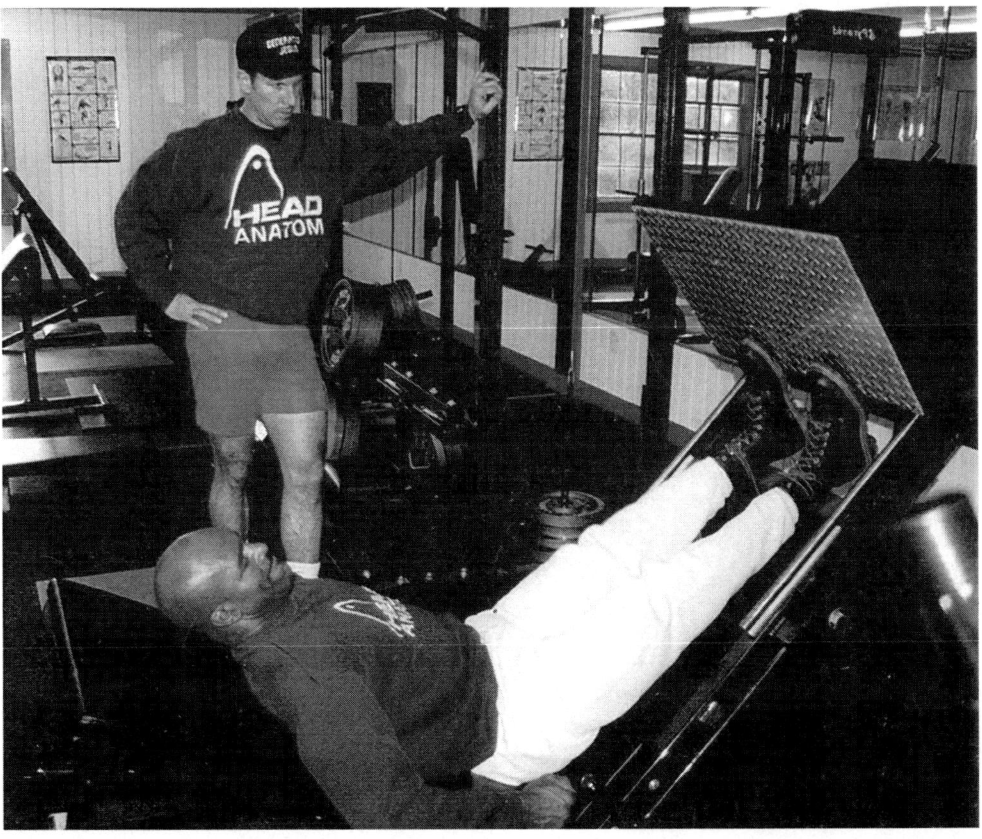

Former world cruiserweight and heavyweight champion Evander Holyfield works the leg press machine as sports performance/fitness trainer Tim Hallmark looks on, 1990s (courtesy Tim Hallmark/timhallmark.com).

on the bleachers and we could see Evander standing by the entrance, wishing all of his teammates good luck as they went out to fight. Evander was about twenty-one at the time, and I thought, what maturity! What amazing character! This guy had been harmed so badly and he showed such dignity the way he was supporting the other fighters. I was just so struck by the way he handled it. I'll never forget it.

Evander Holyfield went on to become an undisputed world champion at cruiserweight and heavyweight. What do you recall about the early years of Holyfield's career when he was with Main Events?

Evander's career is like the background of my kids' early life. My first child was born in '83, my second was born in '84, and my third was born in '89. Evander was always in the background when I was raising them. When he beat Dwight Qawi for the cruiserweight title, Dwight was with Rock Newman. After the weigh-in, Dwight and Rock were walking through the hotel and I overheard their conversation. Dwight said to Rock, "I have tried every trick I know and I can't get to this guy. I can't rattle him." Evander was immovable. Dwight did everything he could to intimidate him and nothing worked.

Early in Evander's career, he used to get tired. I guess it was just a mental block, but he would struggle to get through eight rounds. When he had an opportunity to fight fifteen rounds against Dwight Qawi, they realized that something drastic had to be done. So, they took Evander to a trainer in Houston, Tim Hallmark, who was kind of a strength and conditioning coach. All fighters have strength and conditioning coaches nowadays, but at this time, it was a radical idea. Tim basically took Evander under his wing and put him through a regimen that helped him fight the whole fifteen rounds.

That fight with Qawi had to be one of the toughest fifteen rounds ever. By the time it was over, Evander was completely dehydrated. He was completely spent. Everything he had was out there on the mat. After the fight, I was walking away from the hospital with Dan and he said, "I don't know how much of a career this guy is going to have. He can't sustain this for much longer." He was so beat up in that fight. I said, "I think he just had the toughest fight of his career, Dan. I don't think there will ever be a tougher fight than this." And I don't think there ever was, except for maybe the first Bowe fight. Maybe.

Shortly after Qawi, the time came to build Evander up to heavyweight, because that was the only way to make money. The night Evander knocked out Buster Douglas was one of the best nights of my life. Before the fight, George Benton showed my husband exactly how Evander was going to get the knockout. He was going to wait for the uppercut, and come over the top with the right hand, and knock him out cold. That's exactly what he did. It was planned. It was amazing.

The next day, my daughter Lisa, who was about five years old, just looked at me and said, "Why do you and Daddy keep smiling?" We couldn't stop. That was the turning point for our whole business. After Evander beat George Foreman, Dan said, "Now I know we can pay our investors back. Now I can sleep."

Meldrick Taylor won world titles at junior welterweight and welterweight, but he is best known for his March 1990 unification with WBC world junior welterweight champion Julio Cesar Chavez, Sr. Taylor was defending his IBF junior welterweight title and he lost the bout by twelfth-round TKO. This fight ended in controversy, as Taylor was winning the bout before referee Richard Steele waved it off with two seconds left.

That was a traumatic night. Back then, if you were fighting a Don King fighter, you did not expect to win a decision. That was a given and there was no way around it. We always did what we would call the WBC scoring. If the other guy didn't get beat up or completely dominated, you'd give him the round. We were scoring the Chavez fight as it was happening, and we gave Chavez rounds that we thought he didn't deserve.

Going into the twelfth round, we didn't think Meldrick was ahead. We thought he *should* be ahead, but we didn't think he was. After the fight, I walked over and looked at the scorecards. And the judges had Meldrick ahead! I couldn't believe it! In the days and weeks following the fight, we spent a lot of time looking at the video, because we were going to protest the stoppage. I looked at that video over, and over, and over.... It got to the point where I had nightmares about it. It was one of the worst robberies ever, and it was a prelude to Whitaker–Chavez, which was another huge miscarriage of boxing justice.

Pernell Whitaker is regarded as one of the best fighters of all time, having won world titles at lightweight, junior welterweight, welterweight, and junior middleweight. His September 1993 defense of his WBC welterweight title against former multi-division champion Julio Cesar Chavez, Sr., was ruled a majority draw, but the common consensus was that Whitaker dominated the action.

We told Pernell before the Chavez fight that you're going to know you're winning when it gets so quiet in the arena that you can hear a pin drop. That was what we kept telling him as he was walking into the ring—"Pin drop! Pin drop!" That's what we were waiting for and then the moment came. It got so quiet that you could hear a pin drop.

We were fairly confident that he was winning the fight. Even though it was Don King, it was just so quiet in there. Everybody knew "Pete" had beaten Chavez. There were about eighty thousand people in the Alamodome and they all booed the decision. When the fight was over, we all went out for a meal at a Mexican restaurant. Pete wasn't with us, but the rest of the team was there and we were all wearing "Team Whitaker" jackets. When we walked in, the place got really quiet, and then suddenly everybody stood up and cheered. They were yelling, "Your guy won! He was robbed!" Mexican fans know their boxing. They're not just out there rooting for their guy. If you win, they'll respect you.

That took a little of the sting away, but not too much. Pete was very upset. Everyone was telling him that he won and he said, "Yeah, but that record book is not going to say that." The cover of *Sports Illustrated* featured a picture of Pete with the word "Robbed." It was big news. Chavez's people never gave us a rematch. They just got as far away from Pernell Whitaker as they could.

From the mid '90s to the early 2000s, heavyweight contender Andrew Golota was involved in a number of memorable fights, notably his two 1996 disqualification losses

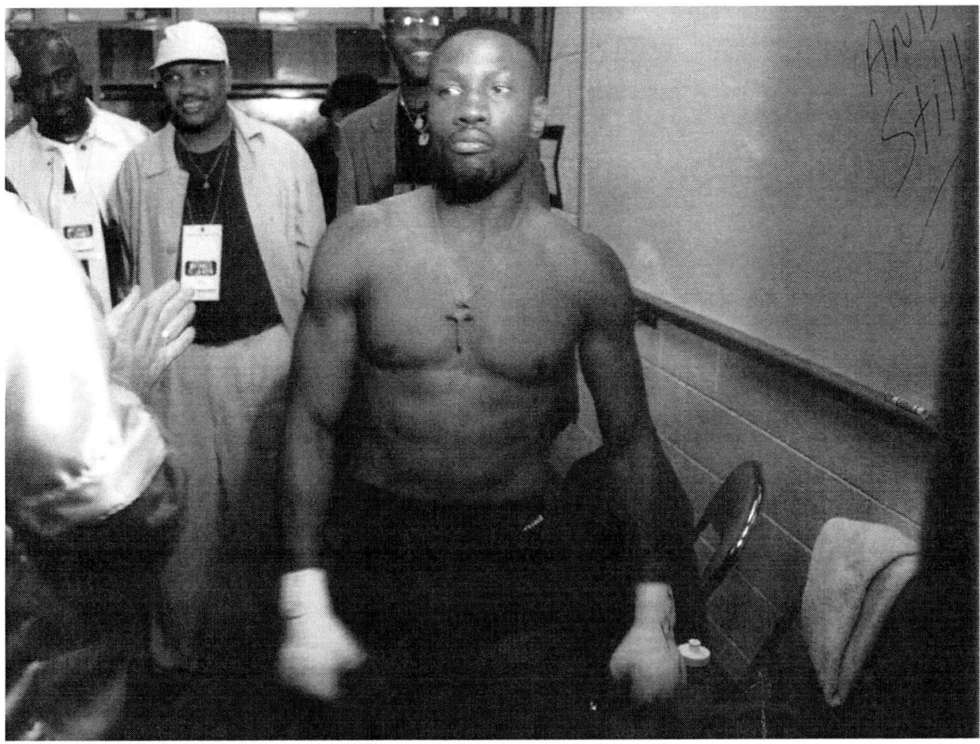

Former four-division world champion Pernell Whitaker, surrounded by team members before a 1990s bout (courtesy Rick Perez).

to former heavyweight champion Riddick Bowe for repeated low blows. Golota was a talented boxer, but he often self-destructed during big fights.

Andrew Golota had all the skill in the world. He would have become heavyweight champion if it wasn't for his mental illness. The problem was that he had panic attacks. Back then, nobody understood what was happening. We all saw him beating Riddick Bowe—winning the fight easily, but then breaking down and hitting him with repeated low blows. That was his way of trying to get out of there. Same thing with Lennox Lewis, same thing with Michael Grant, same thing with Tyson....

We started to understand what was happening after the Lewis fight. I thought I saw him having a seizure in the locker room, but it wasn't a seizure. It was a panic attack. We sent him to a neurologist, who explained that he was having a psychological reaction to being in a high-pressure situation. He thought he was dying. He literally couldn't breathe. We tried to get him help, but he wouldn't accept it. When Andrew was fighting on the lower level, when he wasn't under the bright lights, he dominated. But put him in a big fight and he always fell apart.

In December 1998, at age twenty-one, Fernando Vargas became the youngest boxer to ever win a world title at junior middleweight, with a seventh-round TKO over IBF champion Luis Ramon Campus. In the early 2000s, he had two memorable bouts with accomplished world champions Felix Trinidad and Oscar De La Hoya, where he gave spirited efforts but lost both fights via TKO.

Fernando was the quintessential Main Events fighter. He had a strong Mexican American following on the West Coast. He had personality, he had skills.... He had it all. But he had a style of fighting, where you knew his career wasn't going to last too long. He was very aggressive, almost too aggressive for his own good. Early in his career, a decision was made within the company to put him in with Trinidad. I did not agree with that decision. I was overruled by everyone, including Fernando. There was no dissuading him.

There was also a lot of pressure from the public to make that fight. The perception was that he was ready for this fight, but that wasn't the case. Had he waited two or three years, it might have been a different outcome. He did come very close, but you need experience to win the big fights. And you can only take so many tough fights like that in your career.

After the Trinidad fight, Fernando was more popular than ever. He made a lot of new fans with that performance. We got to the De La Hoya fight, and again, he came so close. Vargas was a guy who was almost as good as those guys, but not quite. He had a good career though. He made millions and millions of dollars, but he never won a major fight. His most respected victory came against Ike Quartey.

Like Vargas, former IBF world junior lightweight and WBC world junior welterweight champion Arturo Gatti was a fighter who won the hearts of the fans, even in defeat. A classic example of this was his May 2002 bout with Micky Ward, a fight he lost by majority decision.

Oh, of course! The Micky Ward loss was the best thing that ever happened to him. The first Gatti–Ward fight took place a month before Lewis–Tyson, so it was kind of lost in the shadows. It was at the Mohegan Sun and the arena wasn't even sold out. But we sat there watching this fight between two fighters whose careers were basically over, and we couldn't believe what we were seeing. It was so brutal!

In this day and age, HBO would never have bought a fight like that. There are a lot of tremendous fights that could happen today, but they don't because there's no platform for them. They aren't the kind of fights that lead to anything significant. But we were lucky that they bought Gatti–Ward, because it turned out to be the start of one of the best trilogies ever.

Sergey Kovalaev won his first world title in August 2013 with a fourth-round TKO over WBO light heavyweight champion Nathan Cleverly. He successfully defended that title eight times, including a November 2014 unification with Bernard Hopkins, where he picked up the WBA and IBF world light heavyweight tiles via unanimous decision. In November 2016, Kovalev lost his titles to former super middleweight champion, Andre Ward, by unanimous decision. He faced Ward in a June rematch the following year, losing by eighth-round TKO.

We were initially approached by Sergey's manager, Egis Klimas, who was just so convincing and so passionate about this young man. He said, "Please just put him in a fight. I don't care who it is. Anybody. You've got to see him. If you don't want him when the fight is over, I'll walk away. I'll never bother you again."

Sergey had previously won a split decision over Darnell Boone. The feeling at that time was that a real prospect should be able to beat someone like Darnell Boone

Former world junior middleweight champion Fernando Vargas (left) faces former two-division world champion Ricardo Mayorga, in Vargas's final fight, 2007. Vargas lost the bout via majority decision (courtesy Bret Newton—ThreatPhoto.com/Pound4Pound.com).

without any controversy. If there was an excuse for their first fight, if he wanted to maintain that he was better than that, this was his chance to prove it. In Sergey's previous fight, six months earlier, there was a tragedy in the ring. His opponent Roman Simakov was killed because of the injuries he suffered during the fight.

Of course, we had concerns. Most fighters are never the same after an experience like that. But when the bell rang, Sergey just obliterated Darnell Boone in two rounds. We had a contract signed within days, and he went on to beat Nathan Cleverly, Bernard Hopkins, Jean Pascal.... When Sergey fought Andre Ward the first time, I thought he clearly won. I just don't understand how that fight was judged the way it was. In my memory, that fight will always be right next to Whitaker-Chavez. The public didn't treat it like the robbery that Whitaker-Chavez was, but I thought they should have.

In the rematch, Sergey clearly didn't deserve to win, although I did not agree with the referee counting him out after a series of low blows. But I can handle the loss in the second fight, better than the loss in the first. After the second fight with Andre Ward, somebody asked me if it felt like it was the end of the world. I said, "No." I thought the world had ended when Holyfield lost to Bowe. That's the advantage of having all this experience. You know it's not the end of the world unless you let it be.

When my husband passed away, I never thought I would be running the business over twenty years later. Next month, Main Events is going to hit its fortieth anniversary. We've been here this whole time. Had Dan survived, I don't think there would have been room for a promotional company like Golden Boy to exist. Dan would have been the person who emerged next to Top Rank. I'm not quite as ambitious as Dan was. I know boxing backwards and forwards, but I've scaled things down. I run things by letting the people around me do what they do best.

My oldest daughter Nicole is here now and she's a reincarnation of her father. In business, we relate to each other the same way I related to her father. She's a natural manager and she handles the day-to-day issues, while I create the themes of the promotions and map out plans for our fighters. It's fun. For the first time in a very long time, we're having fun.

20

Don King: Once and for All

"Me being a promoter of the people, by the people, and *for* the people, my magic lies in my people ties. Bringing back boxing is what my job is and what I'm so enthusiastic about."

At one time, boxing was the number-one sport in America. Like America itself, professional boxing is the land of the free, with an open door for anyone who wants to make his mark. From the 1970s to the 2010s, a certain man with a recognizable face made an especially strong mark, using freedom of speech to keep boxing in the headlines.

Born and raised in Cleveland, Ohio, Don King found his way into mainstream boxing by promoting the 1974 heavyweight world championship fight between Muhammad Ali and then champion George Foreman, staged in Zaire, known as "The Rumble in the Jungle."

From there, King began promoting events with some of the top fighters in the sport, including Roberto Duran, Larry Holmes, Alexis Arguello, Salvador Sanchez, Wilfred Benitez, Wilfredo Gomez, and notably promoting another big event known as the "Thrilla in Manila," which was the third encounter between then heavyweight champion Muhammad Ali and Joe Frazier.

Beyond that, King continued promoting events with some of the best in the game, including Mike Tyson, Terry Norris, Aaron Pryor, Evander Holyfield, Julio Cesar Chavez, Sr., Felix Trinidad, Azumah Nelson, Meldrick Taylor, Mike McCallum, Bernard Hopkins, Gerald McClellan, Marco Antonio Barrera, Cory Spinks, Tomasz Adamek, Ricardo Mayorga, Chris Byrd, John Ruiz, Andrew Golota, Tavoris Cloud, Devon Alexander, and Bermane Stiverne.

In July 2015, one of King's key fighters, junior welterweight Amir Imam (19–0, 15 KOs), scored a fourth-round knockout over Fernando Angulo (29–9, 16 KOs). Around this time, Floyd Mayweather, Jr. (48–0, 26 KOs), who held the WBC and WBA world welterweight titles, and who was considered the best boxer in the world, declared that he would fight one more time before retiring.

Sensing an opportunity, King campaigned to secure Imam as Mayweather's opponent. The potential fight never materialized, as Mayweather went on to win a unanimous decision over Andre Berto (30–3, 23 KOs) in September, while Imam lost his next fight via eighth-round TKO to Adrian Granados (16–4-2, 12 KOs) in November. This interview took place over the phone in July 2015.

Tell me about this potential matchup between your boxer, Amir Imam, and pound-for-pound king Floyd Mayweather, Jr.

Mayweather is a gifted fighter. He's the best in the world. And this young kid Amir Imam is the best *prospect* in the world. I want to see Amir fight Mayweather because you have to compare the guys. They get mad at Mayweather because he knows how to slip, roll, and punch. And you couldn't see a better description, a better depiction, than Amir Imam who can also slip, roll, and punch, but also has the power of Marvin Hagler.

The audience didn't even see what happened when Amir hit Fernando Angulo. They had to wait and see it on the replay. To see the magnificence of this young man and the power he possesses.... He can hit and not get hit, which is what the sweet science is all about. He doesn't have the experience that Floyd has, but he has the gift from God. He has the dexterity and movement of "Sugar" Ray Leonard, the power of Tommy Hearns, the footwork of Roberto Duran.... He has a combination of all those things from the guys that are awesome, undeniable Hall of Fame fighters from his weight class.

Promoter Don King and artist LeRoy Neiman, 2000s (courtesy Marty Rosengarten/ RingsidePhotos.com).

Amir Imam is the only man that has any chance with Floyd Mayweather. It's a class act when you win the admiration of the people. Me being a promoter of the people, by the people, and *for* the people, my magic lies in my people ties. Bringing back boxing is what my job is and what I'm so enthusiastic about.

I understand when I see talent. When people say, "He's too young," or "He doesn't have enough experience," put that aside. Let him go in there and give him the opportunity. It would be one of the best fights that can be seen right now. If he beats Floyd, it would be extraordinary. It would bring all the fans back to boxing. If he doesn't beat Floyd, it would still be a winner for the public to see such a classic display of power, skill, dexterity, lateral movement, and being able to slip and roll. It would be two guys that have this type of ability meeting each other. It would be an irresistible force against an immovable object. Something would have to give.

This is not what they saw in the Mayweather–Pacquiao fight. Pacquiao had already lost four times. This would be two undefeated fighters meeting each other. Pacquiao's job was to go in there and fight Floyd till he falls on the floor. Ain't no give and take, no excuses to make. It's got to be a fight and he didn't do that. Excuses don't count. The public was clearly disturbed about that, but here you've got two undefeated fighters and neither one of them wants to lose. That's what makes fights.

Have you had any communication with Team Mayweather?

I've talked to some of Mayweather's associates. I intend to reach Floyd before I leave Las Vegas. But I'm making a call to give the public something that they want. Be courageous enough to take on a young challenger that I predict is better than anyone out there. Ain't no reservation, ain't no hesitation.... We're ready to step up to the plate and make this a major event. Believe me, the public will be a recipient of one of the best boxing encounters in the century.

Everything with Mayweather is going downhill until he meets someone who has the gift of God, and who fights for the people. Mayweather is a perfectionist. He trains hard, he's dedicated, and he's committed. He doesn't rest on the laurels of his victories. He gets prepared every time. This fight would be the magic of excitement. This man Amir Imam has more than a chance because of his youth, his stature, his esteem.... Let's give the people what they want. Only Floyd can give them that. That's why I want to appeal to Floyd.

Let's make boxing what it's supposed to be—the best man-to-man sport in the world. There's no team, there is no group of people where you can call time out and send somebody in.... If you run out of gas, there is no gas station in sight. You have to deal with what's real right before you. This would be history in the making. It would be a contribution to Floyd's legacy. This is a fight that would really have true danger to him. You can't get around the type of power that was shown on Showtime on July 18.

Angulo made a hell of a fight out of it, throwing punches in bunches. But Amir Imam withstood that danger with his ability to slip and roll and hit him, then follow up because he never stopped his perpetual motion. He withstood that danger with great competitiveness. That's what has me excited and that's why I want to see this fight. Don't retire, Floyd! Take this guy on and the public will say he beat the young, he beat the old.... The good, the bad, and the ugly. I want to see the public have this because of the disappointment from the Pacquiao fight.

Aside from Amir Imam, what else is happening with your stable of fighters?

Trevor Bryan is scheduled to fight Derric Rossy on August 28 on Showtime. They're heavyweights. We're going back to the nuts and bolts of boxing. I thought Bermane Stiverne would do that with Deontay Wilder, and I still think Bermane is the baddest heavyweight out there at this particular time. He didn't get beat by Deontay, he just didn't fight. There's a big difference. He was dehydrated. He went to the sauna every day, trying to get a six-pack.

You don't make excuses, because Deontay is a great fighter. He has the dexterity and the ability to be the champion. He gave a big boost of positiveness to the state of Alabama, which had nothing but negatism in regards to people of color. He stepped up and gave Alabama a new look, but I want to see Bermane get his return match with him. If Deontay beats him again, case closed. If he doesn't, then they can have a rubber match like Ali and Frazier. That third match is what everybody waits to see with great anticipation.

Is there anything you would like to say in closing?

They say a child shall lead them. You got this young kid, Amir Imam, and he can start by going in there with Floyd Mayweather and giving the public what they

Former world light heavyweight and heavyweight champion Michael Spinks (left) and Mike Tyson reunite in 2018 at Graziano's in Canastota, New York, thirty years after their 1988 fight. Promoted by Don King, Tyson vs. Spinks was billed as "Once and for All" since it was a battle between two undefeated heavyweights, with Tyson's heavyweight world titles on the line. Tyson won the bout by first-round knockout (photograph by Tom Patti, courtesy John Scully).

Promoter Butch Lewis, Michigan Boxing Commissioner Dr. Stuart Kirschenbaum, and Don King, 1986 (courtesy Dr. Stuart Kirschenbaum).

want—an electrifying fight that's so exciting they won't have time to go to the bathroom. They can't wink or nothing. They have to sit there glued to their television or wherever they are, if they can't be there live and on the scene in living color. That's what it's got to be. We have to let the people know that we're back on the move to recapture the fans, and bring them back to the greatest sport in the world and that's boxing. God bless the people. I usually say, "Only in America," but I want to send my love to the people all over the world.

21

J Russell Peltz: The Blue Horizon

> "I didn't get into this because I thought I was going to make a fortune. I got into boxing because I love boxing."

Breaking into boxing as a promoter is a tough proposition. Those who try are generally well-connected entrepreneurs with a strong background in business affairs. Being that most promoters have a low success rate, one would be ill-advised to go down this road, unless he is only doing it for the love of the sport.

Born and raised in Philadelphia, Pennsylvania, J Russell Peltz promoted his first boxing event in 1969 at the age of twenty-two, at a local venue called the Blue Horizon.

Having found success at the Blue Horizon, Peltz began promoting fights at the Arena in Philadelphia, as well as the Philadelphia Spectrum.

In the early 1980s, Peltz branched out of Philadelphia and put on events in Atlantic City, New Jersey, eventually promoting televised fights on ESPN and other networks.

Early in his career, Peltz promoted cards with a number of high profile fighters, including George Benton, Bennie Briscoe, Willie Monroe, Bobby Watts, Eugene Hart, Stanley Hayward, Sammy Goss, Jeff Chandler, Robert Hines, Matthew Saad Muhammad, Marvin Hagler, Dwight Muhammad Qawi, Tony Thornton, Frank Fletcher, Marvin Johnson, Charles Williams, Thomas Hearns, Mike Rossman, Charles Brewer, Tyrone Everett, Curtis Parker, Augie Pantellas, Jerry Martin, Charlie Brown, Tim Witherspoon, Roberto Duran, Gary Hinton, Jesse Burnett, Richie Kates, Emile Griffith, and Bobby Chacon.

In more modern times, Peltz promoted fights with Bernard Hopkins, Arturo Gatti, Kassim Ouma, Gabriel Rosado, Amir Mansour, Bryant Jennings, and Jason Sosa. This interview took place over the phone in September 2018.

What is your background in boxing and what led you to become a promoter?

One of my first boxing memories was when I was twelve. I remember being at a dance and telling the girl I was with how disappointed I was that Floyd Patterson had gotten beaten by Ingemar Johansson. The first fight I saw on television was the first fight between Carmen Basilio and Gene Fullmer in August of '59. There were some other fights that stand out—Cleveland Williams against Curley Lee, and also the title fight between Fullmer and Spider Webb in December that year.

One day, I went to the bookstore near my house. I saw what would be called a coffee table book today, but in those days we called them picture books. It was Nat Fleischer's pictorial history of boxing with Sam Andre, who was the photographer. I bought the book and I *became* the book. I read it cover to cover and I suddenly thought I knew more about boxing than anyone in the world.

I kept watching the fights on television, and as a present for my fourteenth birthday, which was December 6, 1960, my dad took me to my first live fight in Philadelphia. It was Len Matthews against Doug Vaillant at the Convention Hall. There were about five thousand people there. When I walked in, I saw the smoke over the ring and I just fell in love. I had an epiphany and I knew that somehow boxing would be a part of my life.

I bought my first *Ring* magazine that year. There was a story about Harold Johnson from Philly and he became my boyhood idol. My dad took me to see him defend his NBA title against Von Clay at the Arena in Philly. Just a couple of months ago, Steve Lott posted a video of that fight. I had the video, but I didn't have the video he had. I watched Steve's video and I saw myself, a fourteen-year-old kid, sitting in the front row next to my dad.

My mom didn't like the fights. She didn't want her little son who was raised in the suburbs to be around fight people, so she told my father that he couldn't take me anymore. By now, '61, '62, I was in the tenth grade. I would tell my parents that I was going to a friend's house, but I would take two buses and the train to the Arena or the Convention Hall, and go to the fights by myself.

Around this time, I decided that I was going to be a sportswriter. I went to Temple University for journalism and I became the sports editor of the daily student newspaper when I was a sophomore. At the end of my junior year, I got a full-time job working on the sports desk, the midnight shift, at the *Evening* and *Sunday Bulletin* which was the oldest afternoon daily in the country.

At the end of August, as I was getting ready for my senior year, the sports editor, Jackie Wilson, came in and said, "Russell, I want to talk to you." I said, "What's up?" He said, "You're going back to school. We'll keep you on one night a week and on the weekends. You'll get your degree, and you can come back and work for us full time after you graduate." I felt like somebody just shot ice water in my veins. I said, "Mr. Wilson…" And I meant it then like I mean it now. I get so emotional when I tell this story. I said, "Mr. Wilson, I'll work for nothing." Meaning, if he kept me on, he didn't even have to pay me. He looked at me and I guess he saw the fear on my face. He smiled that Mona Lisa smile of his and said, "Forget about it. We'll keep you on and we'll pay you."

So, I kept working from midnight to eight. Then I would go to Temple from nine to one, and then I would go home and sleep. In 1968, I won the award for the Outstanding Male Graduate in Journalism at Temple.

The boxing writer at the *Bulletin* was a guy named Jack Fried, who also wrote under the name Matt Ring. He was sixty-five, which was mandatory retirement at the *Bulletin*. I wanted his job, but they gave him an extension on his retirement. So

I'm thinking to myself, do I have to wait for this guy to die before I can be a boxing writer? That's when I started thinking about promoting.

The library at the *Bulletin* was known as "the morgue." It had every single story that was ever printed at the *Bulletin*. I would go through the files about the fights in Philly, and I would write down who fought, what night, how many people came.... In those days, writers used to mark down the attendance, the gross, the net gate after taxes.... And I would make these long lists, mainly on the Blue Horizon, because I thought that would be the most affordable place for me to run fights.

When I was twenty-two, I told the *Bulletin* that I was leaving so I could start putting on fights. They thought it was a joke. There was no such thing as a twenty-two-year-old kid in boxing. Plus, boxing was in a lull in Philly. There wasn't a lot of activity, maybe five or six shows a year.

My future first wife said to me one night, "What makes you think you can be successful doing this?" I had been living at home and I got paid for being an editor of the school paper, plus I had been working at the *Bulletin*. So, I had five thousand dollars saved up. I told her, "It will take me about six months to blow the five thousand, and one day I'll have this little scrapbook to show my kids how their daddy was once a boxing promoter." I got married in August of '69 and I was promoting my first fight in September that year.

In my first show, I got lucky. Bennie Briscoe fought a rematch with Tito Marshall at the Blue Horizon and we sold out. I was making seventy-five hundred dollars a year at the Bulletin, but for this show, I made fifteen hundred in one night. I ran fifteen shows in eight and a half months, and I made the same seventy-five hundred that I made at the *Bulletin*. And I was having more fun.

Professional boxing promoter J Russell Peltz, 2010s (courtesy J Russell Peltz).

One day in the summer of 1970, I was talking to a guy named Jack Puggy. He was a matchmaker and he had been in boxing his whole life. I can still see him spitting on the sidewalk while he was smoking a cigar. He said, "Bennie Briscoe's people offered me his contract for twenty-five hundred. But what do I need a fighter for at my age?" Jack was probably in his sixties. I didn't say anything, but my wheels were spinning. We talked for a couple of minutes, and then I drove real fast to my apartment and called my brother-in-law, who was an accountant. I said, "Arnold, Bennie Briscoe's contract is for sale. You put up the money and I'll promote the fights."

At the time, I was promoting Eugene "Cyclone" Hart, Willie "The Worm" Monroe, and Bobby "Boogaloo" Watts, three young middleweights who went on to have terrific careers. I said, "Sooner or later, they're all going to have to go through Briscoe to become king of the city, and I'll have control of all those fights if you sign Briscoe." So, I called Jimmy Iselin, who managed Bennie Briscoe. I said, "I heard Briscoe is for sale." He knew about me, because I was getting a lot of press for being such a young promoter. He said, "Briscoe owes us eight hundred." I said, "Okay, so it's thirty-three hundred."

I got on a train and I met Briscoe's people at The Palm restaurant in New York. I gave him a check for thirty-three hundred, and he rushed into the kitchen to call Joe Fariello, who was Briscoe's trainer. He said, "We got the deal! They're buying Briscoe from us!" They were so happy, as was I. I went back to Philly, never realizing at the time that Briscoe would become the attraction that he became.

Briscoe fought for me at the beginning of my second season and we started getting too big for the Blue Horizon. We moved to the seven-thousand-seat Arena in West Philly and I was splitting my time between the two venues. In May of '71, I made a fight between "Cyclone" Hart and "Kitten" Hayward. Hart had just knocked out eighteen straight guys. Hayward was a well-known guy and we sold out the Arena.

That summer, I did my first show at the Spectrum. Briscoe fought Juarez de Lima, Hart fought Fate Davis, and Sammy Goss fought Floyd Marshall. I was twenty-four years old and I made ten grand from that show.

Late in '72, the people at the Spectrum called me and wanted to talk. The Spectrum had the Flyers ice hockey, the 76ers basketball, Disney on Ice.... They had everything, but they had a slot they wanted to fill on Monday nights. They ended up hiring me as the director of boxing at the Spectrum, and in '73, we did eighteen shows there. Unfortunately, we lost money on fifteen of them. The vice president of the Spectrum asked me to lunch one day and he said, "Do you think we can turn the program around?" I said, "If I can get the Philly guys to fight each other like they did years ago when boxing was really big here, yes, I can turn it around."

I went around to all the gyms in Philly and posted a notice on the bulletin boards that there was going to be a meeting at Joe Frazier's Gym. About fifty or sixty trainers and managers showed up. I said, "The Spectrum has every major attraction around and they don't need us. Unless you guys are going to start fighting each other, we're going back to the Arena." That was like going back to the ghetto from the Taj Mahal.

I had been wanting to make a rubber match between a welterweight named Alfonso Hayman from South Philly and a kid from North Philly named William Watson. They were 1–1. So, a guy named "Pop" Bates who had Alfonso Hayman came up to me and said, "Okay, we'll fight Watson in the rubber match." The people who had "Lil' Abner," a real crowd-pleasing junior middleweight, said that they would fight "Kitten" Hayward.

Our first show in '74 featured two all–Philly fights and we made a modest profit of about four thousand. Three months earlier, Yank Durham had passed away. He managed Joe Frazier and Willie "The Worm" Monroe, and he was against all–Philly fights. Eddie Futch took over and he knew boxing better than Yank. He agreed to let Willie "The Worm" Monroe fight "Cyclone" Hart, which was just a monster fight the next month in February. We drew over ten thousand people that night and we were on our way.

In '74, '75, '76, '77, and '78, the Spectrum was alongside Madison Square Garden, the Olympic in LA, and The Forum in Inglewood, California, as one of the top boxing centers in the country. All the great black fighters of those years fought for me at the Spectrum—Matthew Saad Muhammad who came up as Matt Franklin, Emile Griffith, Jesse Burnett, Lonnie Bennett, Tommy Hearns.... Bobby Chacon's only fight on the east coast was at the Spectrum. We were just hot those five years.

At the end of '78, gambling was passed in Atlantic City. In 1979, all the big fights that would have been at the Spectrum were getting gobbled up by the casinos. We hit a snag and the crowds started dwindling. In July of 1977, I had promoted the first fight between Matthew Saad Muhammad and Marvin Johnson, which was the greatest fight I ever saw in person. But when it came time for the rematch in April of '79, Bob Arum and also Don King had a stranglehold on the networks. Arum made a deal with me and he ended up promoting the rematch in Indianapolis.

In 1980, the only show I did at the Spectrum featured Jeff Chandler on his way up, which didn't do any business. Ferdie Pacheco took over at NBC, thank God, and he gave a break to guys like me, Murad Muhammad, and Dan Duva. The first fight I got from him was Curtis Parker and David Love at Resorts International in Atlantic City.

Around that time, Bob Arum got the first deal with ESPN, and he announced that fights would take place with Russell Peltz in Atlantic City, Dan Duva in Totowa, Ernie Terrell in Chicago, and Mel Greb in Las Vegas. I was still working at the Spectrum and this hit the papers before I could tell them.

Ed Snider, who owned the Spectrum, got really pissed off, because I was under contract with them. He called me into a meeting, and said I wasn't a team player, and that I had no right to work with Bob Arum. In the middle of the meeting he said, "You know what? If you don't like it here, you can leave. We'll tear up your contract." So, I left the Spectrum and I was the Atlantic City guy for the first year on ESPN.

While I was doing fights for ESPN, we developed fighters like Frank "The Animal" Fletcher and Dwight Braxton, who later became Dwight Muhammad Qawi. Jeff Chandler won the world title in 1980 and the '80s were a really good time. I was doing shows on ESPN, ABC, NBC, CBS...

Arum fired me from the ESPN deal after one year, because I was taking fighters independently to the networks. But I still had a good run, and I was developing fighters like Marvin Johnson, who was a three-time champion, Robert Hines, who won the IBF junior middleweight title, "Choo Choo" Brown, who was the first IBF lightweight champ, Gary Hinton, who was the IBF junior welterweight champ....

I had left the Blue Horizon in '71, but I went back in 1986 to develop talent. Dan Duva called me that year and said he had a USA network date that he was too busy to do. So, in June of '86, I promoted a card at the Blue Horizon which was my first fight on USA. Dan called me a month later with another date, and after that, I got my own deal with USA network.

Everybody in Philly knew about the Blue Horizon, but now the whole country knew about it. In those days, seating at the Blue Horizon was first come first serve. But in '93, I decided to experiment with reserved seating. It changed the size of the crowd and the complexion of the crowd. All of a sudden, we started to sell out in advance. People came because it was the thing to do and the place to be. From '93 to when I left in 2001, we sold out every single show. The capacity crowd was 1,346, plus two hundred standing room. In 1991, I had 2,100 people in there when Tim Witherspoon fought Art Tucker. You literally couldn't move.

At the Blue Horizon, it didn't matter who was fighting. In the semifinal, you could have Fighter A, who was 5–8, and Fighter B, who was 10–7. If I knew it was going to be an action-packed fight, I would make it. I didn't care about ticket sellers. I didn't *need* ticket sellers. We had six hundred season ticket holders. There was another six hundred who didn't pay in advance, but bought the same seats every show. Everybody else was just going to come. People knew they were going to see good fights.

The last USA show was in '98, then ESPN came in. In 2001, the Blue Horizon changed hands twice. I couldn't get along with the new owners, so I left. Bill Cayton had hired me in 1998 as the matchmaker for ESPN. When I got that job, I said to myself, all of those years of making good matches, regardless of the *names* of the fighters, was finally paying off. But after one year, my contract was sliced into quarters and I was relegated to becoming an errand boy. I hung in there because boxing was at a low ebb and I needed whatever I could get. That was probably my most disappointing time in boxing.

Former world middleweight and light heavyweight champion Bernard Hopkins, 2000s (courtesy Marty Rosengarten/ RingsidePhotos.com).

Boxing in the twenty-first century hasn't been really that good for me or for the sport itself. I've had some world champions like Kassim Ouma, and my most recent one, Jason Sosa, who won the WBA junior lightweight title in Beijing when he knocked out Javier Fortuna in June of 2016. That would probably rank as one of my best moments, because it made me feel like I still knew what I was doing. Right now, I work as an advisor to fighters. This was the first year I wasn't even going to take out a promoter's license, except Top Rank came to Philly with Jessie Magdaleno and Isaac Dogboe in April. On that card, I made Bryant Jennings and Joey Dawejko.

I'm not as involved as I once was

and people say to me that I haven't changed with the times. Who wants to? Was boxing better in the '60s or '70s, or is it better today? There's no comparison. Compared to what this sport once was, boxing is completely off the radar.

As you mentioned, one of the first notable fighters you promoted was Bennie Briscoe, a former middleweight world title challenger who fought professionally from 1962 to 1982. Briscoe never won a world title, but he is mentioned in the same sentence as some of the great champions who came out of Philadelphia. Why is that?

Bennie Briscoe worked a full-time job his whole career. First he was in rat control. Later he graduated to trash collector. Before work, Bennie would run five miles and then go to the gym at night. When he retired from the city, he had three months of paid vacation coming to him because he never missed work. I once asked Bennie, "How do you kill these rats? Do you go in and spread poison?" He said, "What are you crazy? We go in there with baseball bats and we club those suckers to death!"

Bennie was a humble guy. He didn't talk trash, he picked it up. He wasn't fancy. And he was never in a bad fight. I think the fact that he never won a world title after three tries probably made people love him even more. He was the poor guy from Augusta, Georgia, who always had it tough. He was an underdog his whole life and he was probably the most beloved fighter in Philadelphia history.

George Benton was a world ranked middleweight out of Philadelphia, who fought professionally from 1949 to 1970. He is known for being one of the best boxers who never fought for a world title. After Benton retired, he went on to become a highly regarded trainer.

George Benton first fought for me on January 13, 1970, at the Blue Horizon. This was toward the end of his career. His opponent was David Beckles. There were five fights on the card. Two ended in the first round, one ended in the second round, and another fight ended in a four-round decision. The fights started at eight and intermission was at eight-thirty. I went to the dressing room and said, "George, do me a favor, will you? Carry this guy for a couple rounds." There I was, a twenty-three-year-old kid, and I'm asking this legend to carry his opponent.

George was a wonderful and friendly guy, but of course, he knocked Beckles out in the first round. His manager at the time was an old time guy named Joe Gramby. He was one of the most brilliant boxing minds I ever knew. He asked me after the fight if they could get another date. I said, "Yeah, I'll get you on in March." But I started thinking about it, and I paid Benton a thousand dollars for that fight. I paid his opponent six hundred, plus travel and hotel, and we were charging three or five dollars to get in. I only made about three hundred on the show. Did I really want to spend sixteen hundred for another main event, when I could get a main event for eight or nine hundred?

For the next month, I noticed that Benton hadn't been coming to the gym. I was kind of hoping that he pulled out or took a different fight. The fight was March 25, and at the end of February, Benton finally came to the gym. I saw him walking up the steps with his raggedy old pale-yellow suitcase, and I said, "What are you doing, George?" He said, "Aren't I fighting for you, Russell?" I said, "I hadn't seen you, I didn't know what was up, I was making other plans...."

So, Benton called his manager Joe Gramby and handed me the phone. Gramby never called me Russell. He called me "Promoter" or "Entrepreneur." He said, "Promoter, George tells me we may not be fighting for you in March." I said, "Well, Joe, you never signed a contract." He said, "What's the matter? Isn't your word any good?" Well, that made me feel like I was two inches tall. I said, "You know what? You're right. Forget about it. You're fighting." So, Benton fought for me against Eddie Owens. It was a tough-ass fight and he won a decision. We lost about eighty dollars on the show, which was my first loser. But I learned an important lesson about keeping my word.

George Benton was a master in the ring. And it's very rare that a great athlete like him goes on to become a great trainer like he did. He never got the credit he deserved for all the work he did with those Main Events fighters—Whitaker, Taylor, Breland, Biggs, Holyfield.... Benton was one of my heroes as a kid and I am so honored to have promoted his last two fights in Philly.

Marvin Hagler is a former undisputed middleweight champion from Brockton, Massachusetts, who fought professionally from 1973 to 1987. What do you recall about the times Hagler fought for you?

In January of 1976, I paid Hagler two thousand dollars to fight "Boogaloo" Watts at the Spectrum. Hagler won that fight, but they gave it to Watts. I was never a guy who wanted a bad decision. I always wanted the judges to call it right, even if it went against a local guy. I was so upset after that fight and I remember screaming at one of the judges.

In March, Hagler came down again to fight Willie "The Worm" Monroe. We had a tremendous snow storm the day of the fight. It was so bad that the film crew couldn't get there. That's a shame, because in my mind, it was the only fight that Hagler ever lost. I didn't think Hagler lost to Leonard, but he lost to Willie "The Worm." Hagler even admitted it the next day. He was quoted as saying, "I still have a lot to learn and Willie's already learned it."

When the fight was over, we were in the back and the Petronelli brothers cornered me. They said, "Listen, Russell, you're working with all these middleweights. Why don't you take us on? We'll cut you in." In response to their offer, I said these words that will forever haunt me. I said, "What can I do for you if you can't beat the guys in Philly?" That's how I turned down ten percent of Marvin Hagler.

Hagler came back to the Spectrum in September and he stopped "Cyclone" Hart. In August of '77, he stopped Monroe in a rematch. And he came back for me again in August of '78 and won a decision over Briscoe. With 14,950 people in attendance, it was the largest crowd ever for an indoor non-championship fight in Pennsylvania history. That was the last time Hagler ever fought for me. After that, Arum signed him because Arum had control of television.

Matthew Franklin, who later became Matthew Saad Muhammad, was a former WBC world light heavyweight champion out of Philadelphia, who boxed professionally from 1974 to 1992. What do you recall about the time you spent promoting some of Muhammad's fights?

Frank Gelb was a manager who had Tyrone Everett. Tyrone's brother Mike was with Pinny Schafer and Pat Duffy. Gelb wanted to have both of the Everetts in his stable, so he bought Mike Everett's contract along with a junior lightweight named Alfonso Evans. Matt Franklin was in that same stable and he didn't want to be left behind. In baseball, they would have called him "the player to be named later." He was a throw-in. Frank Gelb really didn't know much about Franklin. But who did? He wasn't setting the world on fire at that time.

Gelb was my kind of manager. He put Matt Franklin in tough. He sent him overseas where he fought to a draw against Mate Parlov in Italy. In March of '77, he put Franklin in against Eddie Gregory in Philly. That was Eddie Mustafa Muhammad. It was a close fight, but Franklin lost a split decision. Then Gelb made Marvin Johnson and Matthew Franklin for the vacant North American Federation title. That was July 26, 1977. Franklin knocked Johnson out in the twelfth round, the last round. As I said before, I was fortunate to promote the greatest fight I've ever seen in person.

Franklin followed that fight up with "Dynamite" Douglas. It was on the undercard of Roberto Duran and Edwin Viruet at the Spectrum. Franklin got off the floor to stop "Dynamite" Douglas. The following February, he got off the floor to stop Richie Kates. These were the kind of fights you would script for Hollywood. It was like *Rocky*, only it was real life.

Dwight Braxton, who later became Dwight Muhammad Qawi, boxed professionally from 1978 to 1998. He came out of Camden, New Jersey, and won world titles at light heavyweight and cruiserweight. What stands out in your mind about Qawi's early years when you promoted some of his fights?

Braxton was a tough bastard. When he was 5-1-1, we sent him to South Africa early in 1980 to fight a guy named Theunis Kok. Theunis Kok was some hot undefeated star and Braxton knocked him out. Nobody had ever heard of Braxton before that. How could a guy with a record like that do this?

We entered him in the ESPN tournament and he won that. Then we put him in with Mike Rossman. It was his first network appearance. I told Dwight, "You're not going to make any money for this fight, but this fight is going to make you." And of course, after he knocked out Mike Rossman, I lost him. He went with Murad Muhammad and then with Rock Newman. He told me later on that Rock Newman took him for a ride.

Qawi and I got inducted in Canastota the same year, and we got real close that weekend. In his speech, he said that he changed his mind about me. He didn't quite say what he meant, but I think I understood what he was saying. He didn't trust a lot of people and I think he eventually felt better about me. Qawi ended up selling me his Hall of Fame ring because he needed the money, and that's one of the sad parts about boxing. He kept saying, "I'm going to buy it back from you." I told him it wasn't going anywhere. And I still have it.

Bernard Hopkins is a fighter out of Philadelphia, who fought professionally from 1988 to 2016. He won world championships at middleweight and light heavyweight, and he became the oldest man in history, at age forty-eight, to win a world title.

While Hopkins will go down as one of the ten greatest fighters to ever come out of Philly, he was not as beloved as Briscoe and Hayward and other Philly fighters

Former middleweight world title challenger Gabriel Rosado lands a right hand on James Moore en route to a 2008 unanimous decision victory (courtesy Marty Rosengarten/RingsidePhotos.com).

before him. Butch Lewis convinced him to move to Delaware, I guess for tax reasons. Not that there's anything wrong with that, but Hopkins was never a draw when he fought in Philly. The fans just didn't embrace him as a local fighter.

When Bernard Hopkins was coming up, people told me he was good. I hadn't really seen him. When I *did* see him, I was impressed. But Hopkins wasn't always impressive to watch. He was a better fighter than he looked. In the newspapers, I actually picked him to beat Trinidad. Hopkins fought for me twice. I made an offer to sign him and I sent his people a contract. But the next thing I know, he signed with Butch Lewis.

From what I understand, Hopkins got screwed by Butch Lewis and had to sue to get out of his contract. If I'm correct, there was a situation with how the finances were handled with his first fight with Roy Jones. After he got out of the contract with Butch Lewis, he ended up aggravating a host of other promoters. He enjoyed being a renegade and maybe he thought he had to be. I don't think he ever trusted anybody after the Butch Lewis situation.

Arturo Gatti was a former two-division champion out of Jersey City, New Jersey, who fought professionally from 1991 to 2007. What was your involvement with Gatti's career?

I promoted Arturo's brother, Joe Gatti. Dan Duva promoted Arturo. One day, Dan called me on the phone and said, "I have Arturo Gatti and you have Joe Gatti. Why don't we become partners with the Gatti brothers? I'll give you fifty percent of Arturo and you give me fifty percent of Joe." I said, "Okay," and that was the extent of our deal. There was never a piece of paper between us.

But to say that I got lucky would be an understatement. You can't compare Arturo's career with Joe's. Every time Arturo Gatti fought, I got a big check because Arturo made a lot of money. The deal was eventually trimmed to 65–35. Even though it was a handshake deal, Dino Duva honored the agreement I had with Dan, after Dan passed away.

At the Boxing Writers dinner in 2000, Kathy Duva, then in charge, called me over and said, "Russell, I don't understand this. I see these checks going to you each time Arturo fights, but I don't see any paperwork." I told Kathy the story and she said, "If that's what Dan said, then we'll honor the deal." I kept getting paid till Arturo's contract with Main Events ran out, right around the first fight with Micky Ward. They basically said that I had a good ride and that was it. But to have the kind of deal I had based on somebody's word—that's unheard of. Unheard of! There aren't too many people you can do that with.

Gabriel Rosado is a former middleweight world title challenger from Philadelphia, who gained worldwide recognition after suffering some early defeats. Rosado turned professional in 2006 and continues fighting to this day.

I signed Gabe to a two or three fight option when he fought Kassim Ouma in April of 2009. His career was up and down at that point, but everything changed in January of 2012 when he knocked out Jesus Soto Karass. The people at NBC Sports went bonkers and they put him on again in June. He knocked out Sechew Powell, and then we brought him back in September and he stopped Charles Whitaker. All of a sudden, he was the number one contender.

He was in line to fight "K-9" Bundrage, who was the IBF champ, but that wasn't going to happen till July or August. So, I read on the Internet that some fighter had just turned down a lot of money to fight Gennady Golovkin. I called Peter Nelson at HBO and asked if the Golovkin fight was still available, which it was. I told Gabe about it and he wanted to do whatever was going to make the most money. So, we went with Golovkin.

My only regret about the Golovkin fight is that I didn't go to the corner and have it stopped one round earlier. The sixth round was his best round of the fight. He actually nailed Golovkin with some shots in that round, but he was a bloody pulp. In the next round, he really got beat up bad and they had to stop it.

Gabe and I kept working together for his next few fights. After he lost a decision to Jermell Charlo in January of 2014, we agreed to go our separate ways. He ended up signing with Golden Boy. But after he beat Glen Tapia last year, he had a falling out with Golden Boy. He came back to Philly, and we talked, and now we're working together again, with me as his advisor.

How has boxing changed from the time you first became involved to the state of the game today?

I'm one of the few people who have the entire *Ring* magazine collection. About a year or two ago, I did a study. I took a sample of the ratings from 1961—eight divisions, eight world champions.... Actually, one title was split. There were eighty-nine fighters and I looked up their records. Out of those eighty-nine fighters, five were undefeated.

I juxtaposed that with the WBC rankings at that time. I only took the same eight divisions. Obviously, there are a lot more weight classes today than there were in 1961. But there were eighty-eight fighters, and of the eighty-eight, thirty-one were undefeated. Thirty-one undefeated fighters in the rankings opposed to five! What does that tell me? It tells me that nobody is fighting anybody anymore. There are more undefeated fighters walking around in boxing today than any time in history. It's ridiculous!

You know what boxing is like? It's like coming up to the end of the baseball season with no playoffs. That to me is its biggest problem. The guys who buy fights for the networks—they don't want the best fighters, they want the fighters with the best records. Today, fighters like George Benton and Archie Moore wouldn't be on television because of their records.

I think Floyd Mayweather cemented this way of thinking. He was a terrific fighter. I'm not going to knock that. But he was a self-promoter who didn't really take

Former five-division world champion Floyd Mayweather, Jr., who retired with a record of 50–0, 27 KOs, used his undefeated status as a selling point throughout his career, 2015 (courtesy Bret Newton—ThreatPhoto.com/Pound4Pound.com).

chances. A lot of young fighters look up to him and they're trying to follow in his footsteps. Everybody wants to be undefeated. You can't make the fights that I used to make, because nobody wants to take risks until they get million-dollar paydays.

In my opinion, the twenty-first century has not been good for boxing. If you go to a baseball game today, how many of those people can tell you who the heavyweight champion of the world is? How many of them even give a shit? When I was a kid, everybody knew who Sonny Liston was. It was an important thing to be the heavyweight champion. Sports fans know nothing about what's going on in boxing, except for fights like Mayweather–McGregor, which was a farce.

Is it still a money-making sport? Yes, for five percent of the people who are in it. They're making ninety-five percent of the money. But you've got the other ninety-five percent of the sport and they're making five percent of the money.

Next September, September 30th of 2019, it will mark fifty years in boxing for me. I'm going to make it to fifty years, because when I was a kid, I read *50 Years at Ringside* by Nat Fleischer, the editor and publisher of *Ring* magazine. I want to be able to say that I was fifty years at ringside. Boxing has been good to me. I'm one of the lucky ones. I took my childhood passion and turned it into my livelihood. It enabled me to put my sons through college.

Most people are in boxing to make money, not because they love the sport. Very few promoters are diehard fans. I'll make a fight that I know I'm going to lose money on just because I want to see a good fight. There are a few people in this business like me, but not many. I didn't get into this because I thought I was going to make a fortune. I got into boxing because I love boxing. As Bobby Goodman once said, "It's a great sport, but a terrible business."

Announcers and Officials

22

Jim Lampley: World Championship Boxing

> "It was one of those fights where you knew that the two combatants were going to emerge as indelibly linked blood brothers—that what's happening between them is ultimately going to compute to sincere and devoted love."

In boxing, a blow-by-blow announcer describes the action in the ring and offers details about what is taking place. This person's commentary plays a big part in educating the boxing public. Those who tuned into HBO Boxing from the late 1980s to the late 2010s always counted on a very familiar, very reliable voice to help them follow the event they were about to watch.

Born and raised in Hendersonville, North Carolina, Jim Lampley became an enthusiastic boxing fan at an early age. He pursued a career in sportscasting, initially assigned to college football for ABC Sports.

In the mid-1980s, the executives at ABC Sports took notice of Lampley's knowledge of boxing, and offered him an opportunity to be their blow-by-blow guy.

Lampley's start as an announcer of professional boxing coincided with the emergence of then future heavyweight champion Mike Tyson. Lampley called several of Tyson's fights on ABC Sports, and later on HBO Boxing.

From 1988 to 2018, Lampley was HBO's blow-by-blow announcer, calling a number of world championship bouts and meaningful fights, including James "Buster" Douglas–Mike Tyson; Julio Cesar Chavez–Meldrick Taylor I; the Riddick Bowe–Evander Holyfield trilogy; George Foreman–Michael Moorer; the Marco Antonio Barrera–Erik Morales trilogy; the Arturo Gatti–Micky Ward trilogy; and Floyd Mayweather, Jr.–Manny Pacquiao. This interview took place over the phone in October 2019.

How did boxing first become a part of your life and what led you to become the blow-by-blow announcer for HBO Boxing?

My father died when I was five years old. He was a World War II bomber pilot. He was Henderson County, North Carolina's biggest war hero. He was a club champion golfer and course record holder. And he was a huge sports fan. I was his only son. After he died, my mother took the initiative to share with me some of the things that she thought he would have wanted to share with me, if he had still been around.

One graphic example of that was in 1955 or '56, when she took me to her friend's house.

I can vividly remember her walking me down this hallway to a small bedroom. She sat me down in front of this small black and white television and tuned into the *Gillette Friday Night Fights* telecast. It was one of the rematches between "Sugar" Ray Robinson and Carl "Bobo" Olson. She said, "This is what you would be doing if your father were here. So sit here, have fun, and watch the boxing match. And oh, by the way, 'Sugar' Ray Robinson is my favorite fighter." That was my introduction to boxing.

Through the vehicle of *Friday Night Fights*, I spent my childhood watching Dick Tiger, Emile Griffith, "Sugar" Ray Robinson, Carmen Basilio, Gene Fullmer, and all of the star fighters who populated the sport at that time. In 1960, while watching the Rome Olympics, I watched Cassius Clay box and dance and win the gold medal. He was already talking at that point. As a young black man using a slave name to taunt the white establishment in the South, he was the absolute perfect heroic figure for me.

My mother was ardently anti-racist and she made it clear to me that racism was a cardinal sin. It was the one thing I would never think, never feel, never affiliate with. It was important to feel that way, because all around me at that time in the South, the Civil Rights movement was gaining momentum. Among the other things she was directing me to watch on television, besides boxing, were sit-ins, school integrations, and all of the historical elements that were taking place in that part of the world at that time.

Former HBO blow-by-blow announcer Jim Lampley, 2000s (courtesy Marty Rosengarten/RingsidePhotos.com).

I became obsessive about Cassius Clay as his professional career was getting underway. And at the same time, my mother, who now needed to find work as a way to support me, moved us from Hendersonville, North Carolina, to Miami, Florida, so she could sell life insurance to military people in that area. Shortly after moving to Miami, I realized that I was within driving distance of the 5th Street Gym where Cassius Clay trained with Angelo Dundee. On at least two occasions, I persuaded my mother to drive me from our drab community in South Miami to the 5th Street Gym, so that I could watch Dundee train Cassius Clay. Interestingly, I met Dundee and watched him do some work with Willie Pastrano and Luis Rodriguez, but I never met or saw or bumped into Cassius Clay.

I was junior high school age when the build-up began for Clay versus Liston. I saved lawn mowing and car washing money for months, so that I could buy a ticket. I can't remember whether that ticket was a hundred dollars or a hundred and fifty dollars. I wish I still had it. On February 25, 1964, my mother drove me to Miami Beach, and killed time while I sat in the Miami Beach Convention Center and watched Clay upset Liston.

When I got home that night, I got up onto the roof of our house and started shouting, "I shook up the world! I am the greatest of all time!," and all the things that Clay said in the ring after the fight. I was basically tormenting my redneck neighbors, who had been rooting for Liston to shut Clay up. Within forty-eight hours of that, Clay stood on a street corner in Miami and told the media that he had changed his name to Muhammad Ali. That was a tremendous challenge for me.

He was my beloved hero, and he was partially my hero because his name was Cassius Marcellus Clay and what that portrayed in the Civil Rights movement. It probably took me a year or two to adjust to his name change, and to get it through my head that he had the right to his own identity, and that I had to call him Muhammad Ali. It was a real process. Eventually, I got to a point where I could accept that, and it was the first huge lesson he taught me as a human being. Later on, I can't recall that I had a specific position on the Vietnam War, but he taught me that lesson, too. So, with Muhammad Ali, it wasn't just about boxing. He was this person who, from a distance, had an enormous influence on the way I viewed life.

When I was twenty-four or twenty-five years old, I was a graduate student at the University of North Carolina. My name was submitted to make me a candidate for a one-of-a-kind gimmick event—the hiring of a near college age announcer to work on the sidelines of the college football telecast for ABC Sports. I was the ultimate winner of that talent hunt, which went on through all of 1974.

For the first twelve plus years at ABC Sports, the one word I never would have said was "boxing." Howard Cosell called boxing and he called it by himself. It was entirely his product. It would have been crazy for me to say anything at all about my interest in boxing, given Cosell's general feelings about me as an interloper in the business. All I did in regard to that for the next several years was to occasionally go to the executive suite viewing parties to watch closed circuit feeds of the big fights. Sometimes at those viewing parties, I would stand around and talk to people about boxing.

In '85 or '86, I was watching a video feed of Hagler–Hearns. At that point, Cosell had forsaken boxing, famously walking away from it after the Larry Holmes–Randall "Tex" Cobb fight. Al Michaels was calling our delayed broadcast feed of Hagler–Hearns, and I was talking with an executive in the department named Alex Wallau. I barely knew Alex at the time, because he was all about boxing and I was staying away from boxing. But we were standing there watching Hagler–Hearns, and at the end of it, he turned to me and said, "Gosh, you know a lot about boxing. How come you never told anybody?" I kind of gave him a blank look as if to say, "Come on. You know the answer to that."

Not too long after my conversation with Alex, they came to me and said they were trying to refurbish the boxing telecast to prepare for the advent of this young heavyweight from Upstate New York, with whom they were negotiating a deal. That young kid was Mike Tyson. They wanted me to do an audition and call a fight into a video tape machine to see if I had the aptitude to be their blow-by-blow guy.

So, I was sent to Atlantic City to sit at ringside by myself and call a fight between "Smokin" Bert Cooper and Reggie Gross, which ended in a shocking TKO win for Gross. Cooper had dominated most of the fight up to that point, and I learned a lesson that night about how rapidly things can change in a boxing match, and how unpredictable boxing, particularly heavyweight boxing, can be.

All that led to February 16, 1986, when I went to Troy, New York, to cover Mike Tyson versus Jesse Ferguson, which was my first network telecast of a boxing match. It became a very noteworthy boxing match in Tyson's career, because that was the night he said that Cus D'Amato taught him that the purpose of the uppercut was to drive the opponent's nose into their brain. That's pretty much what Mike did to

Former world heavyweight champion Muhammad Ali, then an amateur boxer named Cassius Clay, following a Golden Gloves bout in Chicago, Illinois, late 1950s (courtesy Ray Rodgers).

Ferguson in the sixth round of that fight. I did well enough in the telecast that I became the blow-by-blow guy at ABC, and I called all of the fights on ABC on *Wide World of Sports* on the weekends for the next year and four months.

By that time, my prestige and my position at ABC were withering, because a newly installed department head was doing everything possible to make my life uncomfortable. In fact, I later determined that assigning me to boxing was *designed* to make me uncomfortable. He thought I was a white glove, eastern Ivy League kid who would hate boxing, not having any idea what my life relative to boxing was. On July 2, 1987, I willingly walked away from my contract with ABC, and I took a job working for CBS, where I called pro football and college basketball. I also became the sports director for KTCS-TV in Los Angeles.

By '88, my agent came to me and said that HBO was very interested in hiring me to work the boxing telecast and host Wimbledon. Getting that gig was pretty much my holy grail. At that point, I had a very deep-seated urge to get away from my dependency on commercial television. When you don't have commercial interference, you have much more editorial freedom. And by the way, boxing is the sport in which you have the greatest freedom to tell the truth, because nothing is regarded as debilitatingly outrageous. With boxing, we start at outrageous and go from there. By February 1988, I had agreed on a contract with HBO. And on March 21, 1988, I had my first HBO boxing telecast which was Mike Tyson versus Tony Tubbs.

Mike Tyson won world titles at heavyweight in the mid 1980s and mid 1990s, and was known for his explosive power and take-no-prisoners style. What do you recall about Tyson when he first came onto the scene, and what is your assessment of his career now that all is said and done?

I was schooled to understand that Tyson had an unusual formative background, simply because he was the managerial and promotional property of Jimmy Jacobs and Bill Cayton. They were regarded as extremely knowledgeable, thoughtful, and intelligent people. They were in the process of working with Edwin Rosario, who was a brilliant featherweight fighter. Now they were involved with Tyson, and they already had succeeded at getting local television stations all across the country to show this highlight reel they put together, which was basically a fast-edited view of all of Mike's knockouts up to that point. It was a stunning piece of video tape.

So consequently, people had seen video of this kid knocking people out in spectacular fashion, before ever seeing him fight against a meaningful opponent. Most people never saw him in a meaningful fight until he entered the HBO heavyweight tournament. The tournament was a little bit of a set-up, because none of those guys had any capacity to handle Mike. This was a cakewalk towards becoming the youngest heavyweight champion in the history of the sport. He of course fulfilled the cakewalk, memorably knocking down Trevor Berbick three times with one punch.

I came on board not long after Mike won the championship and started calling his fights. I was overwhelmingly impressed by his power. I understood that he had spectacular attacking skills and that he was a quality defender. But I was also close enough to the situation to see that the portrayal of his overwhelming dominance was a bit of a distortion.

I was still working at ABC the night I watched him go the distance with Mitch "Blood" Green, and he was never anywhere close to knocking Green out. Earlier, I had called his fight with James "Quick" Tillis. A lot of people at ringside had that fight a draw. Some people had Tyson winning by a margin of one round. There were even some scorecards that had Tillis as the winner of that fight. I watched him in the heavyweight tournament when he went the distance with Tony Tucker and "Bonecrusher" Smith. He almost went the distance with Jose Ribalta, which he ended with only ten seconds to go in the fight.

A lot of people were ignoring all of this, paying attention only to the knockouts, and not paying attention to the fact that when he went in with a taller fighter who had a little bit of movement, he was not overwhelming those guys. All of the indications were there, if you paid close attention, that a certain kind of opponent gave Mike lots of trouble. That certain kind of opponent turned out to be James "Buster" Douglas.

Douglas was six-foot-four, two hundred thirty pounds, had foot movement, had an excellent jab, could bring the right hand behind the jab, and was much more dynamic than any of Tyson's previous opponents. A lot of people regard Tyson–Douglas as the biggest upset in boxing history, but the fact is that if you paid attention to what Mike had done against taller fighters with foot movement, you might have said this was a dangerous fight for him. Going in, I thought that there was no way Mike could lose to Buster Douglas. But after it *did* happen, when I put together everything I had seen up to that point, my growing education in boxing led me to realize that there was evidence. There was a design there. There was an indication.

Mike Tyson was part of an era of heavyweight boxing that included Lennox Lewis, Evander Holyfield, Riddick Bowe, George Foreman, and Michael Moorer, all who held world titles at heavyweight at various times throughout the 1990s and early 2000s. How would you compare this era of heavyweight boxing to other eras in the division?

I think you can make the argument that it's the second richest heavyweight era ever, exceeded only by the Ali–Frazier–Foreman era. Generally speaking, for nearly one hundred thirty years, there's only been one great heavyweight at one particular time. That's been the pattern, whether it's Jack Dempsey or Joe Louis. Those guys had very few credible opponents around to fight. But when you have a situation as was the case with Lewis, Bowe, and Holyfield, a legitimate argument could have been made that any of these three guys could be the number one heavyweight.

Tyson was still a part of the picture and the general fan base probably still thought that he was the number one guy. But intelligent reporters who covered the sport knew that wasn't exactly the case. He was coming back from a prison stint and he didn't work as hard as he used to. But the bottom line is that it was a great era in terms of wealth of talent. And ultimately, torturously, over a long period of time, they wound up fighting each other, with the noteworthy exception of Lewis and Bowe.

People who had been to the 1988 Olympic Games, including fighters who had been on the American Olympic Team at the time, had been aware enough to tell me not to waste my time waiting for Bowe to fight Lewis, because it wasn't going to happen. Riddick had more than one opportunity to sign contracts to fight Lennox Lewis and he wasn't interested in doing that. So, Lewis–Bowe was the missing link in that particular era. But at the end of the day, it was a very rich era, and then it got even richer when George Foreman knocked out Michael Moorer. Moorer, by the way, was a really good fighter with a truly outstanding record.

During your time at HBO, Oscar De La Hoya was one of the biggest stars on the network. De La Hoya fought professionally from 1992 to 2008, and won world titles in six different weight classes. What stands out in your mind about the time you called De La Hoya's fights?

The most important thing about De La Hoya was that he accelerated the blending of the Mexican fight culture with the American fight culture. He was an American who was seen by some as a Mexican, because of his name and background. So, he's very important in advancing the general identity of the Latino-American fighter. His Olympic story was an ideal launching pad, which led to his ultimate superstardom. Women would have related to Oscar anyway because of his looks, but to see that this effectively violent athlete was also a tender mama's boy was irresistible.

I was the late-night host at the Barcelona Olympics on NBC in 1992, and we brought him into the studio to sit with me after he won his gold medal. Every woman in the broadcast center was crushing to get into or near our studio, and it was easy to see how appealing he was going to be. Oscar and I became friends, and we had careers that were kind of paralleling each other. I became his video biographer on TV, and in some instances, those calls I made during his fights were very emotional. I think sometimes I was a little overwrought, because of his importance to the sport and because of his importance to HBO.

At this point, I think Oscar himself would acknowledge to you that he probably fell short of maximizing his talent, because his life outside the ring, to some degree, swallowed him up. That's probably the least uncommon personal narrative in boxing. He's typical of a lot of people who became boxing stars, and then squandered some of their talent because of the

Former four-division world champion and HBO commentator Roy Jones, Jr., 2000s (courtesy Marty Rosengarten/ RingsidePhotos.com).

privileges and opportunities that existed outside the ring. But he was still pretty damn good.

From 1993 to 2003, former four-division world champion Roy Jones, Jr., was the most dominant fighter of that time. What is your assessment of Jones's career?

First of all, Roy was a cosmic talent. He did amazing things on HBO. His record is laudable in every way. He showed courage when he lost to Antonio Tarver and fought him a third time. But Roy was not as profoundly oriented to face-to-face competition as the audience wanted him to be. I wish he had fought Dariusz Michalczewski, and I wish he had fought Steve Collins. I wish he had gone further out of his way to prove his preeminence in the light heavyweight division, rather than to ultimately be seen as having avoided a couple of fights that might have further helped him prove his greatness.

I have a hunch that he would have beaten Michalczewski and Steve Collins, but I don't know for certain because I didn't see them in the ring. It's difficult for me to talk about that, because he's one of my closest friends in the world. I love Roy Jones with a great personal passion. And I can't talk about him without making that point, so that you understand my bias. He is a brother to me.

In 2002 and 2003, HBO featured three ten-round bouts between junior welterweights Arturo Gatti and Micky Ward. Ward won the first bout by majority decision, while Gatti won the last two via unanimous decision. These fights are now regarded as one of the best trilogies in boxing history.

This was the ring insider's ultimate gift. Everybody in the sport who knew anything about the sport wanted to see these two guys throw down. That first fight wasn't a fight that was going to get a huge number for our HBO boxing telecast, but everybody in the telecast knew it was going to be the Fight of the Year. Emanuel Steward adequately covered that when he said, "We knew it was going to be the fight of the year, but we didn't know it was going to be the fight of the century!" It was one of those fights where you knew that the two combatants were going to emerge as indelibly linked blood brothers—that what's happening between them is ultimately going to compute to sincere and devoted love.

My favorite memory is that after I finished the telecast, I walked out of the arena, and the first person I ran into was Gatti's manager, Pat Lynch. Pat was as upset as he could possibly be. I said, "Pat, what's the problem? Why are you so bothered?" He said, "I can't believe we lost the fight." I said, "Pat, twenty-four hours from now, nobody outside the Ward family is going to remember who won or lost. That's the last thing anybody is going to remember about this." Anytime there's a fight that great, there're two winners. It doesn't matter who actually won. It's of zero consequence. Micky and Arturo both won. They are *the* great working man's rivalry of their era.

From 2009 to 2015, the boxing public demanded a fight between welterweight world title holders and multi-division champions Floyd Mayweather, Jr., and Manny Pacquiao. The fight ultimately happened in May 2015, with Mayweather winning a unanimous decision. Why was this fight so important to the public and how did it ultimately impact the sport?

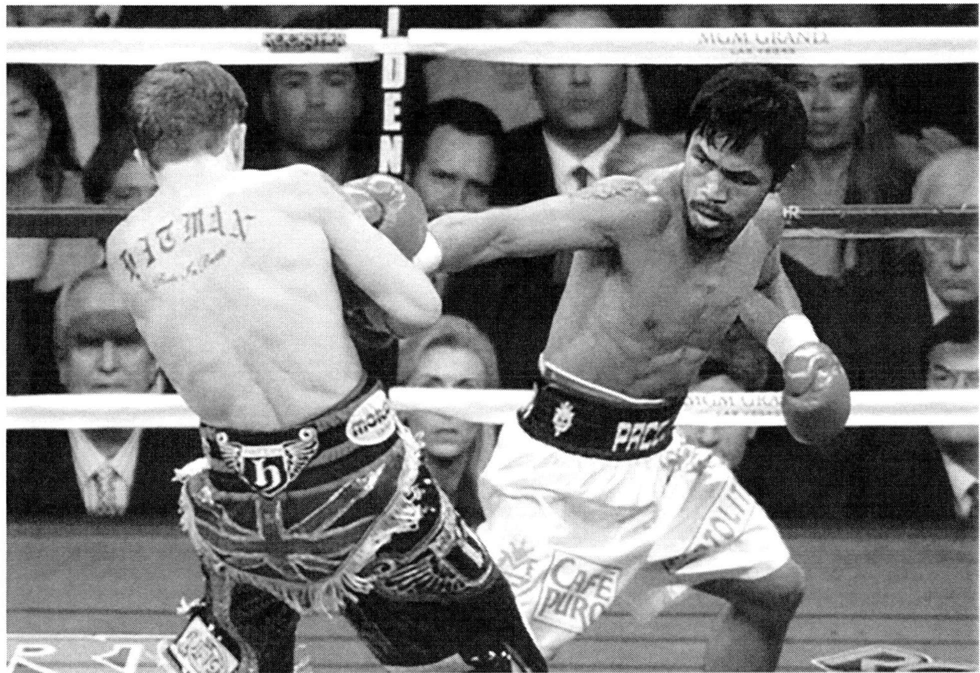

Former eight-division world champion Manny Pacquiao measures up former two-division world champion Ricky Hatton en route to a 2009 second-round knockout. Pacquiao's explosive win over Hatton helped create a public demand for Mayweather vs. Pacquiao (courtesy Bret Newton—ThreatPhoto.com/Pound4Pound.com).

It was important to the boxing world, because the welterweight division had achieved this level of eminence that made clear that it was the central star-making vehicle. When the public started talking about Mayweather–Pacquiao, both fighters had reputations that existed to a certain degree based on their fights with Oscar De La Hoya. Pacquiao had elevated his reputation very overwhelmingly by one-sidedly beating De La Hoya. And his win over De La Hoya was far more one-sided than Mayweather's win over De La Hoya.

This was a classic matchup of fire and ice. One guy was an ultra-violent offensive fighter, and that was Pacquiao. And the other guy, Mayweather, was an ultra-cerebral defensive fighter. So, their styles were right out of the textbook. It was as good as it could get. This was part of the entry into the Internet era, and the self-promotion element of the sport had gone to another level. Mayweather was the master. He precedes Trump as the most meaningful user of social media for his own purposes. This was the early evolution of the phenomenon.

I think all of those things helped make this the giant event that it was. And by the way, almost anybody in boxing could tell you that it wasn't going to be an entertaining fight. Floyd Mayweather's whole method for dominating fights was to eliminate the entertainment factor. He had a calculus in his head throughout his career that winning was more important than pleasing the fans.

Ultimately, this was not a fight that was good for boxing, because even the general public viewer could see that this was a dud. The fight itself did not portray what was interesting about boxing. It portrayed what was *not* interesting about boxing. So therefore, if all around the world there were millions of people who seldom if ever tune into a fight, but because of the public hoopla they tuned into Mayweather versus Pacquiao, they saw something that led them to realize that this is why they don't pay any attention to boxing.

In December 2018, HBO had its final boxing telecast after forty-five years of featuring the sport. Why did HBO get out of the boxing business after having such a strong run?

We're in a different world now. And I think it remains to be seen which economic equations relative to boxing are the ones that will survive and endure and sustain the sport. But it's not hard to see that the streaming model has certain advantages. It creates a global platform. It creates a situation, in which if you get a tiny sliver of the globally available audience, that sliver is enough to make scads of money. Over the long haul, it's potentially a more effective model than the premium pay cable model. And the premium pay cable model was better than the Saturday afternoon network television model. The same can be said for the closed-circuit model.

So at the end of the day, there's a constant evolution in the way that boxing matches are delivered to the public. It looks possible to me that the streaming service model is the one that is going to take hold for the foreseeable future. It wouldn't shock me if we look around in two or three years to see that the premium pay cable model has disappeared from boxing altogether. But I had a great thirty plus years at HBO. The memories are overwhelmingly abundant, and I was lucky for a long period of time to be a part of that.

23

Duane Ford: Through the Eyes of a Judge

"A lot of people get confused with judging. In the amateurs, a punch is worth one point, and a knockdown is worth one point. But on the professional side, whoever gets the snot kicked out of him loses."

Educated boxing fans will often score a fight multiple times, finding themselves with different scores each time. A person's perception of a bout is affected by a number of variables—the reaction of the fans in the arena, the commentators on television, or a biased opinion because of a certain boxer they might favor. At every boxing match, the three judges at ringside are the only people whose job it is to block out all of the distractions and devote one hundred percent of their attention to the action inside the ring.

Born and raised in Las Vegas, Nevada, Duane Ford started his career in professional boxing officiating, first as a timekeeper, and eventually as a judge in the state of Nevada in 1978.

Over the years, Ford has judged some of the biggest fights in Las Vegas, including Ray Leonard–Thomas Hearns I, Salvador Sanchez–Wilfredo Gomez, Larry Holmes–Gerry Cooney, George Foreman–Michael Moorer, Evander Holyfield–Mike Tyson II, Shane Mosley–Oscar De La Hoya II, Jermain Taylor–Bernard Hopkins I, and Manny Pacquiao–Juan Manuel Marquez II.

While most of Ford's work has taken place in the state of Nevada, he has also judged professional boxing in such countries as Japan, Poland, Germany, Mexico, Canada, Panama, Thailand, South Korea, France, and the United Kingdom.

Ford is a former Chairman for the Nevada State Athletic Commission, and has been a lead instructor for the Association of Boxing Commissions (ABC) for certifying other professional judges. This interview took place over the phone in July 2011.

What is your background in boxing and what led you to become a judge?

I've always had a strong interest in boxing. My dad was a huge boxing fan, and I used to lay by the radio and listen to all the big fights like Joe Louis and Joe Walcott.... In college, I did a little fighting. I started going to a bunch of fights and I knew a number of the commissioners who were on at that time. They made me a timekeeper and I did that for a year or so. And then they asked me to start judging and that's how I got involved in it.

What steps does a person have to go through in order to be licensed as a professional boxing judge?

In Nevada, it requires two years of amateur participation. Then they go through a shadowing period. I know people who have been shadowing for two or three years. What they do is they go to the pro fights, and turn their scorecards in to the executive director of the commission, who keeps a record of them and sees how their scoring is compared to the licensed judges. The Association of Boxing Commissions has done a good job of training the new judges and keeping the older officials where they should be. They have great seminars that go right down to the basics and also teach some ideas that are very advanced.

What are the criteria for judging fights? What do you look for and how do you ultimately decide who won the round?

A lot of people get confused with judging. In the amateurs, a punch is worth one point, and a knockdown is worth one point. But on the professional side, whoever gets the snot kicked out of him loses. So, when you compare the amateur criteria and the criteria for the pros, it's like oil and water. On the pro side, you have to look at the punches. What damage are they causing? And if the punches are even and the damage is the same, then you look for effective aggression.

Effective aggression doesn't necessarily mean moving forward. Sometimes you're moving backwards. Look at Earnie Shavers and Larry Holmes. Shavers never took a step backwards that night and he got the heck kicked out of him. Although he did knock Holmes down. So, aggression is getting off first, being quicker… And then there's ring generalship. That's who's in control. So, those are the areas that we look for.

Professional boxing judge Duane Ford (right) stands beside Michelle Corrales-Lewis, the widow of former two-division world champion Diego Corrales, at the announcement of his 2019 induction into the Nevada Boxing Hall of Fame. Trainer Floyd Mayweather, Sr., sits in the background (courtesy Tim Cheatham).

There are a number of fights in boxing that could go either way, where an argument could be made for either fighter. Do you ever feel conflicted when judging a fight?

A judge only judges a round. He doesn't judge a fight. I look at it as a baseball umpire behind home plate. I guess that strike that barely hit the corner is debatable too. But it was the opinion of the umpire that it was a strike. And it's the opinion of a boxing judge when one guy wins the round.

Now, a lot of people complain about the 10-point must. They think it's not wide enough. And some people think they should go to half points, which I think would be ridiculous. There's a situation where a fighter might lose 10–9 in a close round. Or there might be a wider span and the round is still 10–9. But yes, there are some fights that are very, very close.

Of all of the fights that you have judged, what was the toughest to score and what was the deciding factor?

Morales–Barrera I was probably the toughest fight to score. I had Barrera winning, but the other two judges had Morales. I gave it to Barrera just on the basis of one punch. And that one punch made Morales take a knee. It was the last round. That was the toughest by far and I remember it quite well. Barrera would land a punch and he would be winning, then Morales would land and he would be winning, and then Barrera would land and then he was winning.... It just went back and forth.

When judging, do you ever score a round 10–10?

Yes, I have. There's nothing wrong with giving a 10–10 round. And here's where you should use a 10–10 round.... You use it, if you happen to lose your concentration in the middle of the round. Because if you guess who's winning and you're wrong, it's going to take that fighter two rounds to make up for your mistake. So, you use a 10–10 round when you've totally lost your concentration.

The other time is when it's a dead-bang even round. I'm guessing I've done over fifteen hundred world championship rounds. In that time, I might have had two even rounds, maybe three. An even round to me is like a baseball umpire yelling at the pitcher, "It's too close to call! Throw it again!" You've got to make a call.

I've known judges in the past, one of them came from Europe, and it was a twelve-round title fight, and he had seven even rounds. Man, I wish I could judge some tough fights like that—make them all even and only decide on five. But there are even rounds. They're rare, but there are even rounds.

But 10–10 doesn't always mean it was an even round from a judge's standpoint. Look at the Pacquiao–Mosley fight. Pacquiao was winning the round and Mosley knocked him down, so Dave Moretti scored it a 10–10 round.

So, you don't score it 10–8 automatically if there's a knockdown?

Let me ask you the question. Where is that written? It's not. There's a mistaken idea out there that every knockdown is worth two points and it's not true. What we do in the Association of Boxing Commissions at the seminars, we have a beginner's class. It's a basic class, and we teach the people who are just coming into boxing that if a guy is winning the round, and he knocks his opponent down, he wins the round 10–8. You get one point for wining the round and one point for knocking him down. But what do we do about the guy who's losing, who knocks down the guy who's winning? You give him one point for the knockdown and then see what happens from there. So, a knockdown doesn't necessarily mean two points.

Manny Pacquiao (right) defends his WBC world junior lightweight title against Juan Manuel Marquez in their second encounter, winning by split decision, 2008. Judge Duane Ford scored the bout 115–112 for Pacquiao. Pacquiao and Marquez fought a total of four times, because the public was often split about the scoring in each fight. Marquez won the fourth bout via sixth-round knockout (courtesy Bret Newton—ThreatPhoto.com/Pound4Pound.com).

If there are three knockdowns in a round, as was the case in the first fight between featherweights Manny Pacquiao and Juan Manuel Marquez, would you score it 10–6?

Yes.

Some judges wouldn't do that because it takes that fighter so far out of the scoring.

That's their fault for getting knocked down. I don't have to adjust my scoring because a guy gets behind the eight ball. If he gets knocked down three times, he deserves to be down that much as far as points go.

In boxing, a lot of people feel that a challenger has to "take it" from the champion. Meaning, he has to either beat him up significantly or win by a wide margin in order to earn a decision. What are your thoughts on this?

I think that went away with black and white TV. There may be some young judges in boxing who believe that. But in all the seminars I go to, they talk about what advantages the champion has when he enters the ring. And he has absolutely no advantages at all, except one. That one advantage is that if it ends in a draw, he keeps his title. That old story that you have to beat the champion to take his title is not true. There is no champion when you get in the ring. If you notice, the champion takes his belt off and hands it outside the ring. If he was the champion, he would wear his belt. There is no champion in a title fight.

In July 2005, Jermain Taylor defeated undisputed middleweight champion Bernard Hopkins by split decision. Many observers thought that Taylor didn't do enough to earn the victory, but you scored it 115–113 in favor of Taylor. What is your take on that fight?

I remember that fight really well. And where the controversy came to me was the twelfth round. I scored it for Taylor. At the beginning of that round, I saw Taylor landing some good shots on Hopkins. And then they kind of circled around, and they fought, and Taylor was fighting with his back to me most of the time. I couldn't see the punches Hopkins was landing, because they were blocked from where I was sitting. So, I could only score what I saw. I've seen that fight on television a number of times and I think there were about six different angles. And I could clearly see that Hopkins probably won that round. But a judge can only score what he sees. He can't guess.

A lot of boxing fans feel that some scorecards are politically motivated. You hear how Fighter A will have to score a knockout to beat Fighter B, because they are fighting in Fighter B's hometown. And there certainly have been decisions in the past that support this idea. What are your thoughts on this?

First off, I find that statement offensive as a judge. I look at boxing and I look at my past.... And I might have screwed up my personal life a few times. But in boxing, I've never done one thing that I'm ashamed of. A boxing judge can't pitch a no-hitter every game, so they're going to have good nights and bad nights.

Jermain Taylor (left) sizes up undisputed world middleweight champion Bernard Hopkins in their first of two fights in 2005. Taylor won the first encounter via split decision, and the second by unanimous decision (photograph by William Trillo, courtesy Pound4Pound.com).

But I believe that there is some truth to what you just said. There're a lot of new judges who are coming in because they might know someone on the commission, or they might get in only because of political connections. They might not have the ability to concentrate for three minutes, or they might be paying attention to where a guy is from. That really hurts the sport.

I never read anything about a fight before I do it. I don't want to know that the kid was born on a dirt floor, and that if he wins, he can buy his mom a new house. I don't want to know all those things. Because if it's a close round, I'm going to want that mother to get the house. Truthfully and honestly, with me, I never pay attention to where a guy is from. I never pay attention to who his handlers are, or who the promoter is. My job is to go there, decide who won the round, and then forget about that round.

What are some of your favorite fights that you have judged? What fights excited you as a fan, and did that make it difficult to stay focused on the judging?

The fight that immediately comes to mind is Wilfredo Gomez and Salvador Sanchez. In that fight, you had the mariachi bands on one side of the ring and you had the Puerto Rican band on the other. There was so much electricity in the Caesars Pavilion. The hair raised on my arm. I had to really talk to myself to get away from the distractions. There have been many others that I've done that are really exciting. Any of the big fights from the last few years have been great.

I've found through the years that the biggest responsibility of a judge is to stay focused. As a judge, when that bell rings, you can't have your mind wonder anywhere. You have to concentrate for three minutes. I look at a boxing judge as a trustee. A trustee is somebody who holds the values or the goods of another person for safe keeping. When I'm assigned to a fight, I'm honored that both fighters and both camps have chosen me. Therefore I have to live up to that honor and do an honest job.

24

Dr. Stuart Kirschenbaum: Commissioner Emeritus

> "You can't get any lower in life than he did. He had a chance to change it, but something in the dark side of him could never get out to the daylight. That's where Rickey Womack rests."

At one time, professional boxing had very little regulation in the state of Michigan. Certain practices by some of the matchmakers and promoters jeopardized the safety of the fighters. But after a while, things began to change and the sport was ruled under the strictest of supervision.

Born and raised in Brooklyn, New York, Dr. Stuart Kirschenbaum got involved with boxing first as an amateur boxer, then as a judge, and eventually as a commissioner.

From 1981 to 1992, Kirschenbaum was the boxing commissioner in the state of Michigan. During that time, his impact on the regulation and organization of the sport gained him international recognition.

Kirschenbaum cared deeply about the sport and its fighters, as was demonstrated by the fifteen years he spent mentoring Detroit-based light heavyweight Rickey Womack, a promising professional, whose career was derailed because of an armed robbery conviction.

In 2013, Kirschenbaum was appointed by the governor of Michigan to serve as boxing commissioner emeritus, and to act as a special advisor to the governor's office. This placed Kirschenbaum in a category unprecedented in the national boxing arena, by serving under four different governors. This interview took place over the phone in December 2015.

What is your background in boxing and what led you to become the boxing commissioner in the state of Michigan?

The first fight I ever watched was the Marciano–Louis fight. I was a young boy, living in Brooklyn, New York, in an apartment house. My parents had just bought a television. We were one of the first families to have a television and we had a lot of people crammed in the foyer. I have a lot of memories of that. Special events in your life, whether good, bad, or traumatic, seem to burn an imprint in your brain. Watching that fight was an amazing experience. From there, I began watching

Gillette Friday Night Fights with my father and grandfather, and started developing an understanding of the fighters.

As I got older, when I was out of high school, I went to Michigan State University. When I came back to New York in 1965, I was living with my brother who was an entertainer. He was a singer with Jay and the Americans. We used to go to all the fights at The Garden. You could get a ringside ticket for eight bucks. Being on the floor, I used to get spit on by the people in the balcony seats who were chewing on their cigars. If a Puerto Rican fighter lost, all of the rum bottles came flying from the bleachers. The atmosphere made a strong impression on me and I started really getting into boxing. Later on when I was going to New York College of Podiatric Medicine in Harlem, the *New York Daily News* sponsored the Golden Gloves. The application to fight in the Gloves was in the newspaper. I was twenty-two at the time. Boxing was something I had thought about doing, so I decided to sign up.

The application told you where all the gyms were and what you had to do. I went to the Clinton Youth Center at 54th Street and 9th Avenue, where amateurs and professionals trained. This guy Nicky Lyons ran the club. I told him I signed up for the 1967 New York Golden Gloves and he just looked at me. You know that thing where you say, what's wrong with this picture? I was a young Jewish guy going to medical school, not exactly your stereotypical boxer. He put me in the ring right away and he was like, holy God! Look what I came upon! Just from watching boxing and having good coordination, I seemed to have some ability. I had a decent jab, good footwork, I knew how to not get hit.... I was no Tommy Hearns, but it was remarkable for him to see this Jewish medical student who could box.

I went there every day after school. After I finished at the gym, I would go home and study. Sometimes my lips would be a little puffy from being hit in the mouth. When I would drink coffee, the coffee would start dribbling down my face because I couldn't feel my mouth on the rim of the coffee cup. I was getting into this thing. The bug was biting me. I started entering tournaments and beating guys and knocking guys out. It was like a drama out of some crazy dream.

My brother who was in entertainment had a chauffeured-driven limousine take us to these God-forsaken places in New York City. There would be twenty-five hundred to thirty-five hundred people in there watching. They used to save me for the main event. I would watch the fight before me, and one guy would get carried out bloodied, and the other guy would be all exuberant. The crowd would be roaring and I would think, what am I doing? It was very surreal.

In the last fight I ever had, Nicky Lyons told me to just go out there and knock my opponent out. I threw a right hand. The guy slipped my punch and my shoulder dislocated. When I got back to the corner, my corner guy sat me on the stool, put his foot on my chest, and tried to yank my arm back into place. It caused me such excruciating pain. For the rest of the fight I was just jabbing. It was the bravest thing I ever did, if not the stupidest thing. That finished my career inside the ring.

I later came back to Michigan to do a residency in foot surgery. I called the boxing commissioner in Michigan, Chuck Davey, and told him that I wanted to get back in the sport, maybe as a judge. I got licensed and started judging amateur fights. The first amateur fight I ever judged was Tommy Hearns's last amateur fight before

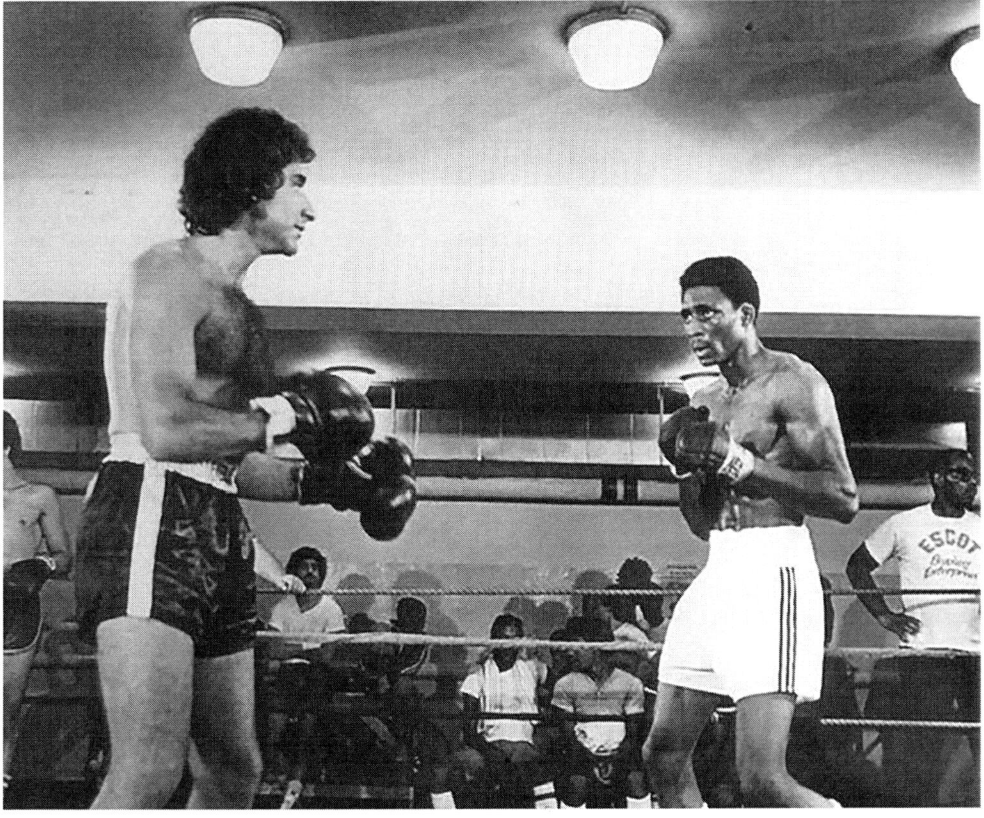

Dr. Stuart Kirschenbaum spars with future five-division world champion Thomas Hearns at the Kronk Gym, 1979 (courtesy Dr. Stuart Kirschenbaum).

he turned professional. I went on to work professional fights and I started getting a good reputation. At that time, the governor was trying to de-regulate professional boxing. I started going to hearings and speaking about the need for safety and regulations. I made an impression and they eventually appointed me to the commission. Within a year's time, in 1981, I became the chairman.

Boxing was very, very busy in Michigan back then. From all those years as a commissioner, I became a recognized presence in the sport. I was one of the founders of the Association of Boxing Commissions and I started implementing changes around the country. I testified in the United States Congress in Washington, D.C., two times, along with Don King, Bob Arum, Howard Cosell, and Bert Sugar, regarding the creation of a federal boxing commission. At that time, I was being considered to be the federal boxing czar, until that legislation was killed.

The recognition I was getting from my position as the commissioner gave me opportunities outside of my duties, like helping the families of Joe Louis and "Sugar" Ray Robinson. I've been very active behind the scenes and I was fortunate to receive the 1993 *Sports Illustrated* Joe Louis Award, as well as the 2010 Joe Louis Brown Bomber Jacket Award. I was inducted into the Michigan Jewish Sports Hall of Fame and I'm a board member of the Emanuel Steward Foundation. In '92, I stepped down from the commission to devote more time to my practice, but I never left the sport. I still try to help the people in boxing as much as I can.

What are some of the changes that you implemented while you were the commissioner?

The first week I was put on the commission, before I was the commissioner, I went to a fight and watched some Detroit fighters fighting these out-of-town fighters. What I noticed was that all these out-of-town guys were wearing the same trunks. They usually got knocked out in the first round and then another guy would come in wearing the exact same pair of trunks.

I went up to one of these guys and said, "Don't you have your own trunks?" He said he didn't and he confirmed that they were all using the same trunks. I said, "Have you ever boxed professionally?" He said, "No." I said, "How did you come to be here tonight?" He told me he was playing basketball and this guy came up and said, "Who weighs 120 pounds? Who weighs 147 pounds? Is there a big guy? Who weighs more than 200 pounds?" The matchmaker was filling up the undercard with these kids and paying them a hundred dollars. I found out that this was the norm. Back then, the commission didn't check records. They just went along with whatever the matchmaker told them.

When I became commissioner, I told the matchmakers and the promoters that I had to approve of each and every fight in the state of Michigan. It wasn't going to be a joke anymore. If you were an opponent and you were brought in from somewhere, you were treated fairly. I used to go into all the dressing rooms before the fights and talk to the out-of-town fighters. I would tell them, "You're in Michigan now. I'm the commissioner and you are allowed to win."

I was very pro-active in almost every aspect of the sport. We started medical and disciplinary suspensions, utilizing computerized record keeping, drug testing.... We began clinics for officials, and we wrote and passed through the legislative process the first complete overhaul of boxing rules and regulations in thirty years. We also abolished single-elimination contests, such as Tough Man contests. We were tough but fair and it was all for the protection of the boxers.

Trainer/manager Emanuel Steward was just starting to build the professional careers of his fighters from the Kronk Gym around the same time you were appointed chairperson of the commission. Tell me about your experiences working with Steward.

Emanuel told me one time that he wanted to pull his guys out of fights in Michigan, because of my tough enforcement of the rules. But in other states, he would hear people talking about Michigan boxing and he started feeling proud of what we were doing.

When I first met Emanuel, we were both on a committee that was naming the Joe Louis Arena and honoring the champion. We formed a friendship from those early meetings. We respected each other, we had friendly battles with each other.... Emanuel was on a fast track and it was a much different track than mine. Emanuel became a star in boxing. Hilmer Kenty was the city's first world champion since Joe Louis, and then you have Tommy Hearns who blew up into something big. He had a lot of terrific fighters and he was a father figure to all of them.

The problem was that Emanuel's popularity would sometimes overshadow

Dr. Stuart Kirschenbaum (bottom right) judges the 1983 IBF world middleweight championship fight between Marvin Hagler and Wilford Scypion, a bout that Hagler won by fourth-round knockout. Referee Frank Cappucino is the third man in the ring (courtesy Dr. Stuart Kirschenbaum).

his fighters. When Tommy Hearns started winning championships and becoming the man in this town, the press would always go to Emanuel for the interview. That became a very sore point. Tommy felt that Emanuel was too much in the limelight. No longer was it a father-son relationship. All of a sudden, the ten-year-old boy who walked into Kronk had become a man, a wealthy and self-confident man, who wanted to assume his own identity.

Tommy eventually left Emanuel over a disagreement, and not until years later did they reconcile. After a while, I think Tommy could see what Emanuel had been doing with him and how strong Emanuel was in his life. At Emanuel's funeral, Tommy gave a eulogy and just fell apart. Only later did he realize what it all meant to him, what Emanuel's caring and protective nature was about, and just what a force in the boxing world Emanuel occupied.

Jackie Kallen, known as "The First Lady of Boxing," managed James Toney when he won the IBF world middleweight championship in May 1991 with an eleventh-round

TKO over Michael Nunn. This was a notable story in boxing and it kept the state of Michigan on the map.

Jackie was a very bright publicist. From the time she was young, she was writing newspaper columns for the local press. She was a pretty blonde and she got a lot of attention. She was very unique. Emanuel Steward took her on as the publicist at the Kronk Gym, where she learned about boxing and became close to all the fighters.

After a while, she moved on from being a publicist. She took everything she learned from the Kronk Gym and started managing fighters. Her first fighter was Bobby Hitz, who was an opponent for George Foreman when George was making his comeback. Bobby's career wasn't going anywhere, but it was Jackie's way of learning the finer intricacies of the sport. Eventually, she saw an opportunity to do something big when she met James Toney. He was a middleweight at the time, trained by Bill Miller. Bill Miller was a very defensive-minded trainer who taught a lot of old-school moves.

James was undefeated and Jackie put him in a fight with Michael Nunn for the championship. He knocked Nunn out in the eleventh round and Jackie Kallen became "The First Lady of Boxing." James got so big, literally and figuratively. His entourage was as big as his girth. I bumped into James a year after he won the title and he was two hundred forty pounds. He loved eating, but he had a lot of skills and was very hard to beat.

When James lost to Roy Jones, he was heavy and out of shape, and he blamed

Dr. Stuart Kirschenbaum with former world heavyweight champion Muhammad Ali, prior to a 1989 press conference regarding the formation of a World Boxing Hall of Fame (courtesy Dr. Stuart Kirschenbaum).

everyone around him for what happened. That was the end of Jackie Kallen and James Toney, but Jackie kept moving. She always had a fighter and she always had connections. She knew how to promote. That was her forte. Wherever Jackie went, it was a great story. Jackie earned her recognition in a sport dominated by men and will always be considered a trailblazer in the history of boxing.

You spent many years as a mentor to Detroit-based light heavyweight Rickey Womack, who eventually fought at heavyweight after spending fifteen years in prison. When did you first meet Womack and how did this relationship evolve?

The first time I met Rickey was at a press conference in Detroit, where Emanuel Steward was announcing the signing of Rickey Womack and Stevie McCrory. Rickey had beaten Evander Holyfield four times out of eight, and he was the light heavyweight amateur champion of the world. Rickey went on to be 9–0 as a pro, and then the shit hit the fan. Around Christmas time in '85, he needed money to buy his girlfriend some gifts. He ended up holding up two mom-and-pop video stores. He pistol-whipped the wife who owned one of the stores and he shot the husband in the buttocks. There were attempted murder charges and he ended up in jail for twelve to twenty-five years.

I followed the story with almost a sad interest. Not knowing Rickey that well, I couldn't imagine how someone of that caliber could do something like this. I started reading more and more about Rickey, and I learned a little bit about his past. He had a very hard upbringing. I don't condone what he did, but I felt like I understood what his problem was. The next thing I know, I got a collect call from a correctional facility and it was Rickey.

I had been mentoring another boxer by the name of Alvin "Too Sweet" Hayes. He had been to prison and he told Rickey that he should give me a call. Rickey and I started having a conversation and he was not the savage beast that you would think he was. He was a feared boxer and now a convicted criminal, but I started seeing the softer side. He didn't really have anyone in his life at this point. His mother was living out of state and Emanuel had stopped having communication with him. I wanted to help him out.

We started talking regularly and I really enjoyed having conversations with him. Rickey spent fifteen years in prison. At this point, he hadn't even been in prison for two years, so this was thirteen years of collect calls. I was Rickey's lifeline to the outside world. He had a picture of my family in his cell. I would go to his parole hearings and speak on his behalf.

As bad as Rickey's crimes were, he was remorseful. He understood what he did. He wanted me to contact the people he harmed, so he could apologize to them. For a man who wasn't educated, Rickey was very articulate. I would make the comparison to Mike Tyson. Tyson wasn't educated, but he could sometimes present himself very well. Rickey and Tyson were actually friends. They were roommates at the Olympic Trials.

Rickey loved to write poetry. I had hundreds of letters and poems that Rickey would send me. One time, Rickey was denied parole and he was so disappointed. He said in this letter, "Doc, you are like a father to me. By the time you get this, I will have taken my life." I had no way of calling him, so I called his twin brother who I stayed in touch with. Days went by and Rickey called and said, "Doc, you're going to be getting a letter from me and I don't want you to open it. I want you to throw it away." This started showing me how unstable Rickey really was.

Rickey became very religious and born again, always quoting the Bible. After his fourth parole hearing, I got a call and he said, "Doc, I'm coming out!" I was happy and excited, but after he hung up, I thought, holy shit! Now what? Rickey had been in prison a long time. He always said, "Time has served me, I haven't served time." That might have been true, but now all of a sudden he was facing responsibilities like rent, phone bills, making his own meals, getting a car.... It's a different life out here.

I picked Rickey up from prison. On the ride home, he saw my cell phone. He had never seen a cell phone before. When we got to my office, he picked up the TV remote control and thought it was another cell phone. He was trying to make a phone call and I thought, this guy has missed a lot of life.

Rickey worked at my office and he was as cute as can be. I had him wearing scrubs and he had this big smile on his face. There were stories around town about Rickey being released and everybody was so excited to see him. After work, I would drive him to the gym. I had Bill Miller training him and he looked unbelievable. He was thirty-nine years old, but it was like time stood still in prison. He had been doing push-ups and pull-ups and he was just a physical specimen.

When he got back in the ring for the first time, he wanted to wear plain black trunks with a towel, a la Mike Tyson. He looked very intimidating. The crowd was going crazy for him, because he was this success story. It was a sell-out crowd at the Cobo Arena in Detroit and he knocked the guy out in the third round. We hugged and kissed, and I felt like the mission was accomplished.

Rickey was back on his feet again, but then things quickly changed. Within days after his first fight, Rickey called me and told me he had gotten married. He had been seeing this girl who had graduated from Notre Dame law school. She tried to take control of Rickey's life, and it became Robin Givens and Mike Tyson. She was telling Rickey that he shouldn't let me run his career and that he should be making a million dollars a fight. Where did this come from? I had Rickey living with his brother and staying on track. Then this girl comes along and the wheels started falling off the cart.

Rickey became very obsessive and jealous with this girl. He kept her locked up in the house and didn't want her talking to anyone. He didn't even want *me* calling the house. When Rickey would go to the gym, she would call me and tell me that he was hitting her and abusing her. Rickey had a very violent childhood. His father used to take the kids in the house and make them eat gun powder to punish them. The trust factor wasn't there. The respect for women wasn't there either, because his mother was abused in front of him. You can sit in a prison cell for fifteen years and think it's all going to come together for you, but you come out into the free world and everything comes back to haunt you.

Rickey's fourth comeback fight was at The Palace. He was the main event. There were about fifteen thousand people there. Tommy Hearns, Michael Moorer, Milton

McCrory, and all the Kronk champions were sitting ringside. On the way to the fight, Rickey asked me if he could cancel. I said, "What are you talking about?! You're the main event!" He said he had an argument with his wife and that he didn't want to fight. I said, "There are certain things in your life known as commitments. You are committed to this and you have to fight. Don't worry. You'll be fine."

Former heavyweight Rickey Womack and Dr. Stuart Kirschenbaum at a 2001 press conference announcing Womack's first fight, following a fifteen-year prison stint for armed robbery (photograph by Dan Graschuck, courtesy Dr. Stuart Kirschenbaum).

We had him against a guy who was not very good. But in the first round, the guy started connecting on Rickey and embarrassing him. Rickey just walked through the fight and wasn't very impressive. Whether he deserved to win or not, I don't know, but they gave him the decision. After the fight, he went back to the dressing room and he didn't want to shower. He just wanted to go home. We got in the car and he asked me if Tommy Hearns saw the fight, and he wanted to know what his Kronk friends were saying about him. Then he said, "Doc, I don't want to do this no more. I'm grateful for everything you've done, but I don't want to do this no more." He got very dark and he said, "You're not going to see me no more. I'm going to be out of your life."

When I dropped him off, his wife asked him how he did. He didn't allow her to go to the fights, so she was there waiting for him. Instead of telling her that he had just won a decision, he told her that he lost. That to me was a real indication that Rickey was unraveling. I was so afraid to leave him at his house that night. He came to see me a couple days later to get his money and I tried to talk him into going back to the gym. It was a good talk and we hugged, but I knew he wasn't in the right frame of mind.

My wife at the time was undergoing cancer treatment. One day in January, she was getting her treatment and I was with her. Rickey went to my office, but I wasn't there. I got a call later that day from one of his trainers. Rickey's wife told this guy's wife that Rickey was looking to kill me and Bill Miller. So, that day that Rickey came to my office, he had a gun. He was looking to put me away. Ironically, my wife's cancer actually saved my life. That night, Rickey started manhandling his wife and throwing her down the stairs. He had this gun and was pointing it at his head. At one point during the tirade, he put the gun between his eyes and pulled the trigger.

I received a call from Rickey's wife telling me what happened. I rushed to the hospital and they had him on a gurney with bloody patches on his forehead. They had him cremated and his ashes were brought to me in a container. I put the container on my office scale and it weighed seventeen pounds. I thought, my God, here's the Rickey that I would push to eat more and more so he could be a heavyweight. Now, he's only seventeen pounds, representative of the life once filled with dreams of becoming heavyweight champion of the world.

For the fifteen years that Rickey and I were together, we cared for each other. I was like a father figure to him. I wanted to see him succeed, but all the darkness, all the skeletons—it was nothing I could clean up. It was a very hard thing to handle. I felt like I failed in so many ways. People tell me there's nothing I could have done. I might have been the only person out there who had no motive for Rickey other than to be in his corner. All I wanted was for him to have a good life.

I look at the fifteen years since his death, I look at the fifteen years before that—that's thirty years of my life that I've had a place in my heart for him. I think about the happy times, the funny times. You can't get any lower in life than he did. He had a chance to change it, but something in the dark side of him could never get out to the daylight. That's where Rickey Womack rests.

I got to meet Mike Tyson years later. He was doing his one-man show at the Fisher Theater here in Detroit. I had heard an interview Mike gave where he was talking about Rickey, and how he was being mismanaged, and how people were ripping him off. I bought a couple of VIP seats to the show so I could meet Mike. I brought with me a couple of articles about Rickey and gave Mike one of Rickey's promo hats with Rickey's name on it. I told him who I was and I said, "Mike, if you get a chance, read these articles and you'll know the true story about what happened with your buddy Rickey at the end of his life." Not too many people know what he went through, what I went through. Our lives were intertwined. It was the unlikely linkage of two so different people, who shared a common ground and love for each other.

Dr. Stuart Kirschenbaum with former world heavyweight champion Joe Louis, following Hilmer Kenty's 1980 ninth-round TKO victory over Ernasto Espana for Espanas's WBA world lightweight title (courtesy Dr. Stuart Kirschenbaum).

You spent several years collecting boxing memorabilia with the intentions of creating a Michigan Boxing Hall of Fame. In 2013, something took place which altered your plans. What happened?

My office in Detroit became a depository to my addiction to the sport and preserving its legacy. When I was commissioner, I understood the historical significance of boxing in the state of Michigan. I kept articles, records, and contracts of everything that was happening. I also had one of the largest collections of Joe Louis memorabilia in the world.

Shortly after Hilmer Kenty won the world championship, I met Joe at a party. He was going through a hard time. He owed money and he was going through some bad things mentally. At the party, people were putting pens in his right hand so he could sign autographs. This was the same right hand that he used to knock out Max Schmeling. Joe could barely hold the pens because of a stroke he had. I was in awe looking at the man, feeling a sense of sympathy and compassion.

Years later after Joe passed, I found his wife Martha in a nursing home. She had no teeth, she was in poor health.... Here in Detroit, we have all these shrines in Joe Louis's honor, and here was his wife who had taken care of the champion after his glory days. She wasn't with him when he had money and was on top of the world. She was with him during the hard times.

I called up some reporters in Detroit and told them the story. Within days, we raised fifteen thousand dollars for her. I was like a guardian to her. After she passed, I made her funeral arrangements. It became a lifelong commitment. Joe transcended the sport of boxing. He was the first African American boxer who whites used to cheer for. He stood for something good and I wanted to make sure that his legacy was preserved forever.

I started buying Joe Louis memorabilia and it became an obsession. I had over five thousand pieces—photographs, clothes, letters.... I had the left-hand glove that he wore in the Schmeling fight, having previously donated the right glove to the city of Detroit. I had just formed a Michigan Boxing Hall of Fame and I was looking for a home for it, so the public could learn about the legacy of Michigan boxing.

In 2013, there was a tragedy in my office. One of the maintenance workers was having an affair with a medical receptionist who worked down the hall from me. If he couldn't have her, nobody was going to have her. He came in one morning, shot her five times, set the building on fire, and shot himself in the head. I stood out there and watched as the building burned down. What I felt more than anything was guilt. My bigger purpose in life was to preserve Joe's legacy and it was going up in flames.

I went there the next day to go through the ashes. I found Joe Louis's glove and it had melted. Afterwards, people would call me and say "Hey, I found an old Joe Louis magazine. I'll send it to you." I'd say, "Don't send me anything." I can't go through that again. I can't start over, because it will never stop. It's like giving an alcoholic a drink. I would be on the Internet looking for that one thing I never had. It was close to fifteen years that this collection was amassed. I try to get past it, but it still haunts me.

I still do everything I can to preserve the legacy of this sport and the great legends in Michigan. I feel like if I don't do it, who will? I watch the clock go by and I know that some day all of this is going to be a thing of the past. This is the type of sport that one day might just be a footnote in history. The people in boxing are what made the sport what it is. They're part of the fabric of life and the history in a country growing out of social injustice, racial discrimination, and inhuman tolerance. We need to remember who these people are and what they meant. That's been my mission and I'm not letting go.

Epilogue: A 10-Count

> "If you're going to work with a fighter, it's because you think they're the best in the world. It has to be like family."

The 1980s and '90s saw a number of exciting matchups, including Evander Holyfield–Dwight Muhammad Qawi I, Julio Cesar Chavez–Meldrick Taylor I, Riddick Bowe–Evander Holyfield I, and Riddick Bowe–Andrew Golota I and II. All of these aforementioned fights had something in common. In the corner of one of the combatants, there was an excitable, protective man with grey hair, who loved his fighters as much as any trainer possibly could.

Born and raised in New York City, later relocating to Paterson, New Jersey, Lou Duva was the first of the Duva family to make his mark in the boxing world.

Duva fought professionally at 147–160 pounds, from 1942 to 1945, compiling a record of 5–10–1. After retiring, he remained in the sport as a trainer, a manager, and a promoter. His first world champion came in December 1963 when Joey Giardello defeated WBC and WBA world middleweight champion Dick Tiger by unanimous decision.

In 1978, Lou Duva's son, Dan Duva, formed Main Events, a New Jersey–based promotional company that started off by putting on local fights, eventually promoting events seen by global audiences. When Dan passed away in 1996, his wife Kathy Duva began running the family business.

Over the years, Lou Duva worked with a number of high-profile fighters, including Rocky Lockridge, Johnny Bumphus, Evander Holyfield, Scott Frank, Alex Arthur, Tyrell Biggs, Vinny Pazienza, Michael Moorer, Andrew Golota, Jose Luis Lopez, Shaun George, Michael Marrone, Arturo Gatti, Zab Judah, Pernell Whitaker, Meldrick Taylor, and Samuel Peter.

This interview took place over the phone in December 2015. Lou Duva passed away on March 8, 2017, at the age of ninety-four.

What is your background in boxing and what led you to train, manage, and promote fighters?

When I was ten years old, I would go to the gym with my brother. I used to go down there and clean up, and some of the fighters there taught me how to box. I started boxing and I learned the sport from all angles. I went into the Army and I turned pro when I got out. I had to stop because there were so many other things I was doing. I was running a trucking company and I had a bail bondsman business.

But I kept going to the gym and I eventually became a trainer. I put a stable of fighters together and I had former fighters working for me as trainers. George Benton was my top trainer. George was one of the top middleweight contenders from Philadelphia. He fought all the best and he beat all the best. He should have gotten a title shot, but he didn't because of politics. My fighters liked learning from him. They related to him. They listened to him. George did what a trainer does and he made champions out of these guys.

My first world champion was Joey Giardello. Joey was a good fighter and when he wanted to fight, nobody could beat him. I had close relationships with all my guys. They were part of my family and we all got along good. I was managing and promoting fighters, and it got so big that my son Dan started Main Events. My brother, my wife—we were all part of it. It was a family affair. I spent time in the gym with the fighters and Dan handled the promotional end of it.

Our first big fight was Thomas Hearns and "Sugar" Ray Leonard in Las Vegas. It was a really big fight and it was good for the operation. We got lucky. We had the right people with us and we did the right things with everybody.

You worked with a number of high-profile fighters in the late 1980s and early '90s, like Evander Holyfield, Meldrick Taylor, Pernell Whitaker, Arturo Gatti, and Andrew Golota. What stands out in your mind about the time you spent with them?

Evander Holyfield was a great fighter and a great person. In the gym, he was tremendous at helping other fighters out. We had a really good relationship. He listened to me and he followed George Benton's instructions. I remember his fight with Buster Douglas very well. I knew he would knock him out in the third round. He had the guts to beat him, he had the background to beat him, and I knew it would happen the way it did. After a while, you get a feeling for a fighter. When you have a lot of experience and a lot of love for them, you know when they're going to deliver. Evander sure as hell delivered! When you talk about a real fighter, he was as real as it gets.

Professional boxing trainer/manager/promoter Lou Duva, 1990s. Duva's friend Rick Perez stands behind him (courtesy Rick Perez).

I have the greatest of respect for Meldrick Taylor. The best fight he had was when he fought Cesar Chavez. He should have won that fight. When Pernell Whitaker was at his best, nobody could beat him. He trained good. He didn't enjoy himself. He trained and that's why he became a great fighter.

Arturo Gatti was a tough guy and he had a lot of tough fights. He was a playboy, but when he came to train, he trained. What he had more than anything was heart and guts. Andrew Golota was a good fighter, who could have been a great fighter. He had a different mind. Before a fight, I would talk to him and say, "This guy likes to do this, he likes to do that...." And Andrew would say, "I know, I know, I know, I know...."

With Riddick Bowe, Andrew was hitting him with low blows. I would tell him to hit the belly, hit him on the shoulder, but don't hit him low. He would say, "Okay." He goes out there and the first right hand he throws is a low blow. I had a heart attack that night! It was one of those little things in my career. I loved boxing. I *still* love boxing.

Do you love the game now as much as when you were actively training, managing and promoting fighters?

No. I loved the game before. I don't have that feeling like I used to. When you had the guys that I had, it's hard to watch boxing today. Tommy Hearns and "Sugar" Ray Leonard, Holyfield and Bowe, Taylor and Chavez.... Today it's Floyd Mayweather and Manny Pacquiao. Pernell Whitaker would put Floyd Mayweather in his back pocket!

Some of the fighters today are overpaid. You have trainers who only want to train a guy if there's enough money in it. Everything is about the money and it hurts the sport. If you're going to work with a fighter, it's because you think they're the best in the world. It has to be like family. With my fighters, I would make sure they kept whatever money they made. I would cook them Italian dinners and make sure they ate right. Those were my guys out there and I had to take care of them.

There's one fighter I'll always remember in my heart and in my soul. That's a kid named Oscar Diaz. He was a tough kid. Not the greatest like Pernell Whitaker, but lots of guts. When he fought, he fought hard and that's all that mattered. I have a place in my heart because of my personal feelings for him and the way he handled things with my family.

Sometimes you have to choose sides in life. Take the good side. Don't take the bad side. Take the good. I had the best guys ever. I still talk to Evander Holyfield and Meldrick Taylor. I'm spending time with my family and if there's something I can do, I'll do it. I'm just making the most of life every way I can.

Return to the Suburbs

While writing my first book, *Ringside: Interviews with 24 Fighters and Boxing Insiders*, I was living in Los Angeles for most of the process. In June 2012, I had just finished my interview with trainer/manager Emanuel Steward and was faced with the reality that I could no longer pay my rent. I had been working as a boxing instructor/personal trainer at a gym in Beverly Hills. In January 2012, the gym was collapsing and I was out of a job. When you live in a big, high-priced city like LA and your earnings only carry you month to month, it's hard to get caught up if you fall behind. I had reached the end of the line, so I had no choice but to return to where I came from—the suburbs of St. Louis, Missouri, where I was born and raised.

Before I moved to LA, I had spent quite a bit of time training fighters. Since I was back in my hometown and reconnecting with the boxing community, I was eager to do it again. While attending some local fights in June 2014, I ran into an amateur boxer by the name of Raymond Handson. Nine years earlier, I trained Raymond for a few weeks and took him to the Ringside Tournament in Kansas City, Missouri. When I saw Raymond at the fights, he had been out of the ring for a number of years. He was about to turn twenty-five years old and he wanted to step up and enter the professional world. Boxing was all he knew, so that was the direction he was looking.

Since Raymond wanted to get back in the ring and I wanted to get back to coaching, we were a good fit. I had access to a boxing gym in the basement of a personal training facility where I worked, so we started training together and he began his second run in the game. Rediscovering boxing as a young adult is a lot different than being a kid who goes to the recreation center after school. Raymond was a nationally ranked amateur as a teenager, but getting in the ring with grown men was a whole new ballgame. As a kid, he would get in shape by riding his bike around the

Doveed Linder spars with middleweight Raymond Handson before one of Handson's 2016 fights (courtesy Andrew Kerman).

neighborhood and sparring with his friends. With me, he had to drive thirty minutes to the gym every day where he was put on a strict regimen.

Before this, Raymond knew very little about the discipline and accountability that an adult needs to continue his boxing career. I could see that he was having a hard time living up to the demands that were made of him. As we trained, he experienced a painful crash course in life. But little by little, I saw a transformation taking place. His boyish grin was replaced by the look of a determined man with the weight of the world on his back. We did a few amateur fights and then he turned professional. In our time together, he had seven pro fights, compiling a record of 5-1-1 with his only loss coming against another 5-0 fighter in a six-round fight that went the distance. I see no shame in that.

After Raymond's last fight, the promotional company that had been giving us fights cancelled their boxing events. Raymond started going to school and I began focusing on other things. I figured my time as a boxing trainer was over, but a couple years later, I got a call from local super middleweight Vaughn Alexander, who had a record of 14-3, 9 KOs. Vaughn is the older brother of Devon Alexander, the former junior welterweight and welterweight world champion out of St. Louis. Vaughn and Devon were two of the top amateurs of their time. In Vaughn's first year as a professional, he was promoted by Don King and had built up a record of 5-0, before doing eleven years in prison for armed robbery and assault.

I met Vaughn shortly before his first fight after prison, because Raymond and Vaughn sparred together. When Vaughn called me about the possibility of training

Raymond Handson jabs Marlon Smith to the body en route to a 2016 unanimous decision victory (courtesy Jimmy Range).

him, I couldn't help but jump at the chance. We had developed a friendship over the past few years and I was intrigued by the idea of training someone with the kind of experience and natural ability that he had.

Vaughn was eighteen when he went to prison, but he was already a veteran of the sport. In the amateurs, he had been trained by Kevin Cunningham, the trainer of former welterweight and junior middleweight world champion Cory Spinks. As a teenager, he was sparring top professionals and going to camps where elite fighters trained. If this game is ninety percent mental, then Vaughn had ninety percent of it down. He was very determined, very serious, and he had a mean streak that served him well in the ring.

As sharp as Vaughn once was, eleven years in prison led to a lot of rust. Like Raymond, he had to rediscover boxing all over again. Vaughn and I spent a few months drilling the fundamentals of the sport and we had a lot of fun doing it. With just a little bit of work, I could see glimpses of a well-schooled fighter who had the potential to reach great heights. In our one and only fight together, Vaughn won a majority decision over an undefeated prospect, scoring a minor upset.

As much as I love training boxers, I tend to dip in and dip out of it. Boxing journalism is something I've done with more consistency. When I came back to St. Louis after leaving LA, I had more than enough interviews for one book. Even though my first manuscript was not yet published, I continued doing interviews for

Super middleweight Vaughn Alexander (left) and junior welterweight Dannie Williams before a 2019 boxing event in St. Louis that featured both fighters (author's collection).

a potential second book. I owe a lot of who I am to boxing—as a person, as a writer, and with everything I do. When I interview people in boxing, I often find nuggets of wisdom and inspiration that help me overcome any hardships and challenges that I'm faced with. That's what these interviews do for me, and I hope they do the same for you.

Index